Praise for *Software Development fo*

"I highly recommend this book for anyone who's ever tried to implement RUP on a small project. Pollice and company have demystified and effectively scaled the process while ensuring that its essence hasn't been compromised. A must-have for any RUPster's library!"

—Chris Soskin
Process Engineering Consultant
Toyota Motor Sales

"A lot of RUP users are looking for examples of practical usage, and this book provides excellent insight on how RUP can be applied in practice to a small project. It walks you through the different phases, from project initiation to completion. The authors have done a good job highlighting both the problems that they ran into, as well as the success they had."

—Per Kroll
Manager, RUP, Rational Software
IBM Corporation

"I loved this book because it is easy to read and full of good stuff that should help software people. It describes how a small team effectively used RUP (Rational Unified Process), a process that is usually thought of as being useful only by large, high-ceremony teams. The authors' straightforward, low-B.S. approach conveys some serious truths and advice. This book belongs on every bookshelf."

—Dan Rawsthorne, Ph.D.
Senior Consultant
Net Objectives

Software Development for Small Teams

The Addison-Wesley Object Technology Series

Grady Booch, Ivar Jacobson, and James Rumbaugh, Series Editors

For more information, check out the series web site at www.awprofessional.com/otseries.

The Component Software Series

Clemens Szyperski, Series Editor

For more information, check out the series web site at www.awprofessional.com/csseries.

Software Development for Small Teams

A RUP–Centric Approach

Gary Pollice
Liz Augustine
Chris Lowe
Jas Madhur

✦✦Addison-Wesley

Boston • San Francisco • New York • Toronto • Montreal
London • Munich • Paris • Madrid
Capetown • Sydney • Tokyo • Singapore • Mexico City

Many of the designations used by manufacturers and sellers to distinguish their products are claimed as trademarks. Where those designations appear in this book, and Addison-Wesley was aware of a trademark claim, the designations have been printed with initial capital letters or in all capitals.

Groove screen shot(s) reprinted by permission from Groove.

The authors and publisher have taken care in the preparation of this book, but make no expressed or implied warranty of any kind and assume no responsibility for errors or omissions. No liability is assumed for incidental or consequential damages in connection with or arising out of the use of the information or programs contained herein.

The publisher offers discounts on this book when ordered in quantity for bulk purchases and special sales. For more information, please contact:

U.S. Corporate and Government Sales
(800) 382-3419
corpsales@pearsontechgroup.com

For sales outside of the U.S., please contact:

International Sales
(317) 581-3793
international@pearsontechgroup.com

Visit Addison-Wesley on the Web: www.awprofessional.com

Library of Congress Cataloging-in-Publication Data

Software development for small teams : a RUP-centric approach / Gary Pollice ... [et.al].
    p. cm.
ISBN 0-321-19950-2 (alk. paper)
1. Computer software—development. I. Pollice, Gary.

QA76.76.D47S638 2003
005.1—dc22

                                                          2003018536

ISBN 0-321-19950-2
Text printed on recycled paper
1 2 3 4 5 6 7 8 9 10—CRS—0706050403
First printing, December 2003

Contents

Foreword

This book is not a textbook on RUP, on agile processes, or on project management —it is a journal from the trenches. It captures the realities of working with a small, distributed team that went through many changes, but managed to complete its mandate: deliver a valuable, working software product to the customer. In it, the combatants tell their story in a direct manner, without any attempt to "spin doctor" it.

I often hear, "We do not need a process, our project is small and simple." You may have this impression, but in the end, you will use *some* process, and most likely that process will be invented on the fly. There is a pervasive impression in our industry that a described process is only good for large companies, running large projects, with hundreds of developers— and then it is only used to make developers' lives miserable. In this book, you will see how a very small group of people, tackling a modest project, can adopt and tailor a described process for their purpose: the Rational Unified Process. They did not add a lot of formality in this adoption. They only selected the elements that would help them, and even complemented RUP with practices from other approaches, such as PSP, eXtreme Programming, and other agile methods.

I also often hear, "Show me how you actually do it." Examples of successful—and sometimes unsuccessful—projects are often key to getting started with a new process. Just diving into a book or a complex Web site and wading through pages of descriptions of an *ideal* way to proceed is too abstract for most of us. Canned, perfect examples that exactly match the theory are not convincing. The great value of this book is that it brings the reader in contact with the reality of an actual project, including its failures, false starts, and limitations, with the authors looking critically at what they did and why it worked or did not. We learn from our experience, and from contrasting our experience with that of others. "Oh, yes, I recognize this pattern; I've been there too. Ah, this is how you worked through it."

This book discusses topics that are not often covered by traditional processes, RUP included. The authors boldly dive into issues dealing with *people*, with the dynamics of forming a team, with communications in a distributed environment, with the use of a collaborative, Internet-based tool, all elements that are an integral part of many small open source projects today.

Finally, this book emphasizes one key practice, often announced in the plan, and often forgotten in the rush to finish: *self-reflection*, sometimes called "post-mortem" or "retrospective." It means stopping for a while, stepping back, and looking at what we did, how we did it, what worked, what did not work, and why. And this whole book is one fantastic example of a very complete post-mortem, done with great candor and humility. This book will not replace all the post-mortems and retrospectives you did not do, but it will give you an idea of what you may have missed.

So, who would use this book and when? Many possibilities: If you are new to modern processes, RUP, agile methods, PSP, and so on, this book will give you the spirit of them, without diving into the details. If you are unsure about the way to handle a small, distributed project, you will learn valuable lessons from a group of people who have asked themselves the same questions you might have asked, who have made choices, right or wrong, and reflected on those choices. Hopefully, you will recognize some patterns, learn from the answers and solutions; this will mean that you make fewer mistakes on your own projects. If you are an expert at these methods, this book will open new avenues—marrying various approaches, scaling down a process, and the value of self-reflection.

I learned a lot about RUP in this book, and came to look at it differently. Thank you Gary, Jas, Liz, and Chris for sharing this experience with us.

Philippe Kruchten
Vancouver, British Columbia
Canada

Preface

The goal of developing software is to deliver something of value to customers. To work effectively, you need to strike the right balance of people, process, and tools. Everyone seems to have favorite tools, techniques, and processes. Software companies sell tools and methods to help you be more effective at building software. Consultants evangelize their methods to convince you that they know how to help your organization and project teams do a better job. We as developers continually learn new techniques and apply new tools to help us do more, in less time, with higher quality.

With over seventy-five years of combined experience working on and observing different software projects, we, the authors, have arrived at a conclusion that some enlightened folks have already figured out: Every project is different, and those things that help one team be a spectacular success might, if not applied with common sense, cause another team to fail miserably. Each team needs to decide how to use a specific process, and then continually adjust to make improvements.

In the face of this continual change, how can a project team know what to change to be most productive? The answer, in our opinion, lies in learning as many different techniques as possible, learning how to effectively use tools that support the different techniques, and determining what combinations work well, and when they work. This suggests an ongoing process of learning.

Good programmers learn from other programmers. They learn by looking at code and reading books on different programming methods. Testers improve by learning their craft from master testers, studying test designs, and learning how to use new techniques and tools. In fact, any individual practitioner learns from others doing the same job and by looking at examples. Each practitioner needs to develop a personal style for working effectively, both as an individual and as a member of a larger team.

Teams too, need examples of how other teams work in order to develop their own style of working together. This book is an example of how a small team developed a software tool. It is a chronicle of what we did and why we did it. We have tried to explain why things worked (or didn't), and we discuss what we'll change next time. Along the way we identify the lessons we learned and offer some ideas for generalizing our experiences.

Your job, as the reader, is to observe what we did and learn from our experiences. If you are working on a small software development project, you will immediately identify with some of our experiences. You may have already faced some of the problems we encountered and solved them to your own satisfaction, or you may still be struggling to find satisfactory solutions. We hope the book provides you with some useful ideas about how to choose and use tools, work with others effectively, and select the techniques that fit your personal and team styles best.

All of the authors have worked in the software industry for many years on different types of projects, from very small ones to very large ones. We all have a passion for what we do. We came to know each other when we worked for Rational Software (which IBM has since purchased). Gary, who started this project, worked on the first Rational Suite project and then changed jobs to work with the Rational Unified Process, or RUP, group. Liz and Chris worked with Gary on Rational Suite and Jas was a member of the RUP group.

We have seen projects succeed with RUP and other processes. We have also seen projects fail using the same processes. We wanted to tell a story of a project that we hoped would succeed. We think we did succeed. More importantly, our customer thinks we succeeded. This is our story and we hope you enjoy reading it.

About This Book

In this book we tell the story of how we worked as a team. We talk about some of the technical obstacles we faced and how we overcame them. We describe some of the patterns we encountered and how we applied them to our team, our project, and our code. We talk about how this small team developed a method for communicating effectively with each other and with our customer. We also talk about the different techniques and methods we adopted, and adapted from several different methodologies, such as RUP, eXtreme Programming (XP), and others.

This book doesn't contain all of the technical details about any specific type of software development technique. It doesn't describe a process. It isn't about writing efficient code, debugging methods, testing techniques, requirements management, or process engineering. Yet, this book touches on all these topics.

The PSP Tools Project

This book chronicles our experiences with developing a working software project, PSP Tools. The goal of PSP Tools is to provide automated support for Watts Humphrey's Personal Software Process (PSP). In version 1, we implemented timers and data gathering tools to support PSP level 1. (For more about PSP, see Appendix B.)

This book contains screen shots, tables, and other snippets showing our progress. We present our experiences, including the final software, to you "warts and all," so that you can see how we actually worked, rather than an idealized interpretation of how we wish we had worked. Our book's Web site, www.awprofessional.com/titles/0321202945, contains all our code plus several non-code artifacts, links to useful sites, and other late-breaking news. We're also happy to hear from you, either about your reactions to the book or about your own experiences developing software. Our email address is psptools@yahoo.com.

How This Book Is Organized

The book is organized as follows:

- Chapters 1 to 3 set the context of the project. We introduce our approach to software development; our views on the importance of balancing people, process, and tools; and describe the PSP Tools project.
- Chapters 4, 5, 6, 8, 10, and 11 describe the project from a team and process perspective. We discuss the different phases of RUP and what we did during each phase.
- Chapters 7 and 9 provide technical details about the code and technology we worked with. While these chapters aren't extensive expositions of the full application, they are designed to give a flavor of the code and explain some of our technical decisions. We hope they will inspire you to download the project from the book's Web site for further exploration.
- The appendixes provide background information about topics with which we assume you have some familiarity: RUP, PSP, and XP.

Who Should Read This Book?

Read this book if you are:

- A *project leader* looking for guidance about techniques for enabling a team to work more effectively, both organizationally and personally. We also discuss tools we used and their alternatives, and we provide practical advice about using a process such as RUP to help foster communication.
- An *individual practitioner (a programmer, tester, or analyst) working on a small project*. This book will help you learn ways to communicate with your team members without unreasonable overhead. It suggests tools that might be useful, and it shows how to apply a process effectively to guide and focus you without also burdening you.
- An *individual practitioner working on an open source project*. This book doesn't focus on open source development, but it does have some parallels with open source experiences. It provides an example of working on a geographically distributed team. It shows how the team accommodated its work styles and tools to account for geographical separation, sets of disparate tools, and working on separate networks.
- Other *individual practitioners* interested in small projects or agile techniques and who are curious about how they fit with other processes, including RUP.

Acknowledgments

This book would not have been possible without the contributions from many people. While we take responsibility for any errors that may appear in the text, we thank the following people who have made the book richer, more interesting, and more honest.

Gary

Thanks to the team. Each one of you has provided insight, knowledge, effort, and support throughout the project. Raj Srinivasan joined us as a tester when we were in need, and produced helpful and focused problem reports. I especially want to thank Philippe Kruchten and Per Kroll from whom I have learned the spirit of RUP and developed my style for using RUP on small projects. Many active members of the agile community have taught me things that I have tried to include in my personal process. I have especially enjoyed my interactions with Bob Martin, Ron Jeffries, and Randy Miller.

I'm sure the rest of the team joins me in thanking the reviewers who provided valuable insights. Besides Per Kroll and Philippe Kruchten, we were fortunate that James Dunion, Magnus Lyckå, Bob Martin, Dan Rawsthorne, and Chris Soskin reviewed our work. We also appreciate the support we have received from Rational Software. Finally, we thank the folks at Addison-Wesley, past and present, who have helped us bring this book together: Paul Becker, Mary O'Brien, Brenda Mulligan, Amy Fleischer, Patrick Cash-Peterson, and our talented and kind copy editor, Rebecca Greenberg. Thank you for your time and your infinite patience.

Liz

Many thanks to my manager, Karl Hakkarainen, who supported and encouraged my work on this project. Thanks also to Gary for leading the project and to all my co-authors—Chris, Jas, and Gary—for being fun to work with while getting the project done. Finally, I extend my appreciation to this book's reviewers whose perceptive, extensive, and funny comments motivated a productive endgame for this project.

Jas

Sincere thanks to Gary, Liz, and Chris (whom I have yet to meet) for your kindness, friendship, insights and support.

Chris

I wish to acknowledge Steve Zerfas, my officemate, for putting up with the conference calls that were part of the PSP Project. He also has heard me say, "On the PSP Project, we did…." more times than any human being should be expected to hear.

I wouldn't have been working on this project without the good graces of my manager, Dave Zygadlo. He was always a good sport about the "midnight project" occasionally creeping into daytime hours.

Finally, I wish to thank my wife, Carmen, for never objecting to the hours I was coding at night, the trips to visit Gary, and for always welcoming Gary into our house when he arrived for a coding session.

CHAPTER 1

In the Beginning

The phone on my desk startled me, breaking my concentration, demanding attention. "This is Gary," I mumbled into the receiver, somewhat miffed that this interruption took me away from dreaming about the "good old days" when life was simple. No, I don't mean that I walked 20 miles in tattered shoes in a foot of snow so I could get to school. I was thinking about how simple programming seemed when I started in the computer industry. I was lamenting the complexities we seem to add for little or no reason today. We do this even for the small projects to which I have always gravitated.

"Gary, this is Russell. Have I got a deal for you!" Russell and I have been friends for years. We worked together in those very same good old days that I was just dreaming about. He is now the development manager of a small company that has been around for a few years and has become successful in its niche. His company builds computer peripherals and the software that goes with them.

Somewhat leery of the "deal," and remembering some of the pranks we've played on each other over the years, I asked, "What do you have in mind?"

"Remember our conversations last year about process and tools and how they can improve a development organization? Well, we've started using the Rational Unified Process and it seems to be helping us. Now my programmers have agreed to try some of the techniques in the Personal Software Process you pointed out to me. My lead programmer looked at PSP and tried it on some very small tasks. He is on board and thinks it will help the organization be more predictable."

"That's great, Russell, but what's the deal?" He certainly had my attention—he'd just mentioned some of the topics I had been thinking about for years. And it turned out that his call hadn't interrupted my reverie after all; my daydreaming had, in fact, been a nice preamble to our conversation.

"Well," Russell continued, "now that the programmers are willing to try PSP, I don't want them to spend a lot of time recording the data and massaging it. We need tools to help automate PSP. I want you and some of your colleagues to build the tools for us."

Now I was really interested. I thought back to some of my conversations with Russell over the last year. One of my beliefs is that a small team can achieve outstanding results building software if it applies the right combination of process and tools. Programmers and other technical practitioners have typically challenged me to prove this assertion. What data did I have to support my belief?

Over the course of my career, I've seen many projects that successfully married process and tools. Most recently, I've worked with, and helped others work with, the Rational Unified Process (RUP). While many of the customers I've worked with are from large organizations, many of them are trying to apply RUP to small teams working on small projects within their organizations. They typically run into trouble applying RUP to smaller projects because they think RUP just does not apply to such projects. I am able to help them get started, but I've always wanted to show them a complete example. An example would be like the proverbial picture worth 10,000 words. (See Appendix A for a brief introduction to RUP.)

Today there are several emerging "agile" processes such as eXtreme Programming (XP) (see Appendix C), SCRUM, Dynamic System Development Method (DSDM), and Feature-Driven Development (FDD). Each of these processes has good advice for practitioners, just as RUP does. They each can point to success stories. They are designed mainly for small teams, but most of them constrain the type of team that should adopt the process (for example, some processes require the team to be co-located). See the accompanying sidebar on Agility.

The challenge for project managers and others working in software development is to decide which parts of all of the different methods work best for them. The best way to accumulate the knowledge is to have personal experience working on projects using each of the processes. Unfortunately, this is not practical. The next best option is to learn how other people have benefited, or not benefited, from applying the different practices. This is similar to programmers learning how to write better code by reading other programmers' code.

We are still missing much hard data on projects. Mostly, people are too busy building software to record the results in detail. Many measurements are done in laboratory-like conditions that don't capture the chaos of the real world. Lab results are often unrealistic because too many variables must be controlled in order to collect a large data set. Perhaps the best data we can get are in the form of well-documented examples.

Agility

Sometime before 2000, the term *agility* began to appear in software development circles. The concepts and principles of agility came from many sources, and different words were used to describe the concepts. In February 2001, the leading proponents of the methods met to discuss differences and similarities. The attendees found they had much in common.

The original Agile Alliance emerged from this meeting and produced the Agile Manifesto (see agilemanifesto.org/). There are four core values expressed in the manifesto, and emphasis is placed upon one of two properties at different ends of a conceptual spectrum. The manifesto asserts that the Alliance values:

- Individuals and interactions over processes and tools
- Working software over comprehensive documentation
- Customer collaboration over contract negotiation
- Responding to change over following a plan

The signatories to the manifesto explicitly state that they believe the items on the right have value, but not as much as those on the left. Some people miss this when they talk about agility and assert that the only things of value are those on the left. This is not the intent of the authors of the manifesto.

If you consider the four value statements as Boolean values—either you have the value or you do not—you end up with sixteen possible combinations. Agility represents one of the combinations.

You might also think of each of the value statements as representing a continuous spectrum. In this case, you have an infinite number of possible combinations. We think this is closer to reality, but it's much easier to characterize a process when you work with sixteen combinations rather than an infinite number of combinations.

Several methodologies claim to be agile. Two of the best known are eXtreme Programming and SCRUM. Our belief is that, when applied according to the spirit in which it was developed, RUP can easily be configured to both embrace the agile values and complement other Agile processes.

I knew that to create a realistic example, I would have to find both an application to build and a small group of colleagues to work on it with me. While creating the example, our group would record what we did and what we decided not to do. After we were done, we could look back and see what worked and what didn't work. An example like this would not be the perfect classroom case study, but it would be a real project, with real results and experiences. I could show it to people to demonstrate how one team applied the spirit of RUP to a small project.

I remember telling Russell about my desire to work on a sample project where we could provide the rationale for our decisions and capture real examples along with all the intermediate artifacts and the final product. And now he was calling to offer me the opportunity I was looking for.

I worried about over-committing myself. "Russell, that sounds great, but you know I have a real job that pays the bills. I'm sure you aren't going to pay my bills for me."

"I knew you were going to say that," Russell said. "That's why I'm calling you now. We aren't starting our next project for at least six months. That should allow you to work a little in your spare time, if you are willing to help your old buddy out. I want the tools ready for my team when we start the new project. It would be great to have the tools before that, so we can try them out, but you have at least six months before we need the first 'real' release." (It turns out that we actually had more than six months. This was helpful because it took us a while to get started.)

Russell continued, "I have some ideas about what the tools need to do for us. I started with the information from the PSP book and the information from the PSP supporting tools specification that was on the SEI Web site.[1] I want to add some features to support the way our team works. We don't need all of PSP implemented right away. We probably need PSP level 1 in the first release."[2]

"Russell, I'll get back to you next week and let you know. I need to talk to some colleagues here and put together a team that can get the job done for you." When I hung up, my mind raced to put together a plan that would allow me to help my friend and, at the same time, see if I was right about trying to make software development fun, like it was in the "good old days."

Meet the Team

I spent the weekend contacting some of the folks from work. I could think of many good candidates, but I knew that most of us were already over-

---

[1] The Personal Software Process (PSP) book is *A Discipline for Software Engineering* by Watts S. Humphrey. The SEI is the Software Engineering Institute at Carnegie Mellon University (see www.sei.cmu.edu/). The specification for tool support on the SEI Web site has been removed since Russell called.

[2] There are several levels of the PSP corresponding to individual engineering maturity. It is similar to the Capability Maturity Model (CMM) defined by the SEI. See Appendix B for an overview of PSP.

committed with work projects and lives outside of work. Luckily I thought of three people who were willing to work on this project. As a group, we share many interests, and we have different but complementary skills. The combination seemed ideal.

Before continuing the story, let us introduce ourselves.

Gary

I'm the originator of the project. I'm the oldest, in terms of age, years in the computer industry, and years spent in school trying to get a graduate degree. I'm also the curmudgeon of the group. In fact, my title at work is Curmudgeon, and that's the job title on my business card. According to the Merriam-Webster online dictionary, a curmudgeon is a "crusty, ill-tempered, usually old man." While I try not to be too ill-tempered, people tell me that I am crusty, and there is nothing I can do about my age.

I've worked in the computer industry for more than thirty years. I started in business systems and then went into more technical areas such as compiler and tool development. Along the way I was fortunate enough to learn a lot about software engineering at places such as the Wang Institute of Graduate Studies, one of the first schools in the country to have a program focusing specifically on software engineering.

I get great satisfaction when a program or system that I work on comes to life and is successful in the marketplace. I have always enjoyed small projects where we seem to get a lot of work done without a lot of overhead. My least enjoyable jobs have been where the project team was large or the organization had a burdensome amount of red tape, usually called *process*. When I look at the enjoyable times, I remember following a process, but one that was a help and not a hindrance. My goal for this project is to deliver high-quality software to Russell and his group. At the same time, I want to capture a real example of a small project where process and tools helped deliver the software and where we had fun working on the project.

Several years ago, I learned of Watts Humphrey's Personal Software Process. I tried it and found that it made me a better engineer, even though I only reached PSP level 1. As a result of using PSP, I was better able to predict my performance and to reduce the number of errors I produced. I readily admit that the PSP bookkeeping was difficult and time-consuming. I always wanted to build tools to make the record keeping and analysis easier.

PSP is a help to me as an individual engineer, but there are very few projects I work on by myself. There is more to building software than programming and measuring myself. When I first saw RUP, I thought it was intimidating. It covers the full set of disciplines required to produce a software product, and it consists of about two thousand Web pages. No matter how you count, that is a lot of information to absorb and put into practice.

As I got to know RUP better I realized that it could work well for small projects. In recent years, I have tried to explain to small teams how they can effectively use RUP. There is a difference, though, in telling someone how to do something and showing them. This was my opportunity to prove it.

Liz

I've been interested in software development practices for most of my twenty years in the computer industry. During my early days as a programmer, I went to school part-time to get a bachelor's degree in computer science. The combination of studying theory at night and applying it by day was powerful.

As a programmer, and later when I switched careers and became a technical writer, I've focused on programmer development environments. My emphasis has always been on making my users successful at their task. In fact, I think of my job as "helping my customers go home at night." I realize that the tools I work on are not interesting in themselves; they're valuable only if they help users do their job more effectively. As a result, I've studied user interface design and have more recently become interested in an emerging field, information architecture, which focuses on the design and presentation of large amounts of information.

Through these two decades of working in the computer industry, though, I've often wondered why we seem to make so little progress toward writing accurate, reliable software in a predictable way. We have new tools, technology, and processes, and yet most software I use seems no better than it did twenty years ago.

So, I'm especially interested in this project. Like Gary, I love the excitement of working on a small team. I have a tendency to try to bypass lots of process if I think I can get away with it. But I like the security offered by a "light-weight" process, especially if it makes sense to me. I'm hoping that the discipline we impose on ourselves during this project results in a predictable schedule, and a usable and reliable software product.

One more note: Although I have been a software engineer in the past, I have not programmed for a long time, and I don't expect to do so on this project. I do, however, plan to help design the tools environment and the user's experience, test the software, and design and write the software documentation.

Chris

When Gary told me about this project, I was immediately interested. I had never heard of PSP, but our development group codes many small projects and we needed to use RUP better. I saw this as a great chance to use PSP and RUP and integrate them into the best coding practices promoted by Steve McConnell in his book, *Code Complete: A Practical Handbook of Software Construction*. I was sold when I learned that we would be developing the system in Java. Our group at work has been coding in C++ for quite a while and is migrating to Java. Participating in two small, separate Java projects at once seemed like a great immersion strategy for me. Immersion and doing is how I learn best.

I have been developing Windows user interfaces for the last eight years. I hope to bring some of that usability knowledge to the project, but my official contribution is in development and testing of the product.

With fifteen years of development experience in C and C++ in four companies, I've seen a lot of failures in software projects and a few successes. This seems to be a common thread in stories that I hear at industry conferences and in books on software development. Maybe this project will help by facilitating a few more successes.

Jas

For me, developing software is like growing a plant. The notion is that from the germ of an idea, one can, over time, and with careful management, cultivate a well-formed functionally useful entity. My experience with software as a developer and user, however, has had me on my knees, in the dirt, and to the point of eating worms.

For a number of reasons, I think Gary's idea to use RUP on a small and useful tool development project is great. I had witnessed the RUP approach of iterative and architecturally centered development salvage a million-line project from oblivion. I was duly impressed. Later I was thrilled with the opportunity to work on developing content for RUP. When Gary approached me with this book idea, I thought "Good, let's see how we apply the ideas that we had spent the previous four years debating and writing about." In another life, I went through a CMM rating process and was intrigued by Humphrey's work on PSP. So onwards to another journey!

Russell

Our customer, Russell, worked with us throughout the project, or at least we pretended that he did. Russell is imaginary, but he is based on real people we have known. In fact, there is a real Russell, who was the starting point for the imaginary Russell. Russell provided a helpful focus for us throughout the project, and Gary "consulted" with him regularly when we had implementation questions. Using an imaginary, composite character based on real user characteristics is often referred to as working with "personas." Alan Cooper popularized this technique in his book, *The Inmates Are Running the Asylum*.

We designed Russell as an experienced project manager. We were building software, called PSP Tools, for use by software developers who work for Russell. Russell wants to help the members of his team improve their personal performance. But Russell and his team must also deliver software. Russell is willing to be a part of our team, as a customer, so that he can ensure that what we build is, in fact, what he wants and needs. He will give us freedom to work around our other jobs, but he does expect to receive valuable software at the end of the project.

Throughout our story, we present many "Russell episodes." We ask you to think of him as a real person. We did, and we feel the end result is better for his "participation."

What's Next?

Now that you have met the team, the trip from starting the project to delivering the code to our customer begins. Sit back and enjoy the ride. When you see something you like, make a note of it. Try it on your next project. If there is something you disagree with, but you have never tried it, consider giving it a try. If you have tried it and it does not work for you, that's okay. Don't use it. Use what works for you and throw out what doesn't work. That should be your motto for applying any process.

In the rest of the chapters, we will take you through our complete experience. You'll see that developing code is only part of the story. We struggled to get started and to settle into a rhythm that worked for us. We will explain our major decisions—what we did, and why we did it that way. More important, we will tell you what worked for us and what didn't.

Like any project team, we made mistakes. No one is perfect. Our goal was to learn from those mistakes so we wouldn't make them on our next project. There are enough new mistakes waiting for us.

CHAPTER 2

Using a Development Process on a Small Project

Most people intuitively know what a small project is. To paraphrase Supreme Court Justice Potter Stewart, you know a small project when you see one.[1] In this chapter, we discuss what we mean when we talk about a small project. We also describe one way to introduce a development process into a small project environment.

What Is a Small Project?

When you first consider a "small project," you might think about the number of people involved; typically, a project with fewer than ten people is said to be "small." You can also measure by the duration of the project, the amount of code produced, the amount of money spent on the project, or the complexity involved.

But we think that the key characteristics of a small project are:

- The level of formality, which usually correlates with the number of people on the project
- The complexity of the new code, which seems to correlate to the number of people involved
- The length of time you have to work on the project

For example, if you're working on a five-person team, and all team members sit in the same office, your communications need to be much less

---

[1] Associate Justice Potter Stewart said about hard-core pornography, "I know it when I see it...."

formal than if you're on a geographically distributed team of 250 people. If you're working on a simple reporting system, you need fewer formal artifacts than you do if you're working on a missile guidance system, and certainly fewer people and fewer lines of code.

There are, of course, exceptions to this general rule. Some projects with few people require high degrees of formality—think of the level of formality you'd need to develop life-support software that complies with government and industry regulations. And some large projects are run very informally.

What About Process on a Small Project?

In general, as size and complexity grow, you need to establish more *rules*. You also need to make sure that people follow those rules to ensure that you all continue working toward the same goal. You need to communicate the goal, as well as other information, clearly and consistently to every member of your team. At some point, as a project grows past being a small project, oral communication is insufficient for much of the information you need to communicate. When we talk about "rules," we're really talking about instituting a process. The process itself can range from very informal to very formal, depending on the needs of the project.

Many small projects have successfully used a process. Because we work, or have worked, for Rational, we're most familiar with RUP and our customers who use RUP. Therefore we decided to use RUP on this project.

Gary once visited a customer where he found a five-person team using RUP on a pilot project. They were really excited about it then, and as it turned out, RUP helped them deliver a successful product. The project manager actually went on vacation during delivery week with absolutely no doubts about whether the delivery would go smoothly—and the manager's confidence turned out to be well-founded. This is just one example of a small project that successfully used RUP.

Benefits of Using RUP on a Small Project

RUP can benefit small projects in several ways.

- RUP provides guidelines about engineering best practices.
- RUP helps you understand the activities, roles, and artifacts you may need on your project and when it's best to use each.

- RUP provides detailed information that helps you effectively apply techniques to your project, if they're appropriate. For example, if you're creating a design model using the Unified Modeling Language (UML), RUP can tell you which diagrams are appropriate and give guidelines about how to structure the model. It can even help you use Rational tools effectively as part of the overall process.
- RUP can help you tailor the process to address specific project issues, for example, in the area of requirements management.

Getting Started with RUP

One of the real advantages of using RUP is that it is flexible. As an example of getting started with it, say you're a project leader, and you're at the beginning of your project. You start with the most important concepts, and then add what you believe your organization needs to be successful. Gary approaches RUP by thinking about the artifacts (requirements, tests, code, and so on) that his project needs, then determining what activities to perform in order to create those artifacts. A key point to remember, though, is that the goal is to build software, not to create artifacts.

Regardless of your project's size, you need to configure RUP for your particular context. Follow the *Spirit of RUP*, as elegantly described by Per Kroll, the director of the RUP product team at IBM Rational Software,[2] in his article in *The Rational Edge*.[3] By following the spirit of RUP, especially on a small project, you will ensure that you have just the right amount of process.

Key Artifacts

Here are the basic artifacts we believe every team needs:

- A *Vision* statement. This helps the project team understand what to build and later helps them know when they're done building it.
- A *Risk List*. What are the *actual* risks you face and how will you mitigate them? When you think about risk, consider these elements of

---

[2] Rational Software was acquired by IBM Corp. in early 2003 and became a part of the IBM Software Group. We will usually say "Rational" even though some of the events described in the book occurred after the acquisition.

[3] Go to www.therationaledge.com and click on Archives.

your project: people, process, and tools. Worry about risks that are real, that have a reasonable probability of occurring. Prioritize risks based on their probability of occurring and the cost associated with them. Yes, it is possible that a member of your team will break a leg skiing and end up in the hospital for the duration of the project. If there is enough cross-knowledge on the project, the impact will be minimal, and the likelihood of such an accident is small—so don't worry too much about mitigating this risk. If you are going to worry, at least worry about things that matter. If a risk starts to look more probable as the project progresses, you can always change your risk list.

- A *Development Case*. This describes how you will adapt RUP to your needs. One important part of a development case is that it explains the responsibilities of each different role on the project. With a small team, of course, each person typically plays more than one role, so it's important to define all the responsibilities carefully.

- *Use cases*. These define a series of interactions between the system and an actor (usually a user) that yield observable results of value. When your team practices iterative development (see the sidebar on Iterative Development), use cases help ensure that you're delivering something of value with each iteration. Use cases serve as the foundation for your requirements. (You can also add nonfunctional requirements that are not based on use cases, such as requirements that focus on response time.) The use cases also serve as a basis for your test plan, your documentation plan, and so on.

  You need to decide whether to express your use cases in UML, in text, or in both. This is a cultural issue, and there's no right answer. Do what's right for your team. You might not need use cases if you were developing a compiler, for example, but we'd use them for most other projects we can imagine.

- A good set of *Tests*. If you're using RUP, then you can begin generating tests as soon as you complete your first use cases. In fact, if you write your tests first based on your requirements, and code to the tests, you can ensure that the software you produce meets your requirements.

- An *Architecture*. This may be extremely informal. Some groups release their first version without a formal architecture, then (assuming success) when they're planning the second version, they start by documenting the architecture so far and how to extend it. Other projects develop an architecture from the beginning. Whether you explicitly set aside time on your project to attend to the architecture, or let the architecture evolve, you have an architecture!

- A *Project Plan*. This should outline the iterations and schedule. Design the iterations so that you address the major risk items during the Elaboration phase (one of the four phases of RUP). This helps you reduce the probability of technical surprises or unexpected rework late in the project.[4]

- A *Glossary*. This should contain definitions to keep your team's language consistent, project-wide. If the team, including your customers and all stakeholders, are familiar with the domain and all of the terms you might use while working on the project, you might not need a written glossary.

Iterative Development

Iterative development describes an approach to developing software that characterizes most modern software development lifecycles. Until the mid-1980s, the typical approach to software development was the *waterfall* lifecycle shown in Figure 2.1. This model works well when you have complete knowledge of the problem at hand and do not experience change during the development period. In the face of the continual change that we experience today when we develop systems, the waterfall model breaks down.

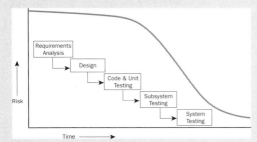

Figure 2.1 The waterfall lifecycle*

continues

---

[4] Magnus Lyckå, who was one of the reviewers of the manuscript for this book, offers a variation. He suggests that you schedule an early Elaboration phase iteration with very simple goals to help the team become accustomed to working together and to working with the process and tools for the project, then schedule the second and subsequent iterations to address the high-risk items. This approach helps teams become familiar with RUP without the added burden of addressing highly complex technical issues. This is especially useful for teams who are new to using RUP.

The waterfall lifecycle has also been shown to be ineffective at driving down risk early in the development period. This characteristic is primarily because testing does not begin until late in the project, when the cost of removing defects is much more expensive than early detection and removal.

In 1986, Barry Boehm introduced his *spiral* model of software development.† Since then, the spiral model has been adopted as the standard approach to developing software, often under different names such as evolutionary software development, or iterative development.

Figure 2.2 shows the way RUP describes iterations. With iterative development, a project is broken up into *iterations*, each of them similar to a complete mini-waterfall cycle. While each iteration may appear to be sequential, like a true mini-waterfall, the actual sequence of activities may be nonlinear. For example, you might work on requirements, then work on analysis and design, then work on requirements again, then testing, then analysis and design, as work needs to be completed.

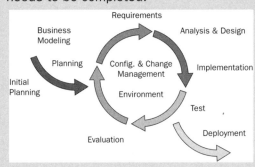

Figure 2.2 RUP iteration diagram†

Each iteration has a goal. In RUP the goal is to produce working software that provides value and can be deployed to a user. Iterations are *time-boxed*. This means that there is a specific time period in which the work is to be done.

If the work is not complete on a specific feature it must be rescheduled for a future iteration or dropped from the product. You do not extend the time frame of an iteration. The time-box feature of iterative development and the continual adjusting of the project plan for each iteration helps you address changes more effectively than with a waterfall model.

Typically, each iteration adds to the work done in previous iterations. For this reason, we say that a process like RUP is both iterative and incremental. We incrementally add to the software until we arrive at the desired product.

One reason that the iterative development model has replaced the waterfall model is that it reduces risk early. This increases the probability that either the project will succeed or you will realize early that you cannot complete the project successfully within the allocated time and budget. Figure 2.3 shows the risk profile for iterative (RUP) versus the typical waterfall risk profile.

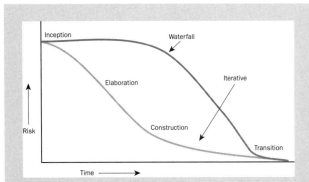

Figure 2.3 Risk profile for iterative versus. waterfall lifecycles

Adopting an iterative approach to software development does not come for free. Making the transition from waterfall to iterative development can be difficult, especially for project managers. We recommend that you read the white paper "From Waterfall to Iterative Lifecycle—A tough transition for project managers" (go to www.ibm.com/software/rational/library/whitepapers/wp-lifecycle.html and select the white paper).

Level of Formality

The artifacts can be as formal or informal as you want, depending on the needs of your business. You might write your vision on a Post-it note and the project plan on a whiteboard. You can keep your requirements on 3x5 cards. And you might have an oral agreement about your development case but not write it down.

As the complexity of a project increases (in terms of the number of people, the amount of functionality, or by any other measurement), you may find that you need to work with these and other documents more formally. RUP provides templates for the artifacts and reports. The latest release of RUP provides two sets of most templates, formal and informal. When appropriate for your team, Rational tools (as well as other vendors' tools) support the process by helping you create and manage the different artifacts.

Also, you can always mix levels of formality. For example, if you're on a three-person team developing the security system for a Web site, communications within the project can be very informal. But when it comes to communicating with other small projects that have an interface with yours, then you may need to be more formal. As a project leader, you should create your own guidelines and adapt elements of the process to meet the needs of your project.

Techniques for Involving the Team

Say you're a project leader and you've identified a process that you think will work for your team. You might start with RUP and configure it specifically for your project team. The next step is to ensure that your team members will follow the process you've configured. The challenge is to keep everyone on track. The following sections provide suggestions for helping your team work with a process such as RUP.

Schedule Workshops

We recommend that you hold a workshop to "kick-start" the project, as described in the RUP guidelines under "Development Case Workshop." This workshop is an opportunity to discuss how your team will use RUP, to show the team how to use the development environment, and to get feedback from the team about how to improve the development process. During this time your group can start gelling as a team—by working together toward a common goal.

We find it beneficial to hold workshops on an as-needed basis throughout the project. For example, during the Elaboration phase of RUP, as you work on developing the architecture, you might hold a workshop on domain analysis. Workshops can help ensure that team members are working with the same basic set of assumptions; they can also help strengthen the team-building effects of the kick-start workshop.[5]

Assign Mentors

Most people learn skills best when they learn from someone else. Since the Middle Ages, apprentices have learned valuable skills from master craftsmen. This learning model is just as valid today. Whenever we learn something new, or venture into unfamiliar territory, we are more successful when we have an experienced guide.

---

[5] See the white paper "Implementing RUP in an Organization—The Volvo IT Approach," at www.ibm.com/software/rational/library/whitepapers/rup-volvo.html.

Your small project can benefit when you engage process and technical mentors. Cultivate an informal consulting relationship with an experienced coworker, or hire a consultant who can provide expertise to your team in a particular area.

Staying on Track

Most of us have been on projects where we start with high hopes for doing things differently, then slowly revert back to the old way of working. There are a few techniques you can use to stay on track and use a process throughout a project.

One real benefit of iterative development is that you always have current data to assess how you're doing. Especially on a small project, we recommend that you schedule short, frequent iterations. RUP tells you that at the end of each iteration you need to do an assessment, even if it's very brief.

- Start with your vision. Are you still pursuing it?
- Assess what worked and what didn't.
- Ask if you have produced working software; if not, plan your next iteration to rectify the situation.
- Are there new risks or requirements, and if so, how do you mitigate or include them? What risks did you mitigate during the last iteration and what requirements did you satisfy?
- Check your project plan. Are you still on schedule? Do you need to adjust the project plan or the process to ensure that you'll deliver on time?
- And, perhaps most important, if something's not working, stop doing it!

The main idea is to continuously verify quality, both of your project and of the process you're following.

For More Information

A good starting point to help you learn more about RUP is the "Process Essentials" topic, available in RUP. If you don't have a copy of RUP, you can evaluate it online at www.ibm.com/software/awdtools/rup. Once you get going, Rational offers plenty of helpful support at the same Web site, including webinars, reading lists, and a discussion forum. So even if you're working on a small project, you still have access to a large development community[6] and many other resources.[7]

Summary

This chapter describes what we mean by a small project. But, like beauty, "small" is in the eye of the beholder. We have given you a brief overview of how to use a process, specifically RUP, on a small project.

---

[6] There is an active community of RUP practitioners on the Rational Developer Network at www.rational.net.

[7] See, for example, *The Rational Unified Process: An Introduction* by Philippe Kruchten and *The Rational Unified Process Made Easy* by Per Kroll and Philippe Kruchten.

CHAPTER 3

People, Process, and Tools

Successful software projects balance the emphasis on people, process, and tools to fit the work at hand. These are not the only characteristics that need balancing on a successful business project. You can probably think of other attributes that are important. We have found that people, process, and tools (or managing technology) are key factors in making a software project successful. How you balance them depends upon your environment and project. This is where the forces of cost, quality, schedule, market conditions, and many others come into play.

This chapter describes our philosophy about people, process, and tools on software projects. We provide specific suggestions, in the form of guidelines, to help you on your own project. We hope this chapter helps you understand where we are coming from and what we value.

Few projects have a perfect balance of people, process, and tools. Usually, one or more will be emphasized over the others, often with good reason. However, when the emphasis is too great on one of the three, project success is seriously jeopardized. We will consider what can happen when things get out of balance at the end of the chapter.

People

Let's get something clear: *Software development is intrinsically a human activity. People are the most important factor for the success of your project!* In fact, people make the difference between success and failure for most team-based endeavors.[1]

---

[1] We originally talked about people being the most important "resource" for your project. When we reviewed this chapter, Chris pointed out that speaking of people as resources takes away the real importance of people. We all agreed. Changing the names of departments from "personnel" to "human resources" has helped add to the dehumanization of the workplace.

There are many books about effective management, including books that are specific to software project management. See the Recommended Reading list at the end of the book for some of our favorites. If you are a software project manager or program manager, these books are great resources for you. We will not address management issues in detail in this book. We spend most of the chapter, however, talking about people. The rest of the book provides details about how we used process and tools on our project. Whether you are a project manager or an individual contributor on your team, you should read this section and consider how your current project team operates.

Harry and Gwen

We introduce this section on people with a short story. You may have heard about or experienced a similar situation, yourself. We assure you that this is a true story that one of our team members lived through.

People can affect a project's success. This story about two smart senior engineers on a five-person project happened a few years ago. There was a critical part of the system that needed to be written before we could move on. The first programmer, Harry,[2] took it upon himself to write this bit of code. Because Harry was the project leader he felt this was his right. Gwen, the other programmer, thought she had a better solution, but couldn't convince Harry. One day Harry wrote some code. That night Gwen checked Harry's code out and rewrote it to do things her way. The next day Harry saw the changes and changed the code back—after having some choice words with Gwen. That night Gwen changed it back to embody her solution. This pattern went on for a couple of weeks. This was bad for the project because it delayed getting some critical code complete. What was worse, was that each time Harry or Gwen changed the code, they broke the system for the rest of us on the team.

Egos and technical reputation came first for Harry and Gwen and the project and team came in a distant second. As you might expect, this project was never completed and it was cancelled without ever delivering a release to the customer. With a slight change in the personnel mix on the project and better management of the personal characteristics of the team, we might have been successful. At least we would have had a better chance.

---

[2] As you would expect, the names have been changed to protect the innocent and guilty.

It's About Communication

At Rational Software, we use the tag line "Software development is a team sport" to describe an approach to software development. As a company, we build tools to help teams. However, the key to success is recognizing that it takes a team to build software, not just a group of individuals with different agendas and different values. Getting the people on your team to work effectively is mainly an issue of establishing good communication between the team members. This leads to trust and respect, which are also necessary people ingredients.

Once two or more people are working on the same project, you have to deal with people issues. Great managers are the ones who enable the people on their team to work most effectively together. Being a great manager is hard work. It's more than just giving your team pizza and great T-shirts—it's helping them to respect each other's abilities, work off each other's strengths, and help them work effectively as a team.

There are some simple people-oriented project guidelines we recommend you consider for any project, especially small projects. The guidelines might seem most appropriate for project leaders to consider, but all team members should look at their project team in light of the guidelines. The guidelines may seem obvious, but we feel they are worth stating explicitly. The following sections present each of these guidelines.

Team Composition

How do you put together a good team? You want people who can get the job done. Does this mean that you need a team of superstars? Not necessarily. The sports world provides examples of teams that have the highest payrolls, the biggest stars, yet end up out of the running for the championship year after year. And, of course, the coach is the one who gets the blame.

Some teams don't have any proven superstars but somehow manage to put things together and come in first. This admittedly doesn't happen often, but we love the stories where the underdog overcomes the odds to become the champion. These stories inspire us and enable us to dream of glory.

The great teams—the really great teams—are more than a collection of superstars. The great teams have a mix of superstars, talented rookies, role players, great coaches, and a great organization. Furthermore, the winning teams keep improving. Teams in business, especially software development teams, are no different than sports teams. Let's look at what we mean.

In software we have superstars. Some of them are great coders who can just sit down, start typing, and produce perfect code. Some are great architects who can understand complex problems and design the right solution. Some are great testers who are able to quickly identify defects and help the developers build better software. Each makes a contribution to the success of the team.

Our experience has been that a software team composed of just superstars cannot be effective for an extended period. There are several reasons for this. The main reason is that egos clash. Regardless of how well people "play well together," there are times when they don't. The Harry and Gwen story earlier in this chapter is an example of this. Experienced programmers have earned their reputations for technical acumen. They like to be the ones doing the hard technical work. They want to have others do the *uninteresting* work.

Product Guideline 1 deals with the composition of the team. It is no easy task to put together a team that has the right mix of skills and experience. As the team forms, make sure that:

- There are senior team members who can lead and teach the more junior members
- The senior members have experience with projects similar to your current project
- The team possesses technical expertise for the most critical aspects of the project

Project Guideline 1 Get the right mix of people on your project

Staff your project with people possessing different skills and experience so they complement each other.

For example, consider beginning a project to develop a new Web site for a company. The site must present the company's catalog to the customer and allow the customer to place orders and enter credit card information. Would you trust this project to a group of engineers just out of school? They may know the basic technologies involved, but they would lack experience in the business aspects of your system. You would make sure that you had one or more experienced engineers familiar with your company's business systems and data assets. You would support them with other, possibly junior, engineers who could provide general programming and technology capabilities.

Provide a Learning Environment

Software developers get excited about solving problems and learning new things. One of the worst fates for a programmer is to implement a system where there are no challenges to meet or new technologies to learn. Maintaining a technical edge is the same as maintaining a competitive edge for software developers.

The most desirable companies for programmers to work in are those that provide a learning environment. Programmers will often join a company because they are promised the opportunity to work on something new. You can make part of your project a learning environment by making sure that everyone on the project has the opportunity to learn. Experienced developers can learn new technologies. Less experienced team members can learn about how software is built from the more senior people.

Project Guideline 2 addresses learning on the project. We recommend that you ensure that there is something to be learned by every member of the team. When you consider the possibilities for learning, it can help you decide which people are most appropriate for your team.

Project Guideline 2 Provide a learning environment

Make sure that every team member has the opportunity to learn on the project. Things to learn can be technical, organizational, or managerial.

There is a hidden trap in this guideline. Sometimes people get so involved in learning that they fail to deliver the product. Project managers need to be alert for the team members who spend all their time learning and forget the primary goal, to deliver working software to the customer.

There are times when a team member does not want to learn anything new on a project. That person has different motivations for joining the team. Project managers should not force everyone to have a learning goal. In general, a project team where people want to learn is more robust than one where people are just trying to get through the project, but there are times when we all want to just do a good job and send the learning parts of our brains on vacation.

Trust, the Glue for the Team

In his excellent book *The Phoenix Agenda*, John Whiteside presents a twelve-step approach to empowering teams. The most important one, in our opinion, is to generate trust. A lack of trust between team members can quickly cause a project to deteriorate to the point where there is little chance for success. The example cited earlier about Harry and Gwen is an example of a lack of trust. Neither engineer trusted the other one.

People often misunderstand what we mean when we talk about trust. Trusting your teammates doesn't mean, for example, that you give a new programmer a critical task, requiring technical skills the programmer doesn't have, and trust they will get the job done correctly. It means that you trust programmers to tell you they are not qualified, or they need help. It means that when they accept tasks, you trust them to do the job right. You trust that they will ask for help if they need it. You trust that the team will provide help when asked (see Project Guideline 3).

Project Guideline 3 Generate trust

Generate trust on the team. Help the team members trust and respect each other.

One of the best stories about trust and teams was told by Susan Butcher, the four-time winner of the Iditarod dog sled race in Alaska. Susan was the guest speaker at the 2001 Rational Users Conference in Denver, Colorado. Susan told of the time when she was out on the trail over a frozen body of water. Her lead dog kept turning to the right, off the trail. She kept demanding that the dog come back on course. This went on for some time until Susan just gave up and let the dog lead. Almost as soon as the dog took the team off the course, the ground where they were heading collapsed into the freezing water—certain death for Susan and the dogs. The words of wisdom Susan gave to us about this incident were: "Sometimes you have to lead, and sometimes you have to let the team lead." What she was really saying is that you have to trust your team.

Disagree Constructively

Some people think that a high-powered team is one that doesn't disagree. Experience has shown us that this is false. Most of the effective teams we have worked with have had significant disagreements between team members about how things should be done. This has, in fact, led to solutions better than any individual had proposed. Healthy disagreement provides the team with a synergy.

Disagreement is good. But when disagreement gets personal and is allowed to get out of hand, it destroys a team. Effective teams are those that have established a way for team members to disagree constructively. They provide a forum for dialog and exploration as well as a way of resolving disagreements. If team members trust each other, disagreements are easy to deal with. People express their opinions, you trust that they are concerned about the team's success, and you work on an agreement. Even if you can't work out an agreement, you have a way of deciding on a course of action and everyone gets behind it.

Project Guideline 4 Allow disagreement

Allow team members to disagree. Provide a way to resolve disagreements.

We can look once again at sports teams for examples of how to handle disagreements. Each team member has some ideas about how best to win. In basketball, the high-scoring shooters want an offensive game where they will pump in basket after basket, not worrying about the other team's score. They are confident that they can meet any challenge by shooting more. This "run-and-gun" style can be effective in many, but not all, cases. There are times when you need to control the ball and slow down the game's pace. You then give the ball to your best ball handlers and put in defensive players who can steal the ball from the opponent and block shots. The coach has the responsibility for assembling a game plan and motivating the team to execute to the plan. The coach also has the responsibility to alter the plan when opportunities arise, or when the existing plan is not working. If a player notices that a defenseman on the other team is playing in a way that allows him to shoot for easy baskets, he tells the coach. The coach makes the final decision. If the situation requires more immediate attention, the team communicates on the floor and adjusts as necessary. Often, a team captain makes the final decision.

The Power of Requests

What motivates you more: when someone *demands* or *requests* something from you? Everyone prefers a request to an order. Requests are the topic of Project Guideline 5.

Project Guideline 5 Ask, don't demand

Make requests, not demands.

When we say that you should make a request, we don't just mean any type of request. Make a *well-formed request*. Gary learned about well-formed requests from John Whiteside when John was Gary's mentor on a project at Digital Equipment Corporation. John calls this type of request a *precision request* in his book referenced earlier in this chapter.[3]

A well-formed request has certain attributes:

- It says *what* needs to be done.
- It says *when* it needs to be completed.
- It says *who* should perform the work.
- When appropriate, it states *where* the work will be performed.

Let's look at two examples of requests. Which is well-formed, and which isn't?

1. "Liz, will you review the Vision document and produce the first draft of the Glossary based upon the domain-specific words in the Vision? Can you send me the draft of the Glossary by noon on Friday?"
2. "Gary, we need to see some results on the architecture soon."

Clearly, the first request is well-formed. It identifies what needs to be done, a Glossary based upon the Vision document. It states who should do the work, Liz. It states when the work is needed, noon on Friday.

The second request is very vague. The only attribute of the well-formed request that it contains is the name of the person. It does not qualify as a well-formed request at all.

There is one other type of statement you should avoid when you are making well-formed requests. Consider the following statement: "John, have your code ready to go by Monday morning."

This is not a request at all. It is a demand. Demands are ineffective. They often have the opposite effect of what you want. People do not react well to demands. They feel they have no control of their own destiny. Remember one thing about well-formed requests: *It isn't a request if they can't say no!* This is important. If you make a demand, you do not allow the other person to give an honest response if they cannot meet the demand. If you follow Project Guideline 3, Generate Trust, you need to trust your teammates to tell you honestly whether they can do the work you request. If they cannot meet your requirements, then you can negotiate a different delivery time, ask someone else, or decide upon a different set of deliver-

---

[3] Chapter 6 in *The Phoenix Agenda.*

ables. If you do not have an environment of trust on your team, these negotiations are impossible.

There is another benefit of using requests. By accepting a request, a person takes ownership. If someone asks you to do something, and you agree, you have a feeling of responsibility to deliver what you promised. If someone tells you that you must deliver something by a certain time, you have no ownership. The task may be impossible. You may have already scheduled a day out with your family. There are any number of reasons why the work may not be done by the specified time. If you are not able to freely agree to deliver the work, you will not take ownership. If you are free to accept or reject the work, you will do whatever it takes to meet your commitments.

It takes practice to make well-formed requests. This is time well spent. Whiteside presents data showing that the number of requests satisfied is approximately constant. This means that a team with an 80% completion rate satisfies 8 in a week that 10 well-formed requests are made, and 40 in a week that 50 are made. This leads to the obvious conclusion that Whiteside states: "To increase your productivity, increase the number of precision [well-formed] requests you make." Clearly, there is a limit to the amount of work that any team can do. When you use well-formed requests, you tend to converge on an optimal request rate for the team.

If you decide to use well-formed requests on your team, set up a simple system to track requests. You can do this with a simple text file or spreadsheet. You might try something more sophisticated, but it is not necessary. Tracking requests allows you to see how well the team is doing with well-formed requests and if there are any problems on the team.

Recognize Achievement

How do you feel when someone says "Thank you?" Most people feel good, as long as they feel the thanks are sincere. They know they have been recognized for something they said or did for someone. One of the most important skills you can develop as a member of a team is the skill of saying thanks; or to put it differently, the skill of recognizing achievement. This is Project Guideline 6.

Project Guideline 6 Recognize achievement

Recognize achievement—sincerely and often.

Sometimes you need to be creative about recognizing achievements. Some people are uncomfortable when they are publicly recognized. You may have to deliver the kudos privately. That's okay. The important thing is that you say thanks and you are sincere about it.

You can overdo recognition. When recognition is not sincere, or it is done habitually for day-to-day accomplishments, it loses its effect. You should say thanks for people doing their job well, even if there are no outstanding achievements or hurdles they have overcome. Just don't do it every day. If you went to work every day and your manager greeted you with "Thank you for the work you did yesterday," how long would it mean something to you? Not very long.

Another example of overdoing recognition can be seen in many companies today. These companies provide different "benefits" to their employees, for example, free lunches, popcorn, pizza, soft drinks, T-shirts, and so on. People feel good about getting these things. However, "familiarity breeds contempt." After a while, people begin to comment that their favorite drink isn't provided, the T-shirts are the wrong color, and a litany of other complaints. What was originally meant to be a way of saying thank you becomes an annoyance.

Be careful and creative about how you thank your team. Make it special. One of the simplest, most special ways is a heartfelt "Thank you."

Process

In some respects, this whole book is about process. In this section we present the process-oriented project guidelines that do not require much contextual information. Those that do require more context in their description are presented in subsequent chapters.

The Prime Directive

Let's start with our fundamental guideline about process, also known as the *prime directive* of process. This guideline is shown in Project Guideline 7.

Project Guideline 7 The prime directive of process

Only do those activities and produce those artifacts that directly lead to delivering value to your customers and stakeholders.

The real trick for the software engineer is to determine which tasks are really necessary. We have a simple way of determining this. We ask the following question about everything we do: *If we don't do this activity, or produce this artifact, will anything bad happen?* If the answer is "no," we don't do it. That seems simple enough. But you have to be brutally honest. It is very easy to fool yourself and tell yourself what you want to hear, rather than recognize reality. You can convince yourself that nothing bad will happen if you don't document your design anywhere except in the code, or if you don't address architecture issues early. You may be able to produce software that works today, but is not sustainable for future releases.

Bob Martin, from ObjectMentor, has a slightly different way of stating the question above. He says that you shouldn't produce the artifact or perform the activity unless something *really* bad would happen.[4] We can quibble over how bad something has to be before you do something, but you get the basic idea.

Address Risk

Another way of thinking about the prime directive leads to the next project guideline. If we're going to do something to avoid a bad outcome, then what we're really saying is that we need to make sure that our process addresses risks. Think about it. Why would you do something if it doesn't address a real risk that you face? Now, not every action you take on a project is directly related to a known risk. That is okay. There are things that you have to do in order to ship your product. If you don't do them, then a potential risk may become an actual risk. See Project Guideline 8.

Project Guideline 8 Have a risk-driven process

Make sure you perform activities and produce artifacts that reduce risk.

Don't Reinvent the Wheel

So, we have to make sure that we do the right things, and don't do unnecessary things. That's great to say, but what things should we consider? If you have ever tried to establish a process in an organization, you know what a difficult job it can be. You may have a wealth of software engineering experience, but it takes time and a lot of effort to put together a coherent,

---

[4] Bob stated this in a posting to the XP mailing list in 2001.

consistent description of what needs to be done. What should you do? Project Guideline 9 will tell you.

Project Guideline 9 Start with a proven foundation

Base your process on proven practices, techniques, and principles.

We're concerned about software reuse. We should also be concerned about process reuse. Starting from scratch and reinventing the wheel, so to speak, is never cost-effective for the following reasons:

- There is too much information to wade through and absorb.
- Once you do uncover the information, you still have to decide how the different techniques work together and how to present the information in a coherent, consistent way.
- Not every idea or technique really works for your project.

Let's consider each of these separately, starting with the amount of information. There is so much information about technology, process, management, and so on, that it is impossible for any one person to keep up with it. Gary reads the mailing lists for XP and agile modeling. About two hundred mail messages appear each day on just these two lists. There is a lot of noise on these lists, but if you want to understand what is happening in the communities, you need to read them. There are usually one or two messages that really have something interesting each day. Add in the articles and books on XP and agile software development and it's hard to keep up with just one area, let alone multiple areas of interest. Now assume that most people have "real jobs," such as developing software. By using a process framework or reusing a process instance, we let others mine the field and distill the interesting information for us.

Next we have the problem of producing a process that is well-defined, consistent, and understandable. What format should you use to present the process to your team or organization? Are there examples and instructions? Is each person on the team forced to look at all of the details, even if they already know what they're doing? There are many more questions and issues to address. When you start from scratch, you have to think of everything. This situation is similar to the software developer who can either develop a set of cooperating classes from scratch or use an object-oriented framework. Smart developers will always start with an existing set of classes and customize them to fit the situation when they can. Smart process engineers (people who configure processes for development groups) start with an existing process and customize it for their needs.

Finally, when you have a set of practices, principles, artifacts, and so on, you need to decide when they apply. We often talk about using best practices. What does that really mean? Are there universal best practices that apply in every situation? Perhaps; however, many, if not most, apply best in certain cases and you need to know when to use the practices rather than blindly follow them all the time. This means that you need to configure your process for specific contexts and projects.

Make Your Process Yours

Tailoring your process means more than just selecting a subset of the practices, activities, and artifacts that might be specified by your process. It means you should select those that fit together in a consistent way. It also means that you should feel free to modify them by removing things that are not necessary (the prime directive) and adding things when necessary. This brings us to Project Guideline 10 and its corollaries.

Project Guideline 10 Configure your process

Tailor your process for every project. Don't assume that every aspect of a process will automatically apply to your situation.

Accepting process guidance blindly is a sure recipe for disaster. You might think of this in the context of a road map. If you want to travel from Lexington, Massachusetts to Cupertino, California, there are thousands of possible routes. You need to decide which is appropriate for your needs. If you go to some of the Web sites that provide driving instructions, you are offered a choice of routes, depending upon your ultimate goal.[5] Similarly, you may choose one process if you are under extreme time pressure because of a rapidly changing market, and another if you have significant overhead imposed on you by customer requirements and regulations.

One thing we have found in our experience is that people tend to configure too much into their process. They think that if they are not sure whether they need something, they should do it. We recommend doing just the opposite, as stated in Corollary 10.1. If you omit something you really

---

[5] The MapQuest site, www.mapquest.com, asks if you want the shortest distance or shortest time route. You could consider many other parameters, based on the sights you want to see or other interests.

do need, it usually shows up quickly and you can add it. If you add something you don't need, you often will just keep doing it and never remove it from your process because you don't know that it isn't necessary. The choice is yours, but we prefer doing less rather than more. We find that the risk is usually small.

Corollary 10.1 When in doubt, leave it out

When configuring your process, if you are not sure whether to do something, don't do it. If you later discover that you need it, you can add it.

How do you decide if you are doing something that's unnecessary or not doing something you need? If you are doing something that is not necessary, you can usually spot it during your iteration reviews. During these reviews you not only assess the work done and progress made, but you evaluate the effectiveness of your process. Some symptoms that can indicate useless work are:

- You produce an artifact that no one looked at.
- You did something that did not lead to delivering software or reducing risks.

Always ask yourself, why am I doing this and who cares?

Configuring your process is more than just deciding what to do, when to do it, and how to do it. It also requires you to decide how formal you need to be. Once you decide that you need to perform an activity or produce an artifact, you should decide how rigorous you have to be. Should you use a tool? Will the artifact need to be modified continually? Who will look at what you produce? These are some of the questions you have to ask yourself to determine how formal you need to be. We find that small teams are usually less formal than large teams. This makes sense because there are fewer lines of communication that need to be established, and those that do exist are usually quite informal—possibly one team member leaning over into another team member's work area and asking a question. Whatever you decide, don't be formal for the sake of formality. Don't lose sight of your primary purpose, to deliver working software to your customer.

How do you configure your process? There are several approaches. We find the easiest is to configure it by focusing on artifacts. That is, we decide what artifacts are necessary to help us reduce risks and deliver the software, then base our process on producing the artifacts. If we know what we have to produce, we can figure out how to produce it. In the next chapter you will see how we configured the process for the PSP Tools project.

Corollary 10.2 Take an artifact-centric approach to process configuration

Configure your process based upon the artifacts you need to produce. Once you know which artifacts you need to produce, you can then figure out how to produce them.

We will see more process-oriented project guidelines in later chapters. The ones presented here are the ones that are most important to understand.

Use Your Brain

We have one final process-oriented guideline, Project Guideline 11. It almost seems silly to mention it, but we have often been surprised by the number of projects that forget to apply it.

Project Guideline 11 Apply common sense liberally

Having a process to guide you in your development efforts does *not* absolve you from using your brain and applying common sense.

People, especially software engineers, are paradoxical. On one hand, they want to be creative and hate being told what to do. On the other hand, they want someone to show them how to do things. The key is that they want to be given the freedom to do things they like to do—the creative activities that challenge their intellect. They are looking for step-by-step instructions for the simple, repetitive pieces they would rather not have to think about. They also want to make sure that the creative parts dominate their time and that they don't spend one second more than necessary on the drudgery.

If you don't consider Project Guideline 11 when configuring your process, you may end up with a process that is too heavy: process for the sake of process. Instead, you want your process to account for the skills of the people on your team, along with your project and organization needs.

When using a process, even if it has been configured, you still need to apply common sense. When the process prescribes something that does not support the people or the ultimate goal, you have the responsibility to question the process element and ensure that it adds value to the project.

Tools

Tools are perhaps the most interesting of the three keys to project success. Adopting tools requires a commitment of time to learn and use them. Sometimes we use tools ineffectively by trying to do too much, or not looking at whether the benefits outweigh the costs. Finally, there are times when we just use the wrong tool. There is an old saying that goes, "If you only have a hammer, everything looks like a nail." We have seen software projects work with only "hammers" and try to build skyscrapers. It just does not work.

We have just a few tool-oriented project guidelines. They are variations on a theme. The first one, Project Guideline 12, sets tools in context of the three keys to successful projects.

Project Guideline 12 Make sure tools are worth the effort

Ensure that your tools support the process and people on your project.

Tools are not an end in themselves. By definition, a tool is something that helps you do your job better. It is good to have a well-stocked tool set and be able to select the ones that will support your efforts. However, you need to make sure that you don't get too wrapped up in using tools for their own sake. We could restate Project Guideline 12 this way: *Just because you have a tool doesn't mean you have to use it.* This doesn't apply only to software tools and software projects. If you look around, you find that we are a society of gadget users. Look in your garage, attic, closets, and other hiding places and you'll find lots of gadgets that are not used, or were used for a while with poor results. Don't fall into this trap with the tool usage on your project.

The advice from Project Guideline 12 leads us to consider a corollary: Just because you are going to use a tool does not mean you have to use all of its features. We believe that there are few, if any, cases where all of the features of the tools we have are really necessary. Sometimes it takes much more effort to use the feature than to adopt another, simpler technique, or skip it all together.

Corollary 12.1 Use only the tool features you need

Use only the features of your tools that make you more efficient.

Our next project guideline (Project Guideline 13) relates tool usage to people (see Project Guideline 2, Provide a Learning Environment). Learning to use the tools properly is important, but is often ignored. We assume that the team members will learn how to use the available tools as they need them. This may be so, but they need to have instruction. The instruction can take many forms: classroom, mentor, books, or online training. Just don't neglect the real time spent in this effort and think it won't affect your project.

Project Guideline 13 Provide time to learn tool usage

Provide instruction on tool usage and schedule the learning time into your project.

The systems we attempt to build today are complex. We need tools that address the complexity and help us understand it. Few programmers today use just a text editor and a compiler. They use integrated development environments (IDEs) that help them construct the components for their application programs. Testers use tools that automate much of the repetitive work of testing, freeing up time to concentrate on developing effective tests.

Using tools effectively takes time. While most people can learn to use a tool with some degree of proficiency by themselves, it is almost always worth the cost to provide some help to them in their learning effort. We only need look around to see the difference in the productivity between *power users* of the tools and those who have only a basic knowledge.

Building Your Own Tools

When should you build your own tools? Should you build your own tools? Project Guideline 14 states our feelings on the subject.

Project Guideline 14 Build tools when necessary

Build your own tools when necessary, but make sure that the benefits outweigh the cost.

Every project needs to customize its process. Projects also have to customize the tools in their environment. In many cases, the tools available to you are excellent, general-purpose tools, but your team has special needs that the tools were not designed to address. If there is a good business case, try to extend existing tools, or build your own tools to do the job. Before you embark on a tool-building subproject, however, we suggest you consider the following:

- Do you really need the features that a special tool will deliver? Is the added functionality something that is nice to have or is it the case that you cannot successfully complete your project without the new features?
- Can you afford the cost of building your own tool and maintaining it? If you build a tool, you must maintain it, just as with any other software product. Project teams and organizations frequently fall into the trap of deciding to build a new tool without considering the full cost associated with it. As soon as you begin to use an internally developed tool, you establish a reliance on that tool. Any problems with the tool must be addressed, and you will probably find that you want to make extensions. Tool-smithing can become a full-time job for one or more team members. This may be all right, but you must be willing to accept the costs.
- Do you need to build a new tool or can you extend an existing one? Many software development tools are designed to be extended. The tool vendors provide an API and documentation for this purpose. This may be your best choice when you decide that you need new tool capabilities for your project.

What Can Go Wrong?

Well-run projects balance people, process, and tools (as well as other things). You don't achieve a good balance by focusing one-third of the emphasis on each area, as shown in Figure 3.1. Instead, consider the parallels to a well-balanced diet. You need to eat some amount of protein, fiber, and fat every day. The exact amount varies with each person. Similarly, the right balance of people, process, and tools varies with each project.

True balance occurs when you emphasize the factors in a way that helps you deliver value to your customer in a predictable, timely manner. Your project team members are working hard, enjoying their work, and gaining

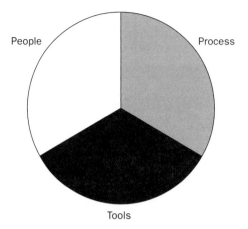

Figure 3.1 A misinformed view of balance

knowledge and satisfaction. You have a process that helps each person know their responsibilities, provides help when needed, and is minimal, or the right size, for the team and the project. You have tools that support the process and the people to help them get their job done.

What can go wrong? Usually you can either pay too much attention to one of the items or too little. In both cases, you will find that your team is not making progress. Whenever this happens, you and the team must determine the reasons for lack of progress and address them as soon as possible. This is where a project manager earns his or her salary. A good manager can accurately measure progress and determine if the team is performing at a less than optimal rate. The manager can then work with the team to communicate the problems and establish a plan for getting back on track.

In the remainder of the book you will find some problems the PSP Tools team encountered and things we tried to correct our problems. Some of them worked. Some did not. They will all give you something to think about and determine if they are appropriate for your team.

Summary

People, process, and tools are important to the success of projects in almost every industry. In the technological industries we work in, they are perhaps even more critical. Yet, intentionally or not, we tend to ignore these issues and assume that they will take care of themselves. We hope that any problems will go away and we take no action to resolve them. The time you spend attending to people issues is time well spent. Of course, you also need to provide just enough process to help your team members rather than hinder them, and equip them with the right tools for the job.

Many people have written about people issues and team development. In this chapter we have provided some of our favorite guidelines. They are not exhaustive, but they can't be. People, process, and tools change continually and, to be good managers and team members, we have to change as well.

CHAPTER 4

Getting Started: The Project Members Become a Team

RUP describes phases of a project, starting with Inception. Perhaps because we were starting a brand new project, we found that we needed some time to come together as a team before we started the Inception phase.

This chapter presents those things we did to address the teamwork aspects of the project. It would be nice if teams were given time to learn how to work well together, and then continue as a team from project to project. Unfortunately, this rarely happens. Our professions experience high turnover in personnel. Organizations often compensate for the possible loss of people by using a matrix-style organization where people are *farmed out* to projects as needed. As a result, the people who work on projects never seem to be able to put down roots and get to know their teammates.

Coalescing into a Team

Gary often repeats a saying commonly used when talking about organizations—that teams "form, storm, and perform." We did assemble the team fairly quickly. But forming the team took a while.

Forming the Team

While working at Rational, we'd all become acquainted with each other. Some of us had worked on small, informal projects together or talked to each other in the course of our work.[1] Some of us worked together on major

---

[1] Chris and Jas, for example, have talked on the phone, but have yet to meet face-to-face.

projects. But we had never before *all* worked together as part of a team; it turned out that getting to know each other—our work styles, strengths, and weaknesses—took some time, more than we had anticipated.

We originally thought we could settle into working as a team fairly quickly; we just needed to decide what to build, assign tasks to team members, and wait for the software to be written. This plan seemed straightforward enough—what barriers could we possibly run into?

When we tried to work together, we found that we really didn't know each other very well at all. We thought we understood each other's abilities and strengths. We assumed that we were each making the same commitment to the project and that we would each be able to act on our commitment. It was not long before reality hit.

We all had good intentions. But we also each had a full-time job and other responsibilities in our lives. In this respect, the PSP Tools project was similar to an open-source project: We were a team of volunteers and we had to respect each other's ability to offer different amounts of time to the project.

When we describe our project, people say that it sounds like an open-source project. In some ways it is, but we think there are many active projects in large organizations that are similar to ours. In fact, there are probably more than you might realize. We see project teams forming and re-forming all the time. The practice of "borrowing" someone from another project for a short time is not uncommon. Managers frequently ask their developers to fit in some small project along with larger projects. All too often, this is done with the suggestion that the smaller project "should not take away from the rest of the work the employees are responsible for."[2]

We also had to learn to say no in response to requests. There were times when it was important to decline a request because we lacked expertise or time. In the beginning of the project, though, we each resisted saying no because we felt that we'd be letting the team down.

Of course, by accepting an assignment that we were unable to complete, we still let the team down. The team members were not disciplined about demanding results by the promised dates. As a result, we had to become more effective managers of our individual schedules and workload.

As an experiment, we tried working with well-formed requests[3] (described in Chapter 3), but soon dropped the practice. Looking back, we were all just as eager to accept well-formed requests as we were to accept-

---

[2] Sometimes a team is formed for a short project that is critical to the organization. These teams are called by different names, such as SWAT teams or Tiger teams, to indicate their urgency.

casual requests, with the same frustrating results. Using well-formed requests did not make it any easier to decline tasks.[4]

We went into the project believing that we could all get started working right away. In retrospect, we realize that we should have held one or two daylong meetings to initiate the project. We were able to justify omitting the meetings because we were a small team. But by trying to save time in the beginning, we ultimately wasted a lot of time in the long run.

On our next project, we'd organize meetings to discuss the nature of the work and the organization of the team, including the following topics:

- *Introductions:* Who are you? What is your background? What are your interests at work? What are you good at doing? What new area do you want experience in?
- *Moving toward a vision:* What are the goals of the project? Can the team produce at least a draft of the team's goals? Who volunteers to polish the draft and send it out for review?
- *Matching the team to the project:* What roles are needed on the project? By examining experience and interest, who is best suited for each role? What are the first deliverables for each role, and when are they due?
- *Establishing ownership of work:* How will we assign work? How does a team member either accept the work or decline it? How do team members support each other?
- *Next steps:* Review deliverables; decide how the team will communicate; schedule next meeting.

Dealing with Employer and Geographical Distribution

On a typical small team, the team members work for the same company in the same location. This was not the case for us. Most of us work in the same town, but one team member lives 3,000 miles away. Another team member travels frequently, and the three of us who do work in the same town work in different buildings that are walking distance apart.

Originally, we all worked for the same company. Part way through the project, Jas left the company but wanted to continue working on this project. We had anticipated several risks but did not anticipate this one.

---

[3] Well-formed requests are also called "precision requests." They are a way for a team to communicate precisely what needs to be done, who should do it, and by when. When they are used effectively, they can help a team work in a highly productive manner.

[4] See *The Phoenix Agenda* by John Whiteside.

One effect of this change was that we lost our comfortable way of communicating. We no longer all shared the same intranet, so we could no longer share calendars, use a common network location for files, or even have access to the same set of tools. We had to find other ways of staying in touch. And we needed to figure out how to continue to work together effectively.

Throughout the rest of the book we return to the topic of our geographical distribution and the problems it caused. This practice is becoming increasingly common, and with more companies encouraging telecommuting and distributed teams, it is sometimes even normal. The main difference between a distributed project in one company and our project is our lack of a common intranet for sharing our tools and data. Solutions exist today that address the intranet problems, and we mention some of them in the final chapter. Although the common intranet problem can be addressed by technology, most other problems are not solved by technology. They are solved by team members who pay attention to people issues.

Most team members enjoy the informality of being able to communicate by talking over the cubicle wall. We had to teach ourselves to pick up the phone and call each other, to have regular meetings, and to use tools to facilitate our communication.

Losing a Member

Throughout most of the book, we talk about our four-member team. For a while, though, we had a fifth member, whom we will call "John." John left the team partway through the project, shortly after we began our Inception phase. What happened? We discuss it here, rather than in the Inception chapter, because it is a team issue, not an Inception topic.

Gary asked John to be the architect. Although John had limited experience in that area, and felt that he wasn't ready for the role, he reluctantly agreed to give it a try. Gary attempted to coach John by urging him to design the simplest thing that could work while keeping in mind future changes, but John seemed to be bogged down by "analysis paralysis." It appeared to the rest of us that John was afraid to do something wrong, so it was very hard for him to get started.

Because none of us were database experts, we identified the design of the database as one of our most important technology risks. We were all concerned about our ability to create a working database application. John had the most experience with databases and he wanted to tackle our database design. This was a good fit for the architect.

During this period we entered into a long cycle. John had difficulty getting started with the database design. He felt that he would fail us if he could not deliver. Most likely, his fears caused him to work slowly and carefully. The team wanted to support John and not pressure him. Our lack of feedback caused John to spend even more time perfecting the design. In retrospect, Gary says that he should have taken more of a leadership role to support John, and also to establish stronger expectations.

And then, John's commitments in his work and his personal life interfered with his ability to deliver work to this project. At the same time, it was hard for John to leave this project because he felt that we were depending on him and he would be letting us down.

We learned and re-learned many lessons on this most human part of the project.

- *Listen to the team.* When a team member says they're not ready to step into a particular role, the manager needs to make a delicate decision—does the team member need to be encouraged to grow into the role or should the manager listen to the team member's response? For a long time, we erred by wishing John into this role, and perhaps by not coaching him enough. In the future, we'll know to be better listeners in this area, and perhaps to be better coaches, but we don't know if we'll have a happier outcome. This is one of the hardest areas of management.
- *Become an effective coach.* During our regular meetings, we'd ask John to produce a piece of work, and he'd say that he'd try. Because we were asking him to work in unfamiliar territory, we could have helped him succeed by having another team member work with him outside of the team meetings. In retrospect, we wish we had tried to use a pairing technique.[5] John worked and lived near other team members, so it would have been relatively easy to arrange times to work with him. In a similar technique, a coach works with a team member to produce a piece of the work together. Together, they create and review the work and produce another piece. By breaking the work down into smaller pieces, the coach can help the learner understand what it means to do this new work—in this case, to create an

---

[5] In a pairing technique, two teammates work together on a specific activity. The most popular pairing method today is *pair programming*, described in Appendix C.

architecture. For more about this, see the sidebar discussion of Couch, Mentor, Guru, Companion.

- *Allow a team member to leave gracefully.* John felt torn between commitments he had made to the team and his personal commitments. We believed John when he said he would perform project tasks, and we held up the project waiting for him to deliver the work. It was hard for him to say no, and it was hard for him to come to the conclusion that he needed to step away from the project in order for us to make progress. We could have helped more by intervening earlier, instead of relying on him to resign; we should have made this a team decision rather than placing the onus solely on John.

Coach, Mentor, Guru, Companion

We feel it is important to have one or more people who act in an advisory role to the team. These people are known by different names, such as coach or mentor, but they all serve the same purpose—to help the team function better as a team. Regardless of what you call these people, we recommend that you identify them and enlist them to help your team as early as possible.

We prefer the term *companion* to describe these people. Many spiritual traditions have the notion of a companion. This is a person who walks with you on part of your journey. The companion has been on this path and knows some of the pitfalls and stopping points along the way. Every path is different, but many are similar. The companion walks with you as long as your paths converge. At some point, your paths diverge and you bid farewell to each other.

The companion on a software development project serves a similar purpose to a spiritual companion. The companion has participated on projects in the same domain, technology sphere, or other area that is common to yours. The companion has learned some of the pitfalls and obstacles you will most likely encounter. The companion can talk about the experiences and relate them to what your team will experience.

The purpose of the companion is not to tell you how to do your job. It is likely that when you expect the companion to give you an answer, no answer is forthcoming. The purpose of the companion is to help you find your own answers and take charge of your own destiny. This is the only way your team can grow and develop its own unique culture.

Who Are Companions?

Companions can come from anywhere. You might discover an excellent companion who is already a member of your team. In organizations where work occurs simultaneously on multiple projects, you might enlist someone from another team. Or, consider hiring a consultant to help your team. We think the best consultants help your team grow and then leave, as compared to consultants who join a team, become the all-knowing oracle, and then perpetuate their own role from project to project.

Wherever you find them, companions need to gain the team's trust. The team must feel comfortable going to the companion with any type of problem and the companion must be a good listener. The companion shares his or her experiences, relating them to the team's current context, and the team takes the experiences and applies them as they see fit.

Look for people you can employ as companions for your team. Engage them to walk with your team on part of the journey that you call your project. Use them as sounding boards and learn from their experiences. When the time is right, thank them for joining you and wish them well as your paths diverge. When you have had a companion, you will look back on the experience and realize that the time spent with him or her was invaluable to your growth as an individual or as a team.

Writing the Development Case

In the Rational Unified Process, a *Development Case* is a description of how you will customize the process for your project. Even on this small, fairly well-defined project, we immediately decided that we wanted to use RUP to help guide us and keep us on track. But we were not interested in process for its own sake.

We started from the premise of Gary's Prime Directive: "Only do those activities and produce those artifacts that directly lead to delivering value to your customers and stakeholders." Another way to think about this directive is to ask "If I don't perform a particular process step, will anything bad happen?" (Read the "Process" section in Chapter 3.) It turned out that we didn't eliminate many RUP steps, but we took a much more informal approach than a larger project might have. For example, instead of creating formal artifacts, we had discussions or wrote informal documents.

As a small team, we were also interested in techniques from the agile community. So Gary and Chris did some pair programming when it was appropriate, and some test-first development (see Appendix C and the sidebar on Agility in Chapter 1), and were pleased with the results. We'll talk more about these points in a later chapter.

We wrote a brief development case using the RUP template. Our development case is available on the project Web site. It is longer than we would like. Most of the length is due to the RUP template. The first five-and-a-half pages contain introductory material and descriptions of how to read the rest of the document. Our team did not need this information, but we recognize that this part of the document can help someone new to the project, or any interested person, understand the purpose and format of the document.

We want to be clear that this is the way *we* decided to document our development case. You can choose to document, or not document, the parts of your development artifacts in whatever way is useful to your team. RUP provides templates that serve as examples and as possible starting points. You must decide what is right for your team.

The next sections describe the key features of our development case.

Conventions Used in the Development Case

Each project team tailors a development case for their project, even if there is a common development case for the larger organization. The Development Case template contains a section that lets you describe how you tailored the Development Case and identify the conventions you used to represent your process.

We focused on artifacts rather than activities; therefore, the main descriptive vehicle in our development case is a table that describes each artifact. Figure 4.1 shows its format.

We created one artifact table for each RUP discipline we planned on using. RUP provides guidance for what to put into the table, but we chose our own style. So, in our Development Case, we described our conventions. These are shown in Table 4.1.

For each discipline, we included placeholders for notes and other issues in the artifact table. The real content that describes our planned process takes up about three pages in the Development Case document. Most of

Artifacts	How to use				Review details	Tools used	Responsible
	Inception	Elaboration	Construction	Transition			

Figure 4.1 Format for the artifact table in the Development Case

Table 4.1 Artifact table explanations

Column Name	Purpose	Contents/Comments
Artifact	The name of the artifact.	A reference to the artifact in RUP, or to a local artifact defined as part of the development case.
How to use	Describe how the artifact is used across the lifecycle.	Decide for each phase whether the artifact is produced or modified significantly. The possible values of this field are: C—create in the phase. M—modify in the phase. Blank—not used or not changed in this phase.
Review details	Define the review level, and review procedures to be applied to the artifact.	Formal—reviewed and signed off by the customer or relevant stakeholders. Informal—reviewed by one or more team members. No sign off required. Blank—no review required.
Tools used	Definition of the tool (or tools), used to produce the artifact.	References to the details of the tools used to develop and maintain the artifact.
Responsible	The role responsible for the artifact.	Describe which role, for example, Project Manager or Developer, is responsible for ensuring that the artifact is completed.

this space is occupied by tables like Figure 4.2, which shows our planned requirements artifacts.

Role Map

Every project distributes responsibilities to team members differently. Few projects have a direct one-to-one mapping between roles described in RUP and actual people and jobs. Therefore, it is important to be clear about what each person is responsible for. On small projects, this is critical because there is a lower threshold to tolerate duplication of effort.

Artifacts	How to use				Review details	Tools used	Responsible
	Inception	Elaboration	Construction	Transition			
Supplementary Specification	C	M			Formal	ReqPro & MS Word	System Analyst
Use-Case Model	C	M			Formal	ReqPro, Rose & MS Word	System Analyst
User-Interface Prototype		C					User-Interface Designer
Vision	C	M			Formal	ReqPro & MS Word	System Analyst

Figure 4.2 Planned requirements artifacts

We recommend that every Development Case have a role map. Table 4.2 shows our initial role map. We simply took the different "Responsible" roles from the discipline artifact tables in the Development Case and created a row in the table for each one. Then we ensured that at least one person on the team was assigned to that set of responsibilities.

Table 4.2 Role map from the Development Case

	Liz	Chris	Jas	Gary
System Analyst			X	
User-Interface Designer		X		
Data Designer				X
Software Architect				X
Integrator				X
Implementer		X		X

Table 4.2 Role map from the Development Case

	Liz	Chris	Jas	Gary
Test Designer		X	X	X
Tester	X	X	X	X
Deployment Manager				X
Technical Writer	X			
Configuration Manager				X
Project Manager				X
Process Engineer				X
Tool Specialist	X	X	X	X

This role map provided an initial guess about how the project would proceed. It helped us ensure that every responsibility was covered and it helped us decide whether anyone was overcommitted.

Artifacts in Our Development Case

You may wonder which artifacts we originally thought we would need to produce for our project. We identified over twenty that we thought would be helpful. We did not create all of them. As we progressed, we found that some of our early assumptions were wrong. Rather than create something just because we planned to do it, we chose to do the right thing and create only those artifacts that were truly helpful.

If you download the material from the book's Web site, you can compare our original Development Case to the following list of those artifacts that we actually produced.

- Vision
- Risk list
- Use-case model
- Design model
- Build
- Component

- Test plan
- Test case
- Test results
- Product (the complete system as it is delivered to the customer)
- Release notes
- End-user support materials
- Iteration plan
- Iteration assessment
- Project plan
- Development case
- Programming guidelines
- Tools

You would probably produce all these artifacts for any project you undertake. You might not produce volumes of paper, diagrams, or data, but you would produce the artifacts in some form. In some cases, there may be existing artifacts that you can just reuse, for example, Tools or Programming guidelines.

Importance of the Development Case

Some people think the Development Case is an important artifact in RUP and others think it should just be part of the project plan. Our thoughts on the Development Case are somewhere in between.

We believe that the Development Case is necessary. Team members need to understand their responsibilities. They need to know what they are expected to produce, what artifacts will be available for their use, and the form of the artifacts. The real question is how much time and effort you should spend creating and maintaining the Development Case.

Our advice is simple. If you have a small team, especially one that has worked together before and has a shared understanding of the process, then the Development Case can be an oral artifact. That is, it can be communicated to the team via discussions. The further you stray from a small, familiar team—whether in terms of size of the team or team members' lack of familiarity with each other or the common process—the more you need to write your Development Case and keep it up to date.

We probably did not have to write down our Development Case. The hour or so that it took was not totally lost, though. It gave our team a good topic of conversation for early meetings.

Reporting on Our Progress

To get a flavor for the PSP, Gary asked each of us to track our time spent on the project in 15-minute increments. We each used Microsoft Word or Excel to keep a diary of our activities. We dutifully recorded meeting time, design time, development time, and so on. This was tedious, and it didn't last long because we found the effort of recording how we were spending our time to be more than we were willing to do. But it did help us understand why it was important to build the tools to assist users with capturing the relevant information.

Gary had been using PSP for a while. Even though he didn't record overhead time, such as time spent in meetings, he did keep track of his development effort. At first, he recorded his time and defects in a spreadsheet. By our second Construction iteration, the tool was stable enough that Gary could use the tool we were building, so he became our first Beta tester.

On all but the smallest of projects, we recommend using specialized tools like a project planner (for example, Microsoft Project), and a change request management tool (for example, Rational ClearQuest). We have used these tools successfully on larger projects. But on this project, we used Groove to keep track of our engineering backlog and defects; for these two items, we created a new Groove discussion tab. This was sufficient, but even on our small project, it became difficult to find information.

Groove

Groove is a collaborative workspace product that helps geographically distributed teams collaborate effectively. When we began the project for this book, Groove was a new product. It consisted of a workspace where we could store files, a calendar, and tools such as an outliner tool and a discussion tool where we could create discussion items and reply to them. Today, Groove includes tools to help with project management and meeting management. Other tools are available as plug-ins from Groove partners.

Groove ships in several editions. The Preview edition is free for personal use and free for a 90-day evaluation for businesses. The Standard edition and the Professional edition are available for purchase. The Preview edition limits the number of workspaces and meetings you can work with. The Standard edition The Professional edition gives you access to all Groove features.

continues

When we talk about a collaborative workspace, we mean a repository that is available to the whole team, regardless of where the team members are located. Additionally, the workspace provides tools that let you perform certain tasks effectively. Groove works as follows:

- Each team member downloads the Groove software and creates an account.
- One team member creates a *project*. A project is a workspace that can have any number of members. The creator or another workspace member with privileges can invite other members to join.
- When you accept the invitation, the workspace is copied from the computer of the person who invited you to your computer, through the Groove server.
- When you create a new file in your workspace, usually by dragging a file into the workspace, or by adding an item to a tool such as a discussion tool, the information is transmitted to the Groove server. If you are not online at the time, it will be transmitted the next time you start the Groove product when you are online.
- The Groove server transmits the new information to everyone on the project. When everyone has the file, it is removed from the Groove server.
- When changes are made to files or any type of item, a similar process occurs. If there are conflicts (for example, two people change the same file), Groove notifies you and copies both files to your workspace.

Groove became our most-used tool for this project. Especially in the beginning, when it was newly released, it didn't always work flawlessly. As Groove matured, it became more robust and indispensable to the team.

Some of our team members have used only the Preview version while others have purchased licenses for the Standard version. The cost is, in our opinion, quite reasonable for what you get. To learn more, visit the Groove Web site: www.groove.net.

We used a stylized way of entering the information. Each headline for a change request had the following format:

```
[status] (priority for defects) Description (assigned) [resolution]
```

The "status" was simply *** (three asterisks) for open defects or engineering tasks; we removed the asterisks when the task was complete. We had a simple Priority scheme for defects:

- P1—Showstopper, can't continue testing.
- P2—Fix as soon as possible, but testing can continue or the customer can still use the product.
- P3—Fix as time permits.

When team members started working on an item, they put their initials after the description, and when the item was resolved, they inserted the build or resolution status. This allowed us to sort the items based on open/close status, and print out reports as needed. Simple, but effective. Figure 4.3 shows a portion of the Defects tab in the Groove workspace.

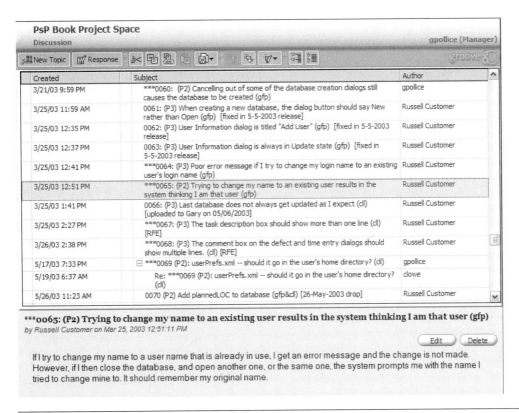

Figure 4.3 Defect tracking with Groove

Creating an Iteration Plan for Inception

RUP is a process that is based on iterative development. If you are not working iteratively, you are not really using RUP.[6] Before each iteration you create an Iteration Plan. The plan does not have to be very detailed, nor does it even need to be a written plan, but it must be one that can be communicated to all members of the team and to all stakeholders.

As our project progressed and we got into the rhythm of regular iterations, we became less worried about creating written plans. In the beginning, though, for the Inception phase, we felt the need to write out the Iteration Plan.

We began with the RUP Iteration Plan template and tailored it to our needs. The plan has these sections:

- *Scope and Objectives.* An overview paragraph for the plan.
- *Plan.* The list of items we expect to complete during the iteration.
- *Resources.* The resources—people, tools, and any other type of resource—we think we'll need in order to complete the planned items.
- *Use Cases.* The use cases or scenarios that we expect to complete for the iteration.
- *Evaluation Criteria.* A list of items we will use to assess the success of the iteration and to determine whether we're ready to start the next iteration.

Figure 4.4 illustrates the Plan section of our Inception Iteration Plan. We used a simple tabular list for our plan.

On a more complex project, we would use a project-planning tool such as Microsoft Project.[7]

RUP 2003 provides help for small, informal projects by including a separate set of informal templates. The informal Iteration Plan template is even simpler than the one we used (see Figure 4.5). You can see how easy it is to plan an iteration. If you communicate regularly with your team, you may even decide not to produce a written plan. If you do create a written plan, using the informal template does not impose any significant overhead.

---

[6] Some people argue that you can consider a project using a waterfall process as a project with a single iteration. We don't think this is worth arguing. You can choose to accept this view, but we think that multiple iterations deliver the best results.

[7] If you use Microsoft Project 2002, RUP provides a compatible project-planning guide that guides you through building a project plan based on RUP activities and artifacts (available on the Rational Developer Network).

Artifact	Due	Responsible	Comment
Initial project plan	10/11/2002	Gary	Through Elaboration, reviewed and agreed upon
Vision and product feature requirements	10/13/2002	Jas, Gary	Reviewed
Supplementary requirements	10/13/2002	Jas	Deferred until needed
Tools environment	10/15/2002		
Clear Case	10/12/2002	Gary, Liz	VOBs
Test environment		Chris	Not completed
Requirements		Jas	Deferred
Project Web site		Gary	Deferred
Initial use-case model	10/15/2002	Jas	Actors and use cases with brief descriptions
Initial risk list	10/15/2002	Gary	Reviewed and understood
Test plan	10/15/2002	Chris	Draft reviewed and agreed upon
Elaboration Iteration Plan	10/15/2002	Gary	Reviewed and agreed upon

Figure 4.4 Planned items for the Inception phase

<Project Name>
Iteration Plan

1. Key Milestones

Milestone	Date
Iteration Start	
Iteration Stop	

2. Iteration Objectives

[Objectives may include creating or refining specific artifacts, addressing risks, or implementing specific requirements, or performing supporting tasks. Some example objectives are listed below.]

Objective/Task	Assigned to
Implement Use Case: Register for Course, Basic flow, Alternative 1, Alternate 2	Fred
Complete Vision	Jill
Detail UC3: Publish Calendar	John
Test all developed requirements	Lance
Create plan for next iteration	Jill
...	...

Figure 4.5 RUP 2003 Iteration Plan template

Summary

On this project, our team understood what we needed to build and we were eager to get started. But it took much longer than we'd predicted before we were a productive team. If we had the project to do over again, we'd spend more time in the beginning focused on the people issues. We'd make it easier for the team to coalesce by launching the project in a more formal way—by holding meetings—instead of expecting things to just "work out." Our experience indicates that spending time in the beginning of the project to create the team will save you time later.

In parallel with attending to the team issues, you need to prepare for the work ahead. Create simple plans that communicate your intentions. Remember: At this stage of the project *all* plans you produce are best guesses rather than accurate statements. Don't spend a lot of time on details; most details will probably change later.

Finally, select your initial process. As with your other plans, this is a best-guess process. It too will change. Most project teams put too much effort into their initial plans; remember that your initial attempt does not have to convey all the details. However, when you've assembled your plans, make sure you communicate them to the whole team and that the team members agree to work with the plans and process you devise.

CHAPTER 5

Inception: We Start to Make Progress

During the Inception phase,[1] you figure out what you need to build, who wants it, and whether they're willing to pay for it. In more concrete terms, you create a vision and business case for the project. We have heard that in Inception you go "a mile wide, and an inch deep." You also need to get agreement from all stakeholders about what you will build. Some of the activities you might undertake during inception are:

- Create a Vision that establishes goals and non-goals.
- Write a first draft of the project's use cases and prioritize them.
- Establish a high-level project schedule.
- Identify risks, and, just as important, figure out how you will address the risks should they occur.
- Establish a development environment (select, install, and configure tools).

During the Inception phase, you do not solve all of the problems that you anticipate. Instead, you want to get a feel for the work ahead by creating a general roadmap. Think about taking a road trip, for example, from Boston, Massachusetts to Vancouver, British Columbia. When you start to plan the trip, you may not need to know the exact route you will travel, but you know the general direction and the places you plan to visit along the way. You might also know how much time you have for the trip. Inception is like this. You want to go broad and not deep. This chapter describes the route we took through our Inception phase.

---

[1] RUP divides a project into four phases. If you are unfamiliar with them, see Appendix A for an overview.

The Vision: Setting Our Goals

A key artifact for the Inception phase is the Vision.[2] The Vision can be represented as a formal document kept under version control or informally—as simple as a Post-it note stuck to a wall. The purpose of the Vision is to get everyone *on board* for the project, headed in the same direction. Vision is a powerful thing. In their book *Software for Your Head*, Jim and Michele McCarthy identify Shared Vision as a key pattern for high-performance teams.

Determining what to build was relatively easy for us because Watts Humphrey had written a high-level specification, or at least a high-level problem and solution statement, in *A Discipline for Software Engineering*. Gary had used the practice for years. Russell knew about PSP from Gary and wanted to use it. So we started the project with an understanding of what to build and needed only to establish boundaries on how much we would build. Throughout the project, Russell helped us identify the feature set and manage changes to it.

Discovering the Extent of the Project: What to Build and What Not to Build

When we started the project, we knew that we wanted to automate the data gathering and reporting for Personal Software Process (PSP) level 1 to help software engineers improve their craft. Our goal was to build a tool that could measure and record planned and actual time spent on specific tasks. This tool would allow a software engineer to compare the estimate against the reality. We also wanted to capture information about defects—where in the process they were introduced and where they were discovered and addressed. We identified the types of data we wanted to capture and report on by selecting tables from Appendix C in Humphrey's book. (For more about PSP, see Appendix B in this book.) Russell also had ideas about what we should build, based upon the needs of his team.

Because we had a solid understanding of what we wanted to build, writing the Vision was a quick exercise. We started with the RUP Vision template and used the document to define the scope of the project. The Vision included what we planned to build (and why). When we released the first

---

[2] The template for the Vision includes more than just a Vision statement. It also includes descriptions of the high-level features of the product. So, when we talk about the Vision artifact, we mean both the Vision statement and a statement of features.

version of our product, we reviewed what we originally thought we would build and compared it to what we actually did build. As we plan each new release, we will use the Vision as our starting point. This doesn't mean that the Vision is static throughout the project. Like most artifacts in a usable process, the Vision is a living artifact that you should change and update when necessary.

On other projects, creating a vision can be more difficult as stakeholders struggle to capture the essence of a large and complex project. However, it is essential to do this work before implementation starts. The Vision is a focusing artifact. It provides the general direction for the team throughout the project. Whenever you are unsure about whether to add a feature or change the way the system might work, the Vision can act as the compass that points you in the right direction. When teams can't agree on the project's scope early, they waste time later by implementing unnecessary features or forgetting to implement necessary ones.

The Vision template contains two small paragraphs, in tabular form, that help focus the team on what they are building and why. Following the format helped us get to the core of our vision quickly, without writing a lot of ambiguous or confusing prose. In our Vision, these paragraphs are part of Section 2, Positioning. The first paragraph is a Problem statement. Figure 5.1 shows the problem statement from our Vision. By filling in the

The problem of	developing software in a predictable and reliable manner
affects	the management of software projects. Specifically, developers are not able to predict reliably how long it takes them to perform development tasks with acceptable quality, which makes it impossible to effectively plan a project;
the impact of which is	users and managers are never sure whether the produced software will meet its requirements, whether the software will be error-ridden, and whether the software will be delivered on time.
A successful solution would be	for developers to become more self-aware of what they do (i.e., the process they follow), how they spend their time, and the kinds of defects they find in their work. Through this awareness, developers would become better estimators.

Figure 5.1 Problem statement from our Vision

For	software development teams
who	need to better understand how and when defects are introduced into their products,
PSP Tools is a	performance metrics gathering and reporting tool
that	helps developers gather and analyze software development metrics.
Unlike	the alternative of failing to gather the data or trying to track it manually,
our product	helps you gather data unobtrusively and provides objective feedback that allows you to improve your individual and team performance.

Figure 5.2 Product Position statement

right column, you describe the problem, who it affects, how it affects them, and what type of solution would ease the pain.

The second paragraph in the Positioning section of the Vision is the Product Position statement. If you could develop software that would solve the problem described in the Problem statement, the Product Position statement describes who would buy it and what would make it unique. The Product Position statement spurs you to focus on your audience early in the process. Figure 5.2 is the Product Position statement from our Vision.

The benefit of following the format of the Product Position statement is that it helps you succinctly capture both the problem you are trying to solve and the value and unique qualities of your solution. The Problem statement and Product Position statement help you communicate your vision to the whole team, including your stakeholders.

Who Are Our Stakeholders?

A Vision is incomplete without an understanding of who the stakeholders are. Who are you building this software for? Who will use it? Why do they need it? The answers to these questions help you identify the right set of people to work with when you gather requirements for the software. Stakeholders are not only customers. They are anyone who has an interest, usually a vested interest, in the success of the project.

The Positioning section identifies customers, or users, of our product. The users are not the only stakeholders, or even necessarily the most important stakeholders. When you build a product for a paying customer, that person is often the most important stakeholder. In many companies, the IT department manager or the manager who orders the software might be the most important stakeholder, sometimes called the *gold owner*.

Whether you have a single gold owner or many paying customers, you will almost always have several stakeholders. It is important to identify who they all are, and how important their input is to the success of your project.

Identifying Stakeholders

On our project, our customer, Russell, found us. There were other stakeholders for this project. Each of us was a stakeholder. We wanted the project to succeed. We wanted to write this story about how we built the software, and to learn some things along the way. For professionals in our industry, the possibility of learning can be a huge incentive. Later in the project, other stakeholders appeared in the form of potential Beta testers.

Writing a Brochure

Jas and Liz decided to write a brochure that captured the essence of what we thought we were building. The brochure was conceived as a marketing version of our Vision. We wrote it by imagining that the implementation was finished and that we were about to ship our product. For Jas and Liz, who were not planning to write code, this exercise helped them understand the Vision. Figure 5.3 shows the brochure.

Gary was initially skeptical about the value of the brochure. He questioned why team members were wasting valuable time on this activity. In hindsight, and with uncharacteristic humility, he wishes we had spent even more time on the brochure. Compared to the Vision document, a brochure provides an easier way to communicate the essence of the product to those not directly involved with building the software. If you are on a project building a new software product, perhaps in a start-up company, the brochure is a great way to convey your vision to potential investors and talent you hope to attract.

In retrospect, Gary says that he should have insisted that we work on the brochure until it captured the spirit of the project. He also should have asked that we each keep the brochure on the wall near our work area. The brochure was, in fact, the high-level vision statement for PSP Tools.

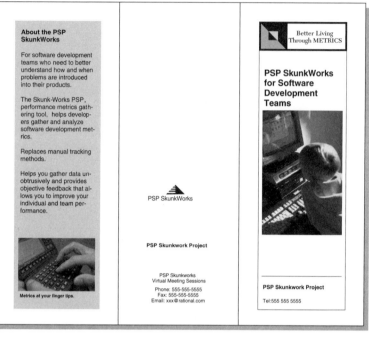

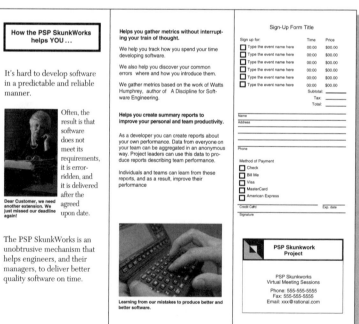

Figure 5.3 Our PSP Tools brochure

Specifying the Features

Even with the brochure, it was important to specify the product's features in the Vision so that we could refer back to them later and use them when analyzing our solution for completeness. We identified features by holding discussions with Russell, reading the PSP documentation, and hosting brainstorming sessions with the development team. Some of the features we identified were not implemented in the first release, but they were certainly part of our shared vision.

Working with and Managing Requirements

We had to decide how to manage our requirements. Was it okay to keep the Microsoft Word documents up-to-date and circulate them, or did we need a more formal system? Specifically, should we use a requirements management tool? Initially, we used Microsoft Word to maintain our requirements. This solution worked for our small project when we were getting started. Especially in the beginning of our small project, with just a single customer, we did not feel that the benefits of using a requirements management system outweighed the very slight overhead such a system would incur.

As the complexity of your project grows, it is useful to capture your requirements in a database where you can assign attributes to each requirement and adjust the attributes as the requirements change. We recommend that project teams establish a way to manage their requirements so that it is easy to find the current status and expectations for any release.

On our project, we eventually decided to switch to a requirements management tool for these reasons:

- We wanted to illustrate the use of a requirements management tool for our readers.
- We wanted to know how much benefit we would get out of keeping traceability information in such a tool.

As you continue reading, keep in mind that the requirements management tool provided much more power for our project than we actually needed. On the other hand, the overhead was so minimal that the tool required us to perform a negligible amount of additional work.

After we wrote the Vision and requirements documents, we imported them directly into Rational RequisitePro (an easy step), identified the specific requirements, and identified the attributes we cared about. RequisitePro is an easy-to-use tool that stores requirements in a database. You can either populate the database directly by entering specific requirements, or, more popularly, by capturing requirements from Microsoft Word documents. It also allows you to attach attributes to your requirements, such as priority, status, and so on. RUP provides guidance on how to manage requirements and determine which attributes are appropriate. Apply common sense to this exercise and make sure that each attribute serves a purpose.

We actually imported our documents into RequisitePro after the Inception phase was over. We waited until the rate of change on the requirements stabilized. Figure 5.4 shows how our Vision document looked after we

5.1 [FEA1 <u>User-definable Activities</u>]

Engineers following any software development process typically have their tasks broken down into different activities such as Planning, Requirements, Coding, Testing, and so on. PSP Tools allows activities to be defined by the user for any given project.

5.2 [FEA2 <u>Record Personal Engineering Statistics</u>]

The Software Engineer is able to record raw data on time spent on a task, size estimates and actual measurement, and defects (predicted and actual). Each of these is described in the following subsections. The basic statistics entered are those entered in the PSP forms (references are from *A Discipline of Software Engineering*, Appendix C):

- PSP 1 Project Plan Summary (Table C34)
- Defect Type Standard (Table C20)
- Defect Recording Log (Table C18)
- Time Recording Log (Table C16)
- Size Estimating Template (Table C39)

5.21 [FEA2.1 <u>Time</u>

<u>Time is recorded in minutes. The user either uses a timer device provided by PSP Tools or uses some other timing device. If the PSP Tools timer device is used, the actual time spent on a task may be automatically added to an open project (see the section on projects). If the time is not automatically entered into a project the user may manually enter the time into a project's data set.</u>

<u>A time entry consists of the following information:</u>

- <u>Date (optional)</u>
- <u>Time spent</u>
- <u>Activity</u>
- <u>Comment (optional)</u>

<u>The activity is one of a set of activities for the project. The user has the ability to define the activities on a project. See section 5.1 for a description of this feature.</u>]

Figure 5.4 Excerpt from our Vision document in RequisitePro

imported it into a RequisitePro project. The text of each feature is high-lighted with a double underline. Notice that we have chosen to identify each feature requirement with the prefix "FEA." When we identified each requirement, we included the requirement's defining text as part of the requirement. This lets us quickly use the features of RequisitePro to iden-tify when requirements change and what other requirements may be affected by such a change.

Using RequisitePro, you can create different views on your require-ments. One of the views is the attribute matrix view. This view provides a concise way of seeing the attributes associated with the specific require-ments, and the value assigned to each attribute. Figure 5.5 is a snapshot of the attribute matrix for our Vision document, taken after we first imported it into RequisitePro and identified the specific requirements.The attribute values shown in Figure 5.5 have the default settings that we assigned to each attribute. Later views show how we modified the values after we eval-uated each requirement.

Requirements:	Priority	Status	Difficulty	Assigned To	Iteration
▶ FEA1: User-definable Activities	Medium	Proposed	Medium		
⊟ FEA2: Record Personal Engineering Statistics	Medium	Proposed	Medium		
FEA2.1: Record time	Medium	Proposed	Medium		
FEA2.2: Record Defects	Medium	Proposed	Medium		
⊟ FEA2.3: Record Size Data	Medium	Proposed	Medium		
FEA2.3.1: Java source counter	Medium	Proposed	Medium		
FEA2.3.2: Count C source lines	Medium	Proposed	Medium		
FEA2.3.3: Count C++ source lines	Medium	Proposed	Medium		
⊟ FEA3: Create a project	Medium	Proposed	Medium		
FEA3.1: Personal Project	Medium	Proposed	Medium		
FEA3.2: Create a team project	Medium	Proposed	Medium		
FEA3.3: Synchronized projects	Medium	Proposed	Medium		
⊟ FEA4: Reporting	Medium	Proposed	Medium		
FEA4.1: Personal reports	Medium	Proposed	Medium		
FEA4.2: Team reports	Medium	Proposed	Medium		
⊟ FEA5: Data access and viewing	Medium	Proposed	Medium		
FEA5.1: Data access security	Medium	Proposed	Medium		
FEA5.2: Project-averaged data	Medium	Proposed	Medium		
FEA5.3: Developer control of access	Medium	Proposed	Medium		
FEA5.4: Anonymous public data	Medium	Proposed	Medium		
FEA6: Statistical analyses	Medium	Proposed	Medium		
⊟ FEA7: PSP Level 1	Medium	Proposed	Medium		
FEA7.1: PSP Level 1 template	Medium	Proposed	Medium		
FEA8: Online Help	Medium	Proposed	Medium		
FEA9: No documentation needed	Medium	Proposed	Medium		

Figure 5.5 Attribute matrix for the PSP Tools features

Defining the Initial Use Cases

As soon as we agreed on the project's vision, we started work on the initial use cases. A *use case* describes important interactions between an actor (usually a person) and the software system. These interactions must yield a result of value to the actor.[3]

Figure 5.6 shows a use-case diagram for the initial set of use cases we identified for PSP Tools. Each use case is represented by an oval. The associated actor is represented as a stick figure.

To create the use case descriptions, we again used a RUP template. We identified the use cases that we thought we'd need to implement, and assigned a title, determined the actor, and wrote a brief description. That's all we needed to do for the Inception phase.[4] As the project progressed, we added information including the basic flow of events (the part that

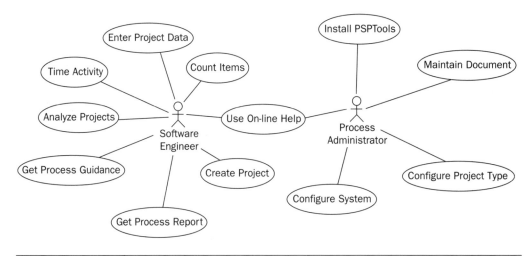

Figure 5.6 Initial use-case diagram

---

[3] RUP contains a couple of definitions of use case in its glossary. One that we prefer is: "A description of system behavior, in terms of sequences of actions. A use case should yield an observable result of value to an actor. A use case contains all flows of events related to producing the 'observable result of value,' including alternate and exception flows."

[4] Depending on the size and needs of your project, you may decide to detail a small number of use cases or scenarios during the Inception phase. On our small project, we placed a higher priority on getting out of Inception quickly and we chose to delve into the details more thoroughly during the Elaboration phase.

describes how the actor and the system interact) and the alternate flows of events (what happens if there's an error or the actor makes a nondefault choice).

We started with many more use cases than we ended up with. During the project we realized that we could collapse multiple use cases into one, and we scoped others out of the project. We reorganized use cases primarily during the Inception phase, while we continued to eliminate features throughout the project. When we exited the Inception phase, our set of use cases was much smaller, as shown in Figure 5.7. We added an actor, Any User, and shortened the names of the two actors we had. We clarified the names of the use cases and collapsed some. For example, we merged the use cases for "Count Items" and "Time Activity" into "Record Personal Engineering Statistics" as alternate flows of events. We also added details such as entering defect information to the use case, something we overlooked in our first attempt at creating a use case model (see the sidebar on Models).

This illustration is an example of a high-level view of the system. You can work with it before you commit your engineers to writing code. As you can see, this system view does not provide much detail, but it does help you understand the relationship between actors and use cases.

The use cases helped us use a common language to more clearly establish the boundaries and different areas of the system. The use cases also

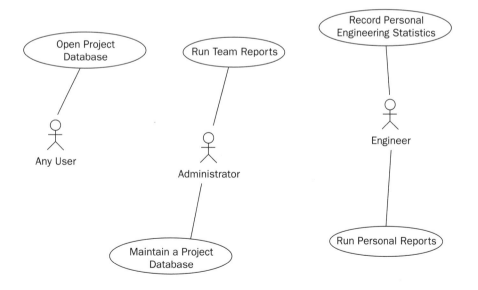

Figure 5.7 Use cases at the end of the Inception phase

Models

A *model* is simply an abstraction of one or more aspects of a system. It is a "complete description of a system from a particular perspective ('complete' meaning you don't need any additional information to understand the system from that perspective)."* One model is never sufficient to describe all aspects of a system.

Models may take different forms. You can use diagrams, physical models (often used in engineering disciplines other than software), mathematical formulae, and so on. In software, UML diagrams may be used to construct one or more models of the system under construction. The source code and its organization form another type of model, called the *implementation model*. RUP describes several types of models and provides guidance on how to construct and represent them.

Models are constructed for a purpose. One purpose is to improve communication and clarity about a system. Another purpose is to actually generate the system, or parts of it, from a model. This practice is known as Model-Driven Development (MDD). There are many ongoing MDD research and development initiatives in industry and academia. One Web site that contains links to MDD material is http://www.iturls.com/English/SoftwareEngineering/SE_mod1.asp.

* RUP 2003 Glossary.

helped all team members understand what work they needed to accomplish, including in the areas of design, implementation, testing, and documentation. It is easy for technical and nontechnical project members to understand use cases. They provide a *communication glue* for the team. By starting with just the names of the use cases and the actors for the use cases, we were able to quickly define what we thought PSP Tools would look like in its first release.

The surprise is that by implementing just a few use cases, we were able to produce a useful, working piece of software. We did not need to write pages and pages of specifications to capture every last detail, though for more complex projects or for risky parts of the implementation, a specification is necessary. Instead, the use cases serve as a way of saying, "When the system is successfully implemented, the user will be able to perform Task X by following these high-level steps."

But notice that implementing each use case implies that the system meets certain prerequisites. For example, "Open Project Database" implies that someone has designed the database, and that there's a way to create and populate a database. None of these steps have real value to the user; hence, they are not separate use cases. They are just stepping-stones to the parts of the system that the user cares about—automating PSP.

Two points are worth mentioning about our use cases. First, we ended up with very few use cases to describe our system. Often people think they need dozens, if not hundreds, of use cases to describe a system. They end up creating many small scenarios or descriptions of behavior that are not, in themselves, a complete sequence of steps that deliver value. Even very large systems can be described by a couple of dozen use cases, each of them richly described with many alternate flows of events.

The second point, and one that we will mention several times while telling the rest of our story, is that we did not become prisoners to format or formality when we created our use cases. Our goal was to build software and we were determined to use the process and its artifacts to help us communicate, not hinder, progress. For a small team, even one that was not located in a single place, this worked fine. Our experience tells us that on a larger team, we would need to adopt more formality for some of our artifacts.

We don't claim that our use cases were perfect. We worked on the principle of making them *good enough* for our purposes. One might question our approach, but in fact most successful projects are just good enough for what they need to be; we think it's wasteful to spend time improving things that do not matter. There are many good resources on use cases that can help you decide how much detail to put in them. We have listed some of our favorites in the bibliography. Enough said about this topic. Let's move on.

A Few Words About Diagrams

Figures 5.6 and 5.7 were clearly produced by a tool. You might wonder if it is necessary to use a tool for your diagrams. As with use cases, our advice is to do what is right for your purposes.

None of our team members are expert modelers. But we use a diagram in a model when it helps communicate information effectively. We sometimes created diagrams on paper or whiteboards. Some of these we kept, some we threw away. At the beginning of the project we threw most of them away. At some point, a diagram matures to the point where it approaches stability. At that point we might commit it to a more permanent, persistent, form by using a tool. Your individual preferences and project needs determine that point.

You also need to decide how to use your model. Many teams use models, as we did, just for communication. Others use models to generate code.

We decided to develop our models to a high level of detail to communicate the key ideas and structures of the PSP Tools software. We decided not to use our models to generate code. Later, we reverse-engineered the code to create class diagrams as a way to document our project. This is a relatively low-cost effort and it had value to us.

We took the view expressed in a paper by David Parnas and Paul Clements in 1986, "A Rational Design Process: How and Why to Fake It."[5] When we were done with the project, we wanted to make it look like we had done everything "right," according to some accepted set of rules. In reality, you can never get everything right over the course of a project. So, at the end of the project, spend some time cleaning up so that whoever works on the project next (including yourself) can understand what you have done. Make it easy to maintain and improve your work.

Gary often created sequence diagrams directly in a tool. He liked the ability to quickly delete objects from the diagram. The tool also made the diagram neater. (If we had to describe Gary's drawing ability, all we can say is that he's a good programmer.)

We began using Rational Rose as the modeling tool of choice. Part way through the project, Rational released XDE (eXtended Developer Experience), a modeling tool that is integrated with a Java development environment, in our case, with the Eclipse integrated development environment (IDE). We chose to switch to the more integrated environment. Because our model was not complex, converting from one tool to the other was easy.

Identifying Nonfunctional Requirements

While most of a system's requirements can be captured through use cases, there are some requirements that cannot be expressed with use cases. We call these "nonfunctional requirements." For example:

- Your product will be sold in another country, so you must design it for international consumption.
- Your product must meet certain performance and quality benchmarks.
- Your product must comply with certain laws or standards, or contain features that allow the product to vie with competing products.

---

[5] *IEEE Transactions on Software Engineering*, Vol. 12, Issue 2, February 1986.

You should create actual nonfunctional requirements for these items so that you can track them, manage them, and, eventually, verify that the system fulfills them.

Project Management

At this point in the project, you know what you are going to build, you have an idea of what you are not going to build, and your use cases provide the starting point to begin analyzing the structure of the software. This is the time to create a project plan, including a schedule.

Prioritizing Requirements

To prioritize requirements, consider at least these points:

- Must one use case be implemented before another? In our case, we needed to implement "Open a Project Database" before "Maintain a Project Database," because you can't maintain a database if you can't open it.
- Do you have to implement the whole use case? Sometimes you only need to implement a single scenario of a use case to enable other work to continue. For example, we only had to implement the basic flow of events on the "Open a Project Database" use case before we could begin working on maintaining the project database.
- Are there architectural or other project risks that can be addressed early? In our case, we decided that implementing the basic flow of "Record Personal Engineering Statistics," along with the alternate flow, "Create a New Task," would help us experience the most project risk earliest in the development cycle. Implementing these scenarios forced us to dive into learning about databases, Java Database Connectivity (JDBC), and other technical areas that posed risks because of our lack of experience with them.
- The most important input to prioritizing use cases is the customer input. What use cases, or parts of use cases, are most important? Which deliver the most value?

Planning

Planning is a continuous activity. Pragmatic planners know that you are most likely to succeed if you plan iteratively, starting at a high level and filling in the details as the project proceeds. RUP presents good advice on how to develop realistic plans. You develop them at different levels:

- You start with an overall plan for your project that does not include dates, at least in the beginning. The project plan describes how you *plan* to accomplish the work that you know about.
- The next level of the plan is developed for each iteration. You want each iteration to be short enough so that you can accurately plan work. If iterations are too long, there is an increasing chance that you will have to make significant changes to the plan before the end of the iteration.

During the Inception phase we developed a high-level project plan.[6] We also developed a detailed iteration plan for just the next iteration. At the end of each iteration, you assess what you accomplished, adjust the project plan if necessary, and make a detailed plan for the next iteration. This process avoids unnecessary and often massive rework of plans.

Once we prioritized the use cases, we assigned them to a proposed series of iterations. We had a rough idea of how long the project would take, the functionality we wanted to put into the project, and some initial guesses on the difficulty. We used this information to create the project plan. Using guidance from RUP, and prior experience, we decided to plan for six iterations: one Inception iteration (our current iteration), one Elaboration iteration, three Construction iterations, and one Transition iteration. This initial plan is only an estimate. You may find later that you need more or fewer iterations.

Starting with Elaboration, we scheduled use cases, or parts of use cases, for each planned iteration, through Construction. This activity is similar to a bin-packing problem. You want to put as many items as possible into the available space. Imagine that you are standing in front of a kitchen table and a set of items. You place items on the table in order of their value. To add an item, you find the appropriate place and push down towards the less valuable pieces to make room. Something falls off the edge of the table, but it's the least valuable item. If the items turn out to be larger than you expect, then again the least valuable items get pushed off the table. This is a simple way of understanding the value of iterative development.

Figure 5.8 is an excerpt from the simple project plan we created. The items in the plan are taken from the iteration plan. The project plan

---

[6] RUP defines a Software Development Plan, which includes the Project Plan. We did not create the more complete Software Development Plan for this project.

Milestone	Artifact	Completion Dates		
		Planned	**Revised**	**Actual**
Iteration 1 (Inception)		10/15/2002		10/15/2002
	Initial project plans	10/11/2002		10/12/2002
	Inception iteration plan	10/1/2002	10/3/2002	10/3/2002
	Working environment set up, including the project repository and project Web site	10/15/2002	Taken out of Inception. Only partial environment by end of Inception.	
	Vision and product feature requirements	10/13/2002		10/14/2002
	Supplementary requirements	10/13/2002	N/A Removed from project until needed.	
	Initial use-case model	10/15/2002		10/15/2002
	Initial risk list	10/15/2002		10/15/2002
	Test plan	10/15/2002	Draft	10/15/2002
	Iteration Assessment	10/15/2002		10/15/2002
Iteration 2 (Elaboration)		12/15/2002		
	Updated project plan			

Figure 5.8 Our initial project plan

"rolls up" the information in the iteration plans and provides additional information, such as planned resource allocation. After our Elaboration phase, we decided not to update our project plan because for our small project it would have meant duplicating work. As we have said before, this does not mean that we did not have a plan. It just means that we decided not to make it a physical artifact. For our project, there was not enough extra benefit to warrant the separate plan.

Along with the overall project plan, which will constantly change throughout the project, we created a detailed iteration plan for our one Elaboration iteration. As in the Inception iteration plan, it contains a list of what we intend to do, who will do it, and when we expect it. It also contains a short description of how we will assess the success of this iteration.

Risk

Risk is a key concept in software development. *Risks* are those things that can cause your project to fail.[7] We want to build and deploy valuable software as quickly as possible. If we try to go too fast, we risk delivering software that has too many defects to be useful. If we go too slowly, we risk not delivering at all, or we risk the customer canceling the agreement. If we adopt new technology or techniques, we risk making mistakes. If we don't adopt new technology or techniques, we risk being left behind by our competition.

The Risk List is a key artifact in RUP. Like most useful artifacts, it is a living thing. You don't just make a list of risks, agree on them, and file them away. In fact, every time we ignored our own Risk List, we ran into trouble. You continually revisit the Risk List to ensure that you are working to reduce risk and that you can deliver working software to your customers.

The Risk List can be informal. However, we recommend that you write it down, and keep it where people can access it, perhaps on a project Web site. Figure 5.9 shows a portion of our initial Risk List. The rank shows the risk's priority. When the rank is 1, we believe there is a high probability that the risk will be realized, and that the effect of that realization will be severe. A value of 5 means that the risk has little probability of occurring or the effect is not severe. If you create a large set of risks, you may choose to assign separate values to the severity of the risk and the probability that the risk will occur. Because we had a small set of risks, we decided to combine the two values. On our Risk List we also included:

- A description.
- An indicator so that we know how to identify the risk, should it be realized.
- A strategy and contingency showing how to either avoid or mitigate the risk. This point is especially important: If you can anticipate the risk, you should also figure out how to keep it from happening or how to minimize its impact, and you should do it before a crisis arises.

---

[7] The RUP 2003 Glossary describes risk as "An ongoing or upcoming concern that has a significant probability of adversely affecting the success of major milestones."

Rank	Description	Indicator	Strategy & Contingency
1	Inexperience with Java database development.	Little or no software produced after the design has been completed for an iteration.	• Formal training class. • Get more time to read books and manuals.
2	Loss of interest in the project.	No progress for more than a month.	See if this is something that can be of interest to the company and get support from within Rational.
3	Bugs in versions of the tools being used. This can cause severe delays and loss of information.	Rework, restart, and recovery actions.	• Unless the bugs are so severe that the tool is not usable in any form, find a stable version of the tool, even if it does not have all the features, and use it throughout the project. • If the bugs are so severe that nothing can be done, do not use the tool in this project.

Figure 5.9 Sample risks

Each team needs to adopt its own standards and decide how to use the Risk List. The important thing is to keep a Risk List and to use it to help your team on the path to success.

Setting Up a Development Environment

During the Inception phase we decided which development tools we wanted to use. The following sections describe what we selected.

Language Tools

We decided to implement code in Java. Chris and Gary were going to write the code, and they were comfortable with Java. Java also provided the multi-platform capabilities that we wanted. Russell's programmers worked on several development platforms.

Choosing a Java development platform was not as easy as we thought it might be originally. We knew that it was possible to just use an editor and command lines to compile and run a program. This is much easier to do on a Unix system than on a Windows system but Chris and Gary used Windows as their main operating system.

We wanted to use an IDE for several reasons. Most IDEs have tools for constructing user interfaces easily. Java UI development can be tricky, especially when handling the different layouts and graphical objects such as trees and tables. So we especially wanted to use a GUI builder.

Most IDEs also provide integrated debugging, execution, and build capabilities. Deciding to use a Java IDE was an easy decision. But it was harder to decide which IDE to use.

There are several Java IDEs available—many good ones are available for free. Our first choice was Forte for Java, now called Sun ONE Studio. We chose the Community Edition. It contained everything we wanted, and it was free. We all downloaded the Java development kit and the Forte software from the Sun Java Web site and began to use it. Our experiences with Forte were mixed. We liked the GUI builder, but the environment seemed sluggish and we had problems with intermittent crashes. We used it throughout the Inception phase and into the Elaboration phase, and then we switched. We discuss our experiences with switching IDEs in Chapter 6.

Requirements Management Tools

The product depends upon good requirements—and requirements continually change. If we have learned nothing else in the last two decades, we have learned that we are fooling ourselves when we think we can capture all of the requirements at the beginning of a project and that they will remain stable throughout the project. Any project, regardless of size, needs a way to manage requirements. When we talk about managing requirements we mean:

- Capturing requirements so they can be transmitted to team members in a consistent manner
- Retrieving and modifying requirements so that changes are easily identified
- Prioritizing requirements to aid the planning process
- Tracing requirements to tests, code, and other relevant artifacts in our development process

We had only a few requirements for the PSP Tools project. We managed them using Microsoft Word documents and a Microsoft Excel spreadsheet. While this worked for us, we recommend a more formal system for any commercial undertaking, such as Rational RequisitePro.

Configuration Management and Version Control Tools

Configuration management and version control is fundamental to developing software for every project, yet many development teams try to work without any configuration management strategy or tools. If we had to choose just one tool for our project, it would be a configuration management tool.

Luckily, we had Rational ClearCase installed on our systems, so the choice was easy. ClearCase is perhaps the most advanced configuration management system available today, and it is useful on both small and large projects. We wanted to do a few basic operations: add files to version control, check files in, check files out, and merge files. Other configuration management tools probably would have worked for us if we had been working on just one project. But you seldom work on just one project.

Testing Tools

With a small team, it is especially critical that all team members become involved with quality and testing. A small team often does not have a dedicated quality staff, so everyone needs to pitch in and help test the software continuously. Even on a larger team, engineers have a responsibility to at least unit-test software before passing it on to the quality assurance department. We decided that different team members would test at different levels.

Chris and Gary were the developers, so they did the unit testing. Liz and Jas did usability and functional testing on the builds. Russell performed the acceptance testing. It is important to involve your user in testing your project from the beginning to ensure that you deliver the right product.[8]

We planned on using tools for all levels of testing. We had to balance the need for tools with the overhead of learning to use the tools. We had to ask what risks we were trying to mitigate by automating the tests and then decide whether it was worth the cost. There were few use cases in the application. Manual testing of the major scenarios would not require a lot of

---

[8] See "Involving Your Customers in Your RUP Project" by Gary Pollice in *The Rational Edge*, April 2002.

time. In fact, in our case, we thought that manual testing would require less time than creating and maintaining automated tests. We opted not to automate the use-case testing.

Gary and Chris wanted to produce clean, error-free code. They decided to create an automated test harness for unit testing. JUnit was their tool of choice. There were many testimonials to JUnit in the literature and in news groups. Gary had some experience with it, and it seemed straightforward to learn. Another point in favor of JUnit was that it was integrated into the Forte IDE. We'll have more to say about using JUnit and our testing in general in subsequent chapters.

Gary also had some experience with Rational PureCoverage, and planned to use it to produce basic code coverage metrics. He was interested in looking at the coverage statistics to determine if there were large pockets of unused, and possibly unneeded, code. If code does not get coverage during tests, it does not necessarily mean that the code is unused. It only means that it is not executed during the tests. However, as you attain a higher percentage of coverage during your tests, you can use the numbers to identify code that either needs testing, or is, in fact, not used at all.

Collaboration Tools

At about this time in the project, we discovered that Jas was leaving Rational. We soon realized that we needed a tool to help us manage communications. Even with just four or five people on the team, we couldn't keep track of which document was the latest, where the documents were, and who had worked on what most recently. We were lucky to have discovered the collaboration tool Groove, which we introduced in Chapter 4. We used Groove throughout the project to track enhancement requests and defects, to place software drops for testing, to make other files (requirements, test plans, instructions, and so on) available to all team members, and to manage our meetings.

Tools in Other Environments

We clearly spent a lot of time setting up our tool environment for PSP Tools. On most projects where you have an established team or environment you spend much less time on tool setup. Small projects that are part of a larger organization will already have an established common set of development tools that are used throughout the organization. You should always look for new tools that will help you do your job better, but you will not have to do much to prepare your basic tool set for your project.

Iteration Evaluation

We planned a single iteration that covered our Inception phase. Our goal was to produce the following artifacts:

- An initial project plan
- Vision endorsed by the stakeholders
- Programming guidelines
- Initial requirements
- The development environment set up and ready for the remainder of the project
- A test plan
- An initial Risk List
- The iteration plan for the Elaboration iteration

We met briefly, evaluated our progress, and declared the Inception phase complete. We achieved our goals. Some artifacts were perhaps in better shape than others. But we were confident that we understood the type of product Russell wanted and that we could build it. Now we were ready to dig in deeper and build the software.

The total amount of work we did for the Inception phase would have taken less than a week had we worked full time on the project. Because we were working on it part time, we took longer. Often project teams spend too much time in the Inception phase. They want to get everything right. They have been trained that the more time you put in up front, the better off you are in the long run. So they agonize over every little detail much too early in the project. We believe you need to be loose at this point and when you find yourself quibbling over details, realize that it's time to move on.

This Sure Sounds Like Waterfall

Sometimes it is difficult to see how a project is really working in an iterative manner, especially during the Inception phase. One criticism that agile practitioners raise is that it seems like we're just gathering requirements—where's the code?!

Following RUP does not mean that you can't write code during the Inception phase. But you don't *have to* write code. We mentioned at the beginning of this chapter that during the Inception phase you are planning your trip. You will spend most of the time understanding your customers and their needs. Use whatever technique helps you in that effort—write code, design storyboards, or produce any other type of prototype, if you feel that the effort will get you closer to understanding the requirements for the project.

In our case, we drew a few diagrams on paper or a whiteboard. We discussed what a possible system might look like. We went broad, not deep. We did not try to capture any detailed requirements.

Summary

Inception is the first phase identified in RUP. This is where you officially begin the project. During the Inception phase, you work with your customers and other stakeholders to agree about what problems you are trying to solve, what type of solution might be appropriate, and whether there is a business value in the solution. From those agreements, you develop an initial project plan with some cost and resource estimates. During the Inception phase you go "wide and shallow" across the complete project. You do not want to get stuck in the details when you know they will most likely change as the project progresses.

You might begin to develop some early approaches to possible solutions. You would do this through storyboards, use cases, and code. The ultimate goal of the Inception phase is to get enough understanding of the problem and the requirements for a solution that you can decide whether it is worth continuing the project and allocating additional resources to it.

Inception is almost always the shortest project phase. Some projects get into difficulties during Inception by trying to go too deep into the details of the solution. Avoid this temptation. As quickly as possible, discover what the problems are, what possible solutions might look like, who wants the product, and—most importantly for commercial projects—whether anyone is willing to pay for it.

> **PSP Tools Inception: less than one week**

CHAPTER 6

Elaboration: We Create the Framework

At this point we knew what we wanted to build. More importantly, we knew what Russell wanted us to build. These were not always identical. Sometimes we let our personal vision cloud our view of what we needed to build to satisfy our customer. In many projects, reality hits home during the Elaboration phase. All of the care and good work that go into writing the Vision and initial requirements cannot guarantee that you will deliver the product within the time and budget allotted.

There are several reasons for this inconsistency. The main problem is that while you are crafting the Vision and eliciting the initial requirements, you are also capturing everything the customer, and other stakeholders, want in the product. In fact, when you prioritize what the product needs to be successful, you create a smaller set of requirements than you started with—sometimes much smaller.

Another problem can be that your team members may not be good at estimating how much they can deliver in the time they have. Even when the team isn't working under a deadline, members often underestimate the effort required to develop product-quality software. (Of course, one reason to build PSP Tools in the first place was to address this very issue.)

We mention the problem of matching reality with expectations at the beginning of the chapter on the Elaboration phase because:

- You often encounter the mismatch during the Elaboration phase.
- It happened to our team.

Elaboration Phase Goals

The milestone at the end of the Elaboration phase is the *Lifecycle Architecture* (LCA) milestone. RUP describes the LCA milestone in terms of evaluation criteria, artifacts, and the state of the artifacts at LCA, as listed in Appendix A. When you first look at the list, you may feel overwhelmed. But remember that you need to do just enough to make your project successful. You don't even have to produce the artifacts in a consistent form if you don't need to.

Toward Stability: Decreasing the Rate of Change

The evaluation criteria for the LCA milestone say the requirements and architecture need to be *stable*. Many people misunderstand how RUP uses the word "stable." In this case, stable doesn't mean "immutable and permanent."[1] RUP uses it to mean "resistant to sudden change of position or condition."[2] This distinction is more than just a semantic quibble. In fact, it is a gateway to understanding the iterative, incremental nature of RUP. If you believe that stability is equivalent to immutability, then you will view RUP as a sequential, waterfall-like process. If, for you, stability suggests that the rate of change exhibits a reducing trend, then you understand RUP as its designers intended.

We expect to revise requirements throughout the project. During the Elaboration phase, you fill in the details of the requirements you identified in the Inception phase, add more as they are identified, and remove some if necessary. But, as you progress through the Elaboration phase the rate of change should decrease.

If you see little or no decrease to the rate of change of the requirements, it may indicate problems. For example, your customer may not have engaged fully with your team, or the business environment may be unstable. If the rate of change isn't slowing, and is unlikely to do so, consider incorporating practices that help you deal with continual *rapid* change effectively. To help manage this type of change, we recommend that you consider such practices as the Planning Game from eXtreme Programming and the daily SCRUM from SCRUM. We consider this approach to be compatible with RUP.

People often ask, "How stable does the architecture need to be?" Again, consider stability in terms of the rate of change. Some might ask whether you should spend time on architecture at all. If there is no architectural risk, then you may not need to spend any time developing your architecture. For example, when you add to an existing system, there is often little risk to the architecture. See the sidebar on architecture to understand our take on it.

---

[1] *American Heritage Dictionary, Second College Edition.*
[2] Ibid.

Architecture

Ask five different software developers about software architecture and you are likely to receive five different answers. We talk a lot about architecture. We work with people who are software architects. Yet, when we are asked to describe architecture, we have difficulty putting together a short *elevator pitch** to get our point across.

Architecture is, in fact, many things and will differ depending on the context in which you are discussing it. RUP provides a definition of architecture in its glossary, which is based on several sources. Part of the definition says that architecture is:

> *The highest-level concept of a system in its environment. The architecture of a software system (at a given point in time) is its organization or structure of significant components, interacting through interfaces, those components being composed of successively smaller components and interfaces.*

There is more to the architecture than just the above definition. The architecture includes the key decisions and rationales to explain why you've selected a certain structure and how the components interact. Some of the architecture may be described by well-known patterns.

Architecture is typically viewed differently by different people at different times. This is analogous to the architecture for a building. The carpenters need blueprints to show them the overall structure, where doors and windows are placed, and so on. Electricians need a different view of the building in the form of an electrical wiring diagram. Plumbers need yet a different view.

Software architecture also needs to be represented through several views when appropriate. For more information, we recommend that you read "The 4+1 View Model of Architecture" by Philippe Kruchten, *IEEE Software*, November 1995.

° An elevator pitch is a term that marketing and sales people use for a short description that you can deliver in the time it takes to ride an elevator. Your pitch must convey key points and convince your listener to buy whatever you are selling (for example, software, request for venture funding, yourself as a job candidate).

Our project wasn't large, and there was little architectural risk. So, what were our goals for the Elaboration phase? They were quite modest. We describe them in the next few sections. Figure 6.1 shows the main parts of The Elaboration Iteration Plan we worked from.

Artifact	Due	Responsible	Comment
Updated project plan		Gary	Through first construction iteration, reviewed and agreed upon
Unit test harness		Chris	Installed and team members trained
Acceptance tests		Jas, Liz	Defined with initial scripts and run for implemented functionality
User interface prototype		Chris	Ready to be enhanced for the product, approved by customer
Software Architecture Document		John	With preliminary design model
Builds and components		John, Chris, Gary	
Test Plan		Chris	One page, describing the general approach
Unit tests		John, Chris, Gary	As per test plan
Documentation and support plan		Liz	Initial draft
Data model		John	Schema defined

3. Resources
Team members will spend at least four hours per week completing their work.

4. Use Cases
The following use cases/scenarios will be implemented during the Elaboration iteration:

- Record Personal Engineering Statistics: Basic Flow of Events with the following alternate flows of events.
  - o Create a New Task.
- Open a project database (with login).

In order to implement the above, a project database must be created. This may be done by implementing the basic flow of events of the use case Maintain Team Project Database.

Figure 6.1 Excerpt from the Elaboration Iteration Plan

Producing an Executable Architecture

Section 4 of the Elaboration Iteration Plan shows which use cases we decided to implement during the Elaboration phase. We selected the most important use-case scenarios for the Elaboration phase by prioritizing the use cases based on the business value and the technical risk. Russell gave us

	Use Case	Bus. Priority	Tech. Priority
1	Open Project Database	2	1
2	Record Personal Engineering Statistics	1	2
3	Run Personal Reports	3	3
4	Run Team Reports	4	5
5	Maintain a Project Database	5	4

Figure 6.2 Use case prioritization

input on business value. Gary and Chris determined the technical risk. Figure 6.2 shows how we ranked the use cases. Using our priorities, we identified those scenarios most likely to exercise the architecture.

We will have more to say about the executable architecture and the Elaboration phase engineering work later in this chapter.

Adding Some Details to Requirements

We didn't expect to complete the details of every use case by the end of the Elaboration phase. We expected, however, to create enough details for those use-case scenarios we planned to implement in this phase.

We created use case details as follows:

- We wrote text in the use case document. The text described the high-level interaction between the actor and the system (PSP Tools).
- We produced a few sequence diagrams that showed the objects involved in the scenarios and how they would collaborate.

We find that combining text and pictures conveys ideas effectively. The pictures can give you a high-level understanding at a glance, while the text helps you dive deeper into the details. Also, keep in mind that people absorb information differently. Some people work well with visual images and actually understand the text better as a result of studying the images. Other people need to read the text first before the pictures make sense. By providing both types of information, you enable a more diverse audience to contribute to your project.

Figure 6.3 illustrates the level of detail we wrote for the basic flow of events for the Open Project Database use case. We describe the use case as

Any User	PSP Tools
1. Select **Open....**	
2. Specify a project database and select **OK.**	3. Open the project database. If an error occurs, display an appropriate error message and end this use case.
4. Enter the user name and optional password and select **Login**. Select **Cancel** to end this use case with no state change.	5. Ensure that the user name and password (if present) are for an existing member of the database. If not, display an appropriate message and allow the user to be added to the database. If the PSP User decides not to add the new user, end the use case; otherwise, proceed with **Alternate Flow of Events: Add New User to Project Database.** If there is an existing user, proceed with the next step.
	6. Make the database the current database for the user. Close any open database. Display the appropriate view of the data in the project database for this user.

Figure 6.3 Basic flow of events for Open Project Database use case

a dialog between the actor, Any User in this case, and the system. At this point we didn't need more detail and we weren't concerned about exceptions or alternate flows of events.

The use-case description format we used in Figure 6.3 is one that Gary learned from Craig Larman's book *Applying UML and Patterns*. The simple presentation helped all of us. It made it easy for Russell to quickly read and understand what the software was supposed to do at the user level. It had enough information for Gary and Chris to work from. And it provided information to Liz and Jas who were designing tests and planning documentation. For us, writing more details at this phase would not have been productive.

Gary used the Rational XDE and Rose tools to capture his thoughts in sequence diagrams and then used the diagrams to communicate with Chris. Figure 6.4 illustrates one of the diagrams he created for the scenario described in Figure 6.3. The object names in the diagram aren't necessarily the final names, but they reflect the responsibilities of some of the objects, like openManager, and the way we planned to organize our code.

Notice that the sequence diagram may not be as detailed as some you might have seen. We strived, throughout the project, to create just enough documentation to help us communicate and to build the software. Russell didn't care about documentation; he cared about software his team could use.

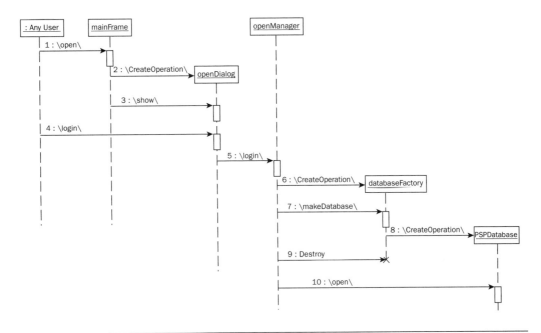

Figure 6.4 Partial sequence diagram for opening a project database

We cared about satisfying Russell. We certainly believe that some documentation about how the software was built is useful. We just made sure that we weren't documentation prisoners.

Creating Tests and Test Plans

In RUP, quality is a way of life. It begins early and continues throughout the complete lifecycle. We all agreed that we wanted to deliver solid software that would give our customers few problems.

We approached testing from two directions for the Elaboration phase. First, Chris and Gary planned to develop and run unit tests. They decided to use the JUnit test framework[3] and to try the *test-first* practice described in eXtreme Programming (see Appendix C). Liz and Jas planned to work on software acceptance tests. They started with the use cases. They also

---

[3] See www.junit.org for information on the JUnit test framework.

engaged Russell as much as possible to ensure that the tests they developed reflected his expectations.

Test planning proved to be a bit of a sticking point for us. We thought we should have a written plan so we could refer to it as we evaluated the different iterations. We wanted to ensure consistency in our testing across iterations.

Chris volunteered to write the test plan. He started with the Test Plan Template from RUP. The template was large and included many sections that weren't helpful to our project. Chris' first draft had ten pages of words, with little or no content. He ran into one of the problems we often see when people work from templates—they think all the sections are important and necessary.

Chris and Gary discussed the template and decided on a course of action. They wrote a simple statement describing how the team should approach testing.

Each class will have corresponding unit tests. No code will be checked into version control unless all unit tests pass.

Acceptance tests will be run and will pass before any software is delivered to the customer.

This test plan was small enough to fit on a large Post-it note that we could pin on the wall. It conveyed everything we needed to know. It didn't specify in detail how to write our tests. It didn't specify what tools to use or the structure of the tests. For our four-person project, this was *good enough*.

Liz and Jas collaborated on defining the initial acceptance tests based on the use cases. Liz then took the lead and produced the acceptance tests. Russell reviewed the tests with the rest of the team and we used the tests to assess the Elaboration iteration plan's success. Liz wrote an acceptance test plan for the Elaboration phase. She was most comfortable writing ideas in a document, but she made sure not to get caught up in making the document perfect. She wrote the test document with enough information so that a tester could run the test and determine if the program behaved as expected. Figure 6.5 is an excerpt from the Elaboration Acceptance Test document. It shows a sequence of tests to run for the basic flow of events of the Open Project Database use case.

When the document was created we didn't know the exact commands, message text, or the look and feel of the program. The use-case description provides enough guidance to write the test. The test in Figure 6.5 can be

Actions:
1. Select **Open Project Database**.
2. At file dialog prompt, specify a project database.
    a. Already a member — you're in.
    b. Not a member — add yourself.
    c. Not a member — change your username.

Preconditions:
At least two databases exist.
App is started.

Tests:

Test ID	Select database	Member?	Expected Result	Next step
2.0.1	Select database: AccTest1	Yes	Display view of data for DB1.	Test 2.0.2
2.0.2	Select database: AccTest2	Yes	Display view of data for DB2.	Leave app open
2.0.3	Select database: AccTest1	No	Prompt for next step	Opt to add self, Leave app open
2.0.4	Select database: AccTest2	No	Prompt for next step	Opt to switch user id, leave app open
2.0.5	Select database: AccTest2	No	Prompt for next step	Opt to cancel, exit app.

Figure 6.5 Excerpt from the Elaboration Acceptance Test document

restated as the following sequence of operations through some scenarios of the use case.

1. Open the database AccTest1. You are a member.
2. While AccTest1 is open, choose to open a different database, AccTest2. You are a member.
3. While AccTest2 is open, open AccTest1 again, but try to log in as a user who isn't a member. The application should let you add yourself to the project database.

4. Switch one more time to AccTest2, as a user who isn't a member. This time, don't add yourself, but change to a user who is a member of AccTest2.
5. Finally, re-open AccTest2, but cancel out of the login and exit the program.

This sequence allows a tester to verify a significant number of combinations from the scenario for logging into a PSP project database.

Don't Forget Exploratory Testing

Exploratory testing is a good idea for any project. Regardless of the amount of test planning you do, you are likely to uncover more defects, in a short time, by doing exploratory testing.

Exploratory testing is "purposeful wandering: navigating through a space with a general mission, but without a prescribed route."[4] To get started, select a specific subset of the functionality to explore and *try a few things* to see how well the software meets your expectations. You may find some problems. You may find some surprises. You can scribble some notes and use them to design some more formal test cases and tests.

Russell and Gary were very good at exploratory testing. With each new build, they were able to quickly uncover major problems in the added functionality.

Unit Testing

Setting up the development environment for unit testing was simple. Chris and Gary downloaded JUnit, installed it, and made the `junit.jar` file a part of their development project's CLASSPATH.[5] It really is that easy!

Writing the tests and getting them to work is not so easy. Gary had previously used JUnit, but Chris hadn't. Our intention was to write tests for our classes before we wrote the implementation code for the tests. For some types of classes, but not all, this is a straightforward process. We compromised this practice a lot as we proceeded. We wrote tests first for many of our data object classes. For some classes we wrote tests later. Our GUI

---

[4] From *Lessons Learned in Software Testing* by Cem Kaner, James Bach, and Bret Pettichord.
[5] Java uses the CLASSPATH environment variable to identify the location of libraries and other files needed to execute a Java program.

classes never had unit tests written for them. See Chapter 7 for more details on our unit testing.

It isn't clear to us what effect the compromises we made had on the quality of the final product. There are several practices that have been recently introduced by the agile community. Some of them, like writing tests first, make sense. At the time we are writing this, actual empirical evidence is sparse. There have been a few experiments run on test-first programming (or test-driven design), with mixed results.

Gary recently taught a graduate class in empirical software engineering at Worcester Polytechnic Institute (http://www.wpi.edu). They ran an experiment and found some evidence that test-first was beneficial, but the evidence was not conclusive.[6] We think the practice has merit, but suspect there is a significant learning curve before one gets good at it, as is the case with many practices.

Creating the PSP Tools Architecture

There was little architectural risk for our project. That didn't mean that we just started coding. Indeed, we designed an architecture, albeit an informal one. Chris and Gary met for a couple of hours in a room with a whiteboard and sketched out the user-visible parts of the application. This exercise helped them develop a shared understanding of what the user interface would look like. During this exercise, they also brainstormed about how to lay out the Java code.

They decided on a main PSP window, divided into two panes. The left pane would contain a tree view of all the tasks in the database for the *current user*.[7] We weren't sure exactly how to present the tree view, but we decided it would contain information for the current user only. We weren't sure whether we would change the display for an administrator; the requirements at that point called for a user with special privileges who could, for example, produce combined reports. Rather than trying to nail down the details, we came to a general understanding of the view and decided to defer a more specific design of the user interface.

The right pane was to contain the details of the item selected in the tree view. The major items in the database were tasks (which were really

---

[6] The Web site for the course is www.cs.wpi.edu/~gpollice/cs562-s03.
[7] The *current user* is the term we used to identify the person who had logged into the PSP database.

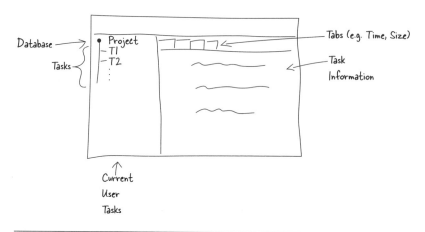

Figure 6.6 Initial sketch of the user interface

projects), times, and defects. But the times and defects were both associated with specific tasks, so it seemed natural for the right pane to contain task details.

During the design session, Chris and Gary drew a few diagrams on the whiteboard. Figures 6.6 and 6.8 show what they drew.[8] They describe some of the more important parts of the application. They also represent the thinking at the beginning of the Elaboration phase. In subsequent chapters we see how the thinking changed, and discuss the reasons for the changes.

One could hardly call the sketch of the user interface in Figure 6.6 detailed, but it was a good starting point. When we compare it to the final main window from PSP Tools shown in Figure 6.7, it is surprisingly accurate. We weren't sure what the tabs would contain, how many tabs there would be, or exactly what would be in the tree for each task. At this point, we also weren't sure about how the different actions, like creating a new task, would be invoked. We were confident, however, that we would be able to get the right level of presentation—perhaps not at first, but incrementally and iteratively—as we proceeded through the Elaboration and Construction phases. You can see in Figure 6.7 that we included buttons for many of the actions rather than forcing the user to work with menu selections exclusively.

At our design meeting we also took time to lay out the major packages for our code. The sketch in Figure 6.8 can be used as part of the design

---

[8] The diagrams have been copied from the notes Gary took at the session.

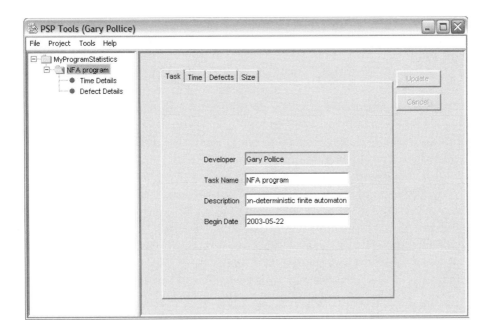

Figure 6.7 The actual PSP Tools user interface

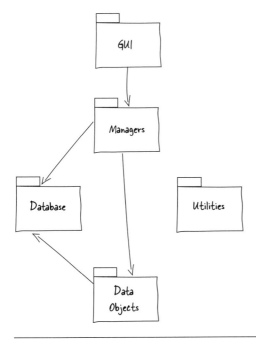

Figure 6.8 Initial package distribution layout

model and part of the implementation model described in RUP. Our plan at the outset was to not worry about making the models look good. That is post-production work to us. While the customer worked with the product during and just after the Transition phase, we would schedule time to decide what we needed to turn into a persistent form for the next release.

We have mentioned this attitude of deferring things before. Liz calls this "programming by procrastination." It may sound like a bad idea, but it is another way of stating what some members of the agile community mean by "You aren't gonna need it" (YAGNI) and "Do the simplest thing that could possibly work." We think the real benefit of taking this approach is that it starts you moving and keeps you moving, especially during those times when you are tempted to spend too much time trying to get everything just right before continuing. The more experienced you are, the more you know how to achieve the right balance of appropriate caution and moving ahead. The best way to learn is by making mistakes yourself, or by working on a project with more experienced people to learn how they balance the risks to make decisions.

Login: Not as Simple as We Thought

We spent a lot of time during the Elaboration phase trying to decide how users would identify themselves to the system. This common problem is faced by both large and small software product teams. It isn't clear if there is an ideal solution that fits every case. Our preference was for a PSP Tools user to open a database and have the software automatically recognize the user. We thought we could use the user's login name, which we could obtain from the system software.

This wasn't a perfect solution. We imagined scenarios when the user would want to be logged in under a different name. For example, if you work on different projects in your organization, you might want different login names for each project, but you would not log in to the operating system using different names. So you would want distinct user names when using PSP Tools only.

We struggled with another question. Do you log in to PSP Tools or do you log in to a specific PSP Tools database? We considered scenarios that involved a single user who wanted to use different databases and different login names, for example:

- If you log in to PSP Tools, when you open a database, what happens if you are not a member[9] of the database? Do you need someone who is a member of the database to add you?

- If you close one database and open another one, what happens if you aren't a member of the second one? Will it ask you to log in again or does it retain your original login ID?
- What happens when you use different system login names, for example, if you use different computers on a regular basis?
- Different privileges might be associated with your user name. Do you retain those privileges when you switch from one database to another?

These are difficult questions to answer, and it is even more difficult to arrive at a solution that satisfies all of the issues. We eventually decided that you log in to a specific database. When you open a database you will be asked to log in, even if you use the identical user ID and privileges for the database you are closing. This was a sufficient solution, relatively easy to implement, and we decided that in the normal use of the product, changing databases would be an infrequent occurrence.

When you open or create a new database in PSP Tools, you log in. For the first database opened or created in a PSP Tools session, the login name defaults to the user name obtained from the system. You can override this setting when you log in to PSP Tools. From that point on, as long as you don't quit PSP Tools, every time you open or create a new database, the default user ID becomes the last user (login) name used.

Changes to the Tool Environment

Two significant changes occurred in our tool environment during the Elaboration phase. We switched our primary development platform—our Java programming IDE—from the Forte Community Edition to Rational XDE (and the Eclipse IDE). And, we started to use Groove more extensively. We discuss the reasons behind these changes, and their ramifications, in the next few sections.

Forte to XDE—Good-bye to the GUI Builder

Rational introduced a new tool, XDE (eXtended Developer Experience), that:

---

[9] We used the term *member* of a database or project to indicate someone who was able to modify the contents of a project database.

- Enables easy integration of UML models and code
- Lets developers forward- or reverse-engineer applications with little effort
- Keeps code and models synchronized automatically

While Gary and Chris are not *advanced* modelers, they do appreciate the value of a diagram and thought it would be beneficial to use the XDE diagramming features.

There were other reasons for switching from Forte to XDE. Chris was beginning to use XDE as his development environment at Rational, and he was looking forward to learning more about the environment. Gary had less-than-optimal experiences with Forte and was looking for an IDE with which he was more comfortable. The Forte environment hung on several occasions and also had a significantly "sluggish" feel. However, Chris didn't experience these problems, so perhaps they were due to the configuration of Gary's computer. Since then, Gary has upgraded to a professional version of the operating system and the Forte platform has evolved, giving us reason to believe that he wouldn't experience the same problems today.

A side effect of switching IDEs was the loss of a GUI builder. Forte has a nice tool set for creating user interfaces. With Forte, you construct a user interface by dragging the visual components to windows, defining behavior by modifying component properties, and writing the methods to implement the behavior. Other integrated GUI builders behave similarly.

We were anxious about giving up the Forte GUI builder because it was easy to use. There is a comfort in working in a visual environment without worrying about the underlying mechanisms. It turned out that with Eclipse, we had better control over the final look and behavior of the user interface, as well as an assurance that the resulting code was portable to different development environments.

IDE GUI builders typically generate highly stylized code, with comments that are often cryptic to humans and used by the GUI builder to recreate the code. There are often sections of code that you are forbidden to modify; if you do, the IDE might not be able to recreate the components correctly. If you switch to a different development environment with its own GUI builder, you may not be able to recreate your user interface with the new tools. Some environments also have their own visual components, such as custom layout managers. If you use one of the custom components, you are locked into using that environment or its libraries.

In fact, when we switched from Forte to XDE, we were able to use the Forte GUI code as a starting point. Fortunately, we hadn't gotten very far with GUI design in Forte, and we had made minimal use of Forte's unique features.

You might wonder whether we traded one set of problems for another when we switched environments. We felt that we made a good choice in our switch. Rational XDE is built on the open-source Eclipse environment. This allowed us to use just the Eclipse environment for our code development, other Eclipse plug-ins such as the JUnit plug-in, and the XDE product when we wanted to work with UML diagrams. We decided not to generate code from our diagrams, but to use diagrams for human communication. Therefore we avoided locking ourselves into specific coding conventions imposed by the tool.

The lessons learned: Do not rely on features specific to one development environment, especially its GUI builder. Learn how to develop the user interface from the basic components. Find an environment that lets you develop generic code quickly and reliably. Proceed cautiously if you do use features that are unique to your environment.

New Uses for Groove

Until the Elaboration phase, we used the Groove workspace as a vehicle for sharing documents and informal communication between the team members. During the Elaboration phase, we found new uses for Groove.

Even though Chris and Gary both worked at the Rational Lexington, Massachusetts campus, they were in different buildings, and Gary often traveled or worked from home. They needed a way to record and assign engineering work between them. They created an *engineering backlog* (a term used in the SCRUM methodology).[10] It is simply a list of tasks we needed to perform to realize the requirements in our software and satisfy Russell, our customer.

They added a tab to Groove that we called "Engineering Backlog."[11] This was a simple discussion tool that comes with all Groove editions. Each engineering task was set up as a separate discussion item. They used a stylized form to identify open items, who was responsible, and when items were implemented in the code. Figure 6.9 shows what the engineering backlog looks like. This approach worked well for our two developers. For a larger system or for more people, we recommend using a more formal work assignment mechanism.

---

[10] See *Agile Software Development with SCRUM* by Ken Schwaber and Mike Beedle.
[11] In Groove, you add another tab to a workspace when you add a tool. You can have several copies of the same tool in the workspace, giving each copy a different name.

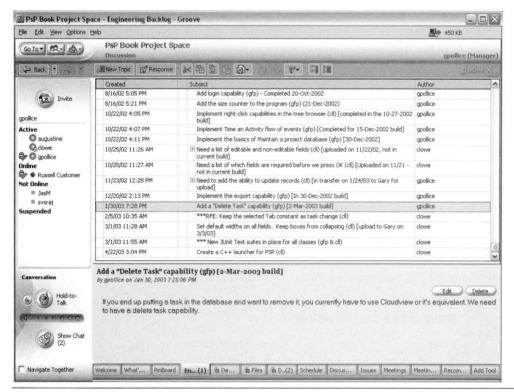

Figure 6.9 Project engineering backlog

Deferring Database Creation

When you consider the use-case scenarios we decided to implement in our Elaboration iteration plan, you might wonder how we created a database. After all, the only database-related use case we planned to implement was Open Project Database. But we believed that adding database creation code to the iteration would not address any additional technical risk and it would delay the Elaboration phase.

We chose to use a standard database implementation, one that supported JDBC and the SQL query language. So, we created an SQL script to populate a database. This solution was sufficient for the time being. The script, `createdb.sql`, used a series of `create` and `insert` SQL statements to create a database with a few initial records. We used this script during the Elaboration phase to test code and to ensure that we were meeting our goals.

We started designing the application using the PointBase database that comes with the Forte environment. When we changed to use Rational XDE, we decided to switch the database implementation as well. We decided to use the Cloudscape database, delivered as the JDBC reference database implementation with the J2EE platform.[12] For the J2EE 1.3.1 release, we found a useful utility program called Cloudview that let us interact directly with the database.

These tools proved to be invaluable in the beginning because they allowed us to verify whether the code we wrote was working. For example:

- Because we implemented only minimal functionality, we didn't yet have the ability to use the PSP Tools code to query the database. Using Cloudview, we performed early versions of the queries that we later implemented in our code.
- During early acceptance testing, Jas and Liz used Cloudview and the scripts Gary wrote to create the databases they needed.

We recommend that you use a general-purpose tool such as Cloudview for the database management software you choose to work with.

An Alternative to the Database

There are different schools of thought about whether you need to design and implement database code during the Elaboration phase. An alternate approach to the one we took is to defer the database implementation until you absolutely need it. In the meantime, you can define the interfaces for accessing the data and create alternate data provider classes. This follows good design practice, which says you should separate the responsibilities between the physical representation of the data and the classes that access the data.[13]

By creating alternate data storage classes you might be able to create a simpler system than if you start with a more complex solution, such as a database. For example, for PSP Tools, we might have started by using a simple file-based data store for the project database. This would have worked for a single user, but not for multiple simultaneous users. Later, we would have needed to do some amount of rework when we finally added the database.

---

[12] J2EE and the Java SDK can be downloaded from http://java.sun.com.

[13] There are several good books that describe the best object-oriented design principles. In this book, we will not address these topics in detail.

However, we had the requirement for multiple simultaneous users, so we implemented the database early in the project. Also, database design and implementation was a major risk for the project's success. None of us had any recent, useful experience with database software. A goal of the Elaboration phase was to prove to ourselves that the database would not be a blocking factor for finishing the project. In the end, it was a relief to have implemented the database early. It was also a good decision to defer writing the final creation and query code because these aspects of the project didn't pose technical risks.

Database Design

It turned out that implementing the database was quite simple. Our data model for PSP Tools isn't complex. Figure 6.10 shows a UML representation of the data in our database.

This diagram illustrates the usefulness of UML diagrams. It took about five minutes to capture the information in XDE, and the diagram shows a lot in a small space, for example:

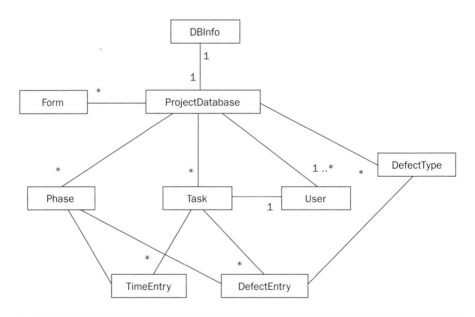

Figure 6.10 PSP Tools data model

- There is one DBInfo object for the project database. (The DBInfo object records the properties of the database, such as the name, description, and so on.)
- There must be at least one User in every project database, but there can be more than one.
- A project database can contain any number of Tasks.
- Each Task has time entries and defect entries associated with it.
- Every Task is associated with exactly one user.

The diagram could be more detailed or more consistent, but the level of detail was enough for Gary to create a working database and communicate to others how the database was structured. In fact, the `createdb.sql` script shows that there is a separate table for each of the classes in Figure 6.10.

Scope Management: Cut Early and Often

At the beginning of this chapter, we said that reality hits home in the Elaboration phase. You begin to see what you can and cannot do in the time you have, with the budget allocated, and the resources available. Even though our project was a part-time project with no fixed end date, we were forced to confront the limitations of what we could do and what we were prepared to do.

The best example of this brush with reality came early in the Elaboration phase. In retrospect, our vision was grandiose. We planned to create a general-purpose PSP tool that would allow the user to select specific processes for a given database. We envisioned users selecting a process from a menu when they created a new project database. The software would then populate the database with the correct tables, phases, and other data needed to support the process. In the PSP description as defined by Watts Humphrey, there are different levels of PSP and different forms and data items that are recorded for each level. The purpose of PSP is to become better at estimating and delivering quality, so it is natural to assume that as engineers improve, they will want to use a higher level of PSP implementation.

We even thought it would be a great idea to let users create their own forms and develop their own personal process. The emphasis here is that *we* thought it would be a great idea! Russell didn't care. Russell wanted an implementation of PSP level 0.1 or 1.0 that his engineers could use, and he wanted it sooner rather than later. Our loss of customer focus cost us significantly as we began to design the system.

We spent time brainstorming different ways of representing the flexible solution that *we* wanted. We considered ways of creating dynamic schemas for the database, representing forms via XML, creating a form editor for the user, and other creative ideas that never made it into the release. Not only did they not make it into the release, but the time and effort spent on thinking up the ideas and possible solutions took time away from building the system our customer wanted.

There is a critical lesson learned from this experience: Keep your focus on your customers' needs. Build what they want, not what you want.

The ultimate Vision for PSP Tools didn't change. What did change was our plan for the first release of PSP Tools. To tie this realization back to tools, a requirements management tool allows you to quickly change the attributes, such as the release number, for requirements captured in the Vision. Changing the release number to something greater than 1.0 takes it out of the initial release but retains it in the overall Vision.

Because we used Rational RequisitePro, it was easy to change the requirement attributes for the release number and the status of the features. Making these changes helped us maintain a clear and shared understanding of which features we expected to deliver to our customer for the initial release.

Figure 6.11 shows a screen shot of a part of the attribute matrix for the feature requirements specified in our Vision document as we exited

Requirements:	Priority	Status	Difficulty	Assigned To	Iteration	Release
FEA1: User-definable Activities User-definable Activities	Medium	Proposed	High			2
FEA2: Record Personal Engineering Statistics Record Personal Engineering Statistics	High	Approved	Medium	Gary and Chris		1
FEA2.1: Record time Time Time is recorded in minutes. The user either uses a timer device provided by PSP Tools or uses some other timing device. If the PSP Tools timer device is used, the actual time spent on a task may be automatically added to an open project (see the section on projects). If the time is not.	High	Approved	Medium	Gary and Chris	C1, C2	1
FEA2.2: Record Defects Defect Tracking The product provides the means to keep track of defects. Defects are entered for an open project. Defect data consists of:	Medium	Approved	Medium	Gary and Chris	C2	1

Figure 6.11 A portion of the feature requirement attribute matrix

the Elaboration phase. Notice the change in the release for the FEA1 requirement. Release 2 at this point represents the next, or some other future, release. The Vision document didn't change. It still reflected our vision of what we wanted to include in PSP Tools. The attributes changed to reflect what we would deliver for this release.

What Do You Mean You Can't Install The Product?

Every software project has concerns that are outside the realm of producing code. Sometimes these issues are pushed aside—we forget about them, or we don't believe that the concerns will develop into problems. During our project, an issue cropped up early and we ignored it. In retrospect, we should have attended to it earlier. The issue was: How does the end user install the software?

The lack of an installation utility didn't seem like a big deal to Gary and Chris. They just needed to build the software. With the required runtime components installed on their computers, the code ran fine. Surely, everyone could load the Java runtime software and the J2EE distribution. Gary wrote a simple script called `runPSPTools` that started the software. Of course, the software had to be in the same directory as the script, the runtime components had to be installed in the right directories, and a couple of environment variables needed to be set. How hard could that be? After all, each of us was an experienced professional in the software industry, and we were comfortable experimenting with early versions of new tools.

Testers and other quality professionals will quickly recognize what happened. How often do engineers say, "It works on my machine, you must have done something wrong?" This phrase seems to be etched on developers' minds. They use it when someone is unable to get their software working. Gary should know better because he tries as much as possible to act like a naive user when trying out someone else's software. When it came to the installation of the PSP Tools product and the required supporting software, he regressed. He was too close to the software and had difficulty seeing the problem.

Two events occurred that should have given Gary notice that installation wasn't as trivial as he thought. First, he spent over an hour with Liz one day helping her set up her machine so she could run the software and begin testing. Liz reports that even after getting Gary's help, each time she wanted to start the tool, she first had to look up the steps. During part of the project, she realized she was avoiding starting the software because it was too hard to work with.

Next, Jas had trouble getting the software to work when he installed it from the build drop area we set up on Groove. Jas turned to Gary; through a series of chat sessions on Groove and one or two phone calls, he got the software working. Gary knew that he needed to address the installation, but he kept deferring it. These events were just *one-time* occurrences, so it wasn't really *that* important.

Actually, it was that important. As soon as we finished the Elaboration phase, more people wanted to try the software. They needed to install it without problems, and we didn't have a satisfactory way for them to do it. Jas worked with people who tried to install the software and gave up in frustration. Jas kept requesting a better installation experience but Gary still deferred the work. Because we weren't ready when potential users wanted to use the software, we missed an opportunity to get early feedback.

Creating a usable installation process actually was very simple, but Gary didn't want to think about it. He wanted to write the code for the product and see the functionality from the critical use cases materialize. Without an acceptable way to install the software, however, prospective users would never get to the use cases. A well-known lesson in software product development is that if a customer, or potential customer, tries your product and fails to use it the first time, you may have lost that customer forever. You certainly have lost the customer's trust and have to work especially hard to get it back and convince him or her to give your product another try.

How could we have avoided this problem? The simplest way would have been to make installing the software a use case in our requirements at the beginning. It isn't clear whether we would have prioritized it as a critical one in our Inception phase, but we would have thought about it and when the need arose, we would have had some idea of how it might work. In Chapter 8, you will see that the problem wasn't hard. In fact, it took Gary less than an hour to produce an acceptable install solution. A lot of damage had been done by that time. Hopefully the potential users will give PSP Tools another try.

Assessing the Elaboration Phase

At the beginning of this chapter, we stated the Elaboration phase's goals. How did we do, and were we through with the Elaboration phase? We didn't complete everything we identified in the Elaboration iteration plan.

We spent little time updating the overall project plan. Gary pulled together an initial software architecture document. Liz drafted a support and documentation plan. Most of the documents were not used as we progressed. The reason is simple: We talked to each other regularly and kept brief lists of what we needed or were doing on Groove. And this was (yes, you guessed it) good enough for this project.

What about the LCA (Lifecycle Architecture) milestone—did we get there? Yes we did. At the end of the iteration, we were able to present Russell with an executable architecture. More importantly, we were able to use it as the basis for upcoming iterations, and we could talk in terms of what we had produced. We reduced the risk of working with a database. It really wasn't that hard. Our requirements changed somewhat during the Elaboration phase, mainly because we scoped out some of the things we hoped to deliver for the initial release. But the requirements had stabilized enough so that we understood what work we needed to complete to finish the project.

We wrote a short iteration plan for the first iteration in the Construction phase. This was the last plan we wrote down. (There will be more to say about this in Chapter 8.) We declared victory and began our march through the Construction phase.

Reviewing the Executable Architecture

During our Elaboration phase assessment, we wanted to review the executable architecture at one of our regular team meetings before showing it to Russell. We wanted to look at the software and step through the use cases and scenarios together. There are several communication tools that allow you to share views of working software, such as Microsoft NetMeeting and WebEx software. However, some of us were working with slow connections; using group communication software with such connections can be painful.

We found a solution to our problem with a software tool that allowed us to record a session with the executable architecture and share that session with the team. We used the *Viewlet* technology from Qarbon, Inc.[14]

Gary recorded a Viewlet of using the PSP Tools software, stepping through each of the expected scenarios. He added comments to the Viewlet that helped the team understand what was included and excluded from the software at that point. After he compiled the Viewlet, he placed it on Groove and the team used that to explore the software together. Figure 6.12 shows a snapshot from the Elaboration phase review Viewlet.

---

[14] See www.qarbon.com for information on the Viewlet technology.

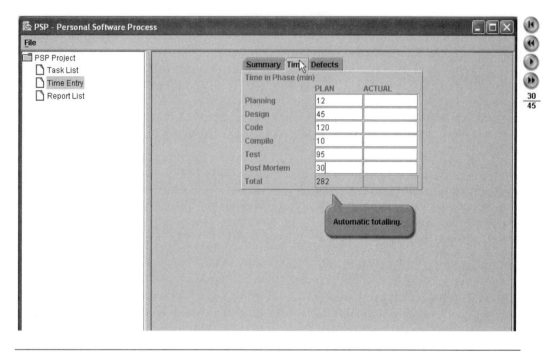

Figure 6.12 Snapshot from the Elaboration phase review Viewlet

Viewlets are a great way to demonstrate your work, or to document and train people on your software. We included the Elaboration phrase review Viewlet on the Web site for the book.

Summary

In the Elaboration phase, you drive down the biggest technical risks and set up your project for success. You want to make the Construction phase as smooth as possible, knowing that there will always be changes. You spend some time addressing the architecture along with other technical risks and develop an executable architecture. This lets you show your stakeholders a candidate architecture that you are able to implement. Just as important, you are able to show them working software.

The PSP Tools project was simple, but we identified some technical risks involving the database technology. We selected just enough of the requirements—use cases and scenarios—to implement in order to give us the confidence that we would be able to deliver software to our customer that satisfied his needs as we understood them. We also were able to reason about our solution and understand how it might be enhanced in the future to meet changing requirements.

PSPTools Elaboration: 3 weeks

CHAPTER 7

Elaboration Details

The previous chapter on the Elaboration phase discussed the phase from a high-level project view. For readers who want more information about the actual software development work that we performed, this chapter presents a more detailed view of the technical aspects of the Elaboration phase, including these topics:

- *Getting started*—How we structured the code, the conventions we adopted, and other administrative details that helped us.
- *Starting to implement the user interface*—Getting the user interface up and running wasn't too difficult, but when you haven't explored all of the capabilities of the Java Swing classes, there can be some surprises.
- *The database*—This presented the highest technical risk to the project because neither developer had much experience designing or extracting data from databases, especially with Java.
- *Testing*—Chris and Gary decided to use a test-first approach as much as possible. We talk about how we set up the tests and what we actually did during the Elaboration phase.

Beginning the Elaboration Phase

Before the Elaboration phase, Chris and Gary explored some of the technologies they would be working with. They met several times to discuss how PSP Tools might look, what the database needed to do, the tools they wanted to use, and so on. Now it was time to act on the decisions they made.

Which Java Platform?

We could use any one of several languages to develop PSP Tools. We knew we wanted one that would allow us to deploy to as many customers as possible, which meant we needed the program to run on many different computing platforms. We chose Java mainly for this reason, and for the fact that we were comfortable with programming in Java.

Java is more than a language. Sometimes we feel that if you create an acronym of any three or four letters starting with "J" you have identified yet another Java-related technology (for example, JDBC, JNI, JNDI, JMS, and so on). Simply put—*Java is BIG!* Our first task was to decide what parts of the Java platform to use.

If you stick to just the Java platform, the options for building GUIs (graphical user interfaces) are Swing and the more basic AWT (Abstract Window Toolkit), a graphics toolkit. The Java Swing components are designed for building GUIs for desktop applications, while AWT requires you to do more work. Many people have concerns about the performance of the Swing components, but we felt that performance wasn't a major issue for the PSP Tools user interface. Other graphic toolkits are available, but each would require additional startup time and would require us to distribute an additional library with PSP Tools. Swing seemed to be a good choice.

When we started PSP Tools, the Java 1.4 platform was in Beta testing. Some of the new features might have been useful, but we chose to use Java 1.3.1 instead. We know that Beta software is likely to change and that it is not as mature (that is, reliable and stable) as released versions of the software. In general, we recommend that you not base your product on Beta versions of any software or tools *unless it is impossible to deliver your product without it*. We think this is just a matter of applying common sense, yet it is amazing how many projects have Beta-quality or early releases of software on their list of critical needs in order to deliver their own product.

What About the Database?

The database was the other important technology we needed. The Java platform helped us here with the Java Database Connectivity (JDBC) API that is part of the Java 2 Enterprise Edition (J2EE) platform. JDBC gave us a standard, well-defined way of working with a database with Java. And, the J2EE distribution comes with the Cloudscape database DBMS as a reference implementation. In theory, if we were able to get the program working with Cloudscape, using only the JDBC API, we should be able to easily slide in a different DBMS in future releases. So, J2EE version 1.3 was our choice for the database technology.

Other Development Tools

We (Chris and Gary) decided to use two other tools at this point in the project. Rational ClearCase was a simple choice for our version control needs. We were both familiar with it and it was available to both of us on at least one of our computers.

Like Java, ClearCase is big. But once you set it up, it is very easy to use the few ClearCase features you work with regularly. It takes a little more effort to perform some of the advanced operations with ClearCase, but knowing those operations are available when you need them does bring development teams peace of mind.

Neither Chris nor Gary is a ClearCase administrator. We enlisted the help of one of the Rational ClearCase administrators to set up a VOB (versioned object base) for our project. The VOB is where all versions of a system, or part of a system, are stored. Once you have the VOBs you need, each team member who needs access to the files sets up a *view* onto the VOBs. The view selects the appropriate versions of each file based upon a specification, called a *configuration specification.*[1]

ClearCase was overkill for PSP Tools. Yet, once it is set up, it is just as easy to use as any other version control or configuration management software tool. We had confidence that regardless of how our project grew, ClearCase could handle our needs and we wouldn't have to worry about switching tools.

The second development tool we selected was the Forte for Java Community Edition IDE. We already discussed the selection of IDEs in Chapter 6 and will not repeat it here.

Source Code Structure

We wanted our code structure to be as simple as possible, but no simpler. It should be easy to explain what the different packages and files contain, and it should be easy to remember the description.

We organized the PSP Tools code in two ways. The first was in terms of layers. Although the product was simple and didn't require a complex

---

[1] For more information on ClearCase, see the Rational Web site, www.rational.com, or look at the book *Software Configuration Management Strategies and Rational ClearCase* by Brian White.

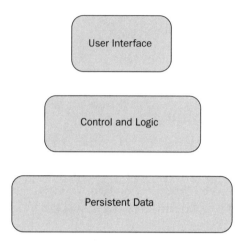

Figure 7.1 PSP Tools layers

architecture, we wanted to have a good base for future additions. We chose to think of the application in three layers, shown in Figure 7.1. The layering scheme is simple, but it gave us an initial cut at where we needed to locate the different packages we created and the classes that went into the packages. Initially we were not sure whether there would be a single package in each layer or whether some layers would have multiple packages.

Layers are one way to look at the architecture of a system, but understanding the layers is not sufficient to understand how the system is structured. As we began to design the different classes we wanted, we added some packages to the layers. Figure 7.2 shows the packages we ended up with.

Due to the simplicity of the application, we ended up with one package per layer except for the persistent data layer. There are also some packages outside the three main layers. We could consider these packages as a *utility layer*, but in general they were not so cohesive that we felt they deserved the layer label. The utility packages contain *helper classes* that are used by the other layers.

Figure 7.2 also shows the main dependency arrows for the packages in the layers. A dependency is "A relationship between two *modeling elements*, in which a change to one modeling element (the independent element) will affect the other modeling element (the dependent element)."[2] A good design

---

[2] UML glossary, version 1.5.

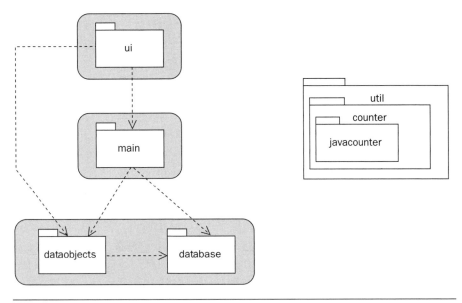

Figure 7.2 Final PSP Tools packages

practice is to avoid two-way dependencies. We actually have some mutual dependencies that we will talk about when we discuss the Construction details in Chapter 9. The arrows in Figure 7.2 show the ideal dependencies.

The PSP Tools User Interface

Developing a user interface is its own special art. There are many guidelines and standards to follow, some of them contradictory when you develop for multiple platforms. Neither Chris nor Gary is an expert user interface designer. However, we have had some training on what makes a usable UI and applied that knowledge to the PSP Tools user interface. This section describes some of the challenges and our approach to designing the UI.

The User Interface Ripple Effect

On most projects, the UI will go through several iterations and revisions before it is ready to ship. These continual changes have two significant consequences.

First, UI changes can affect your testing effort. If your test scripts are executed manually, they are very susceptible to simple changes in the UI. For example, if the text of a menu item or button changes, the test script must be changed so the tester knows which selection to make or button to push. Keeping the tests in synchronization with the code can be time consuming.

If you are using automated test tools (and we highly recommend that you do), you need to make sure that you design your tests in such a way that cosmetic changes to the UI require little or no change to the tests. This often means that you need to do more than use a record-playback testing tool. You need to read the script that the tool produces to ensure that it accommodates changes to the UI in the best possible way. Sometimes it is better to write the test script without recording the initial test gestures. In any case, the test tool you use should work on the specific objects in a way that does not identify the object by the text on a label or some other textual or positional property of the object.

The second item that is affected by UI changes is the documentation. When the text of a visible item on the screen changes, the documentation may require an associated change. When you move, add, or remove items on the screen, the screen shots that you might want to include in the documentation immediately become obsolete.

These self-defense tips will help you avoid many last-minute documentation changes:

- Negotiate with the project leader to establish a UI freeze date that's earlier than the documentation and code freeze dates. Even if you agree to a week-long grace period, that gives you enough time to catch and correct last-minute changes. This technique also helps raise engineers' awareness of the impact of UI changes on your work.
- Write in a top-down fashion, starting with organization, then working on use cases, and writing the conceptual information. Fill in the details about using the user interface as late as possible in the project.
- Minimize your use of screen shots, using them for significant milestones in long procedures or to visually describe a procedure that's difficult to explain in words. When you do use screen shots, capture only the relevant portion of the screen, not the entire screen or desktop.
- Work closely with the QA team. Because the documentation and the tests should be based on use cases, your documentation can serve as one of the test cases for the product. In return, it is helpful to ask

testers to review your work. This collaboration helps both the writers and the testers work more efficiently because it eliminates duplicate work. More importantly, your customers benefit by receiving a more bug-free product with more accurate documentation.

■ Maintain a sense of humor and an attitude of flexibility. You can minimize last-minute changes but you can't eliminate them entirely.

Our First UI

The Elaboration Iteration Plan identified the use cases and scenarios we planned to implement: Create a New Task and Open the Project Database. We were most concerned with the code in the control and logic and in the persistent data layers. We felt the highest risks to the project's success were in the code in these layers. But we had to show the complete sequence of operations, so we could not completely ignore the UI.

We had an idea of what we wanted the application to look like (see Figure 6.6), but we were unsure about the details. For the Elaboration phase we deferred these details and only created enough of the UI to show that we had successfully implemented the planned functionality. The user interface we created early in the Elaboration phase is shown in Figure 7.3.

The UI in Figure 7.3 is not suitable for delivery to customers. It has just one menu, usually a sign that the full functionality is not implemented, or that it is a *very* simple application. Further, the tabbed panes take up too little space in their enclosing pane. The text fields are not large enough

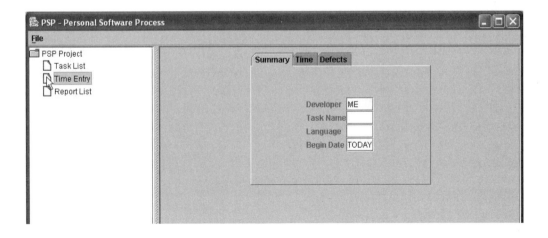

Figure 7.3 UI early in the Elaboration phase

to display much information. We were not sure what the tree in the left pane would look like, but at this point we thought there would be separate folders in the tree for tasks, time entries, and reports. If you take a moment to think about what we needed, this UI required more work. We needed to show defects. And, in general, it is not clear what you can or cannot do by just looking at this UI. Yet, there is enough of a framework for the UI that we could build upon it and modify it easily.

Exploring the UI Code

There are a few Java Swing components that are key to understanding the structure of the user interface. If you are an experienced Java programmer, you can probably skip to the end of this section, but for those of you who are new to Java, or to Swing, you will find our explaination helpful for exploring the code on your own. The key Swing components for the main PSP Tools window are shown in Figure 7.4.

We began developing the user interface with the GUI builder from the Forte IDE. While it was easy to create the components and make them

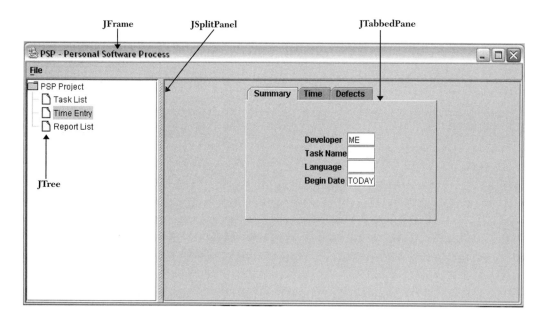

Figure 7.4 Key Swing items in the PSP Tools main window

work, we found that the generated code wasn't always easy to understand, making it difficult to modify when we were not working with the GUI builder. We also found places where dependencies on Forte libraries were inserted into the code. Even before we decided to switch to the Eclipse IDE, we began writing our UI code without resorting to the GUI builder.

Creating and composing the Swing components identified in Figure 7.4 involved more than just creating objects and gluing them together. Each component requires initialization and customization. When we refactored and rewrote the code to remove the GUI builder dependencies, we made sure that each constructor called an `initialize` method that did the work of initialization and customization. The initialization for the JFrame, which is in our class `PSPMainFrame`, is shown in Listing 7.1.[3]

Listing 7.1 PSPMainFrame initialization code

```
/**
 * Initialize the frame by setting default behaviors such
 * as the default close operation, and so on.
 */
private void initializeFrame()
{
      setDefaultCloseOperation(DO_NOTHING_ON_CLOSE);
      setTitle(APP_TITLE);
      setupMenus();
      setJMenuBar(menuBar);
      addWindowListener(
          new WindowAdapter()
        {
            public void windowClosing(WindowEvent evt)
            {
                doFileExit();
            }
        });

      int width = PSPUserPrefs.getWidth();
      int height= PSPUserPrefs.getHeight();
      if (width == 0 || height == 0)
```

continues

---

[3] The code you can download from the book's Web site may look slightly different. Chris and Gary planned on making a final review and refactoring pass through the code before packaging it for the site.

```
        {
setBounds(INITIAL_X, INITIAL_Y, INITIAL_WIDTH,
  INITIAL_HEIGHT);
        }
    else
        {
        setBounds(INITIAL_X, INITIAL_Y, width, height);
        }

    mainPanel = new JPanel();
    /*
     * DO NOT remove the next line. It seems to do nothing, but
     * it is necessary to get the pane into memory.
     */
    JRootPane rootPane = getRootPane();
    getContentPane().add(createSplitPane(),
          BorderLayout.CENTER);


  }
```

Notice that the code only creates the split panel. The tree and the tabbed panes are not built. They will be added to the left and right sides of the split panel when a database is opened or created.

One technique we used consistently is shown in Listing 7.1, where we add the window listener. We need to add an instance of the `Window-Adapter` class to the set of listeners attached to the window. This enables us to recognize when the user clicks the close box in the upper right corner. The default behavior is to simply exit the application and close the window and any of the window's children. We want to override this behavior by calling the `doFileExit()` method[4] to gracefully exit the program when the window closes.

We only need one instance of this specific window adapter class. Rather than creating a separately named class, the Java language lets us create an *anonymous class*. The anonymous class is declared inline as shown. The

---

[4] The name `doFileExit` follows a naming convention we use for methods that are called from menu selections. In this case, the name tells us that this is the Exit command selected from the File menu.

only method we need to override is the `windowClosing()` method, which we declare in the anonymous class definition.

The `PSPMainFrame.java` file contains quite a bit of code since it is the main interface for the PSP Tools user. Most of the code, especially the code developed during the Elaboration phase, is not very interesting. After the frame is initialized, the main frame waits for the user to do something by interacting with it. This interaction occurs in one of the following ways:

- Making a menu selection
- Clicking on an item in the tree, if a tree is displayed in the left panel
- Closing the window and exiting the program through the close box
- Selecting a tab in the tabbed panel, if one is displayed
- Entering data from the keyboard into one of the fields in a panel

There are other gestures the user might make, such as minimizing and restoring a window, but these are handled directly by the Swing class instances and require no intervention on the part of our code.

We use a simple approach to handling menu commands. We have an `ActionListener` class object attached to each menu selection. The `ActionListener` is responsible for "listening" to what is happening in the application, and when the event that it is listening for occurs, it invokes some action. We install the `ActionListener` when we create the menu command. The menu commands are created when we set up the menus. The third statement in the method in Listing 7.1 calls the `setupMenus()` method, which is shown in Listing 7.2.

Listing 7.2 Setting up the PSP Tools menus

```
    /**
     * Set up the menus for the application.
     */
    private void setupMenus()
    {
        menuBar = new JMenuBar();
        menuBar.add(createFileMenu());
        menuBar.add(createProjectMenu());
        menuBar.add(createToolsMenu());
        menuBar.add(createHelpMenu());
    }
```

It is easy to add a new menu to the main menu bar. You add a method to create the menu and add the returned menu to the menu bar. The more interesting code is in the methods that create the menus. They are the ones that create the specific action listeners. Listing 7.3 shows the section of code in createFileMenu() that adds the menu item for opening a project database. All of the menu items are added in a similar fashion.

Listing 7.3 Adding the Open item to the File menu

```
// Open Project Database
JMenuItem fileOpen = new JMenuItem("Open...");
fileOpen.setMnemonic('O');
fileOpen.addActionListener(
    new ActionListener()
    {
        public void actionPerformed(ActionEvent evt)
        {
            doFileOpen(null);
        }
    });
fileMenu.add(fileOpen);
```

The sequence we use to add an item to a menu is as follows:

1. Create the new JMenuItem with the appropriate label.
2. Set the mnemonic (that is, the key that is used with the system-specific "mouseless modifier"—usually Alt) to select the menu item.
3. Add the action listener, using an anonymous class.
4. Add the menu item to the appropriate menu.

We will close this section by providing an insight to the tree that appears in the left pane of the UI. Trees are very powerful and provide a visual model that users are familiar with. We often see file systems presented in a tree form. Trees in Java require the programmer to know a little more than most of the other Swing components. However, if you just need to perform standard tasks with your tree, Java makes life a little easier for you. We chose the easy way, shown in Listing 7.4. The "easy way" means that you use a default tree model, which is sufficient for modeling the tree node behavior and appearance for most applications.

Listing 7.4 The PSPTree constructor

```java
/**
 * Default constructor.
 */
public PSPTree()
{
    super();
    model = new DefaultTreeModel(rootNode);
    setModel(model);
    getSelectionModel().setSelectionMode(
        TreeSelectionModel.SINGLE_TREE_SELECTION);
    putClientProperty("JTree.lineStyle", "Horizontal");
    setShowsRootHandles(true);

    //Listen for RMB clicks
    addMouseListener (myMouseListener);

    //Listen for when the selection changes.
    addTreeSelectionListener(new TreeSelectionListener()
    {
        public void valueChanged(TreeSelectionEvent e)
        {
            DefaultMutableTreeNode node =
(DefaultMutableTreeNode)getLastSelectedPathComponent();
            if (node == null) {
                return;
            }

            Object nodeInfo = node.getUserObject() ;

            if (nodeInfo instanceof Task) {
                (Task)nodeInfo.setTopTab(
                    getRequestedTab());
                JPanel newPanel =
                ((Task)nodeInfo).getPanel(nodeInfo);
                ((PSPMainFrame)getTopLevelAncestor()).
                    setRightPane(newPanel);
                ((PSPMainFrame)getTopLevelAncestor()).
                    setMenuFor(PSPMainFrame.PSP_TASK);
                ItemID = ((Task)nodeInfo).getTaskID();
                tm = null;
            } else if (nodeInfo instanceof PSPTimeSummary){
```

continues

```
// ...
} else if
                    (nodeInfo instanceof PSPDefectSummary) {
                        // ...
                    } else {       // this is the Root Object
                        // ...
                    }
            }
        });
```

We will populate the tree after we create it. The constructor shown in Listing 7.4 creates an empty tree that has a default tree model. Trees, like many other graphical objects in Swing and other graphical frameworks, have a separate data model for which the graphical object provides a view on that data. A JTree object (PSPTree is a subclass of JTree) requires a model that is a class implementing the TreeModel interface. If you want standard behavior, which we do, you can use the DefaultTreeModel, which is defined in the Swing framework. We need to set the property in the tree model that ensures that only a single item in the tree can be selected at any time.

We finish the constructor by adding a listener that is a TreeSelectionListener. This object listens for events, such as mouse clicks that select a tree item, and takes appropriate action. In our constructor, we look to see if the node is a task, time summary, or a report. For formatting purposes, we inserted comments instead of code where there are repetitive types of code segments. The final version of PSPTree looks different since we reorganized and refined the UI.

The PSPTree class has several methods that handle the actions invoked by the tree selection listener. If you want to understand how the tree is structured, study the loadTasks() method. When a project database is open, this method is called. It asks the database object to return the items (tasks) for the current user, and these are added individually to the tree with the proper structure. The root node of the tree is kept as a private variable in the PSPTree instance.

There is a lot more code to the PSP Tools UI than we have shown here. But this is not a book on Java. There are several books available that can help you to get better information than we can provide here. We want to give you a feel for the code so that you can explore for yourself and understand it enough to begin to modify it for your own needs.

The PSP Tools Database

One approach to developing our application was to defer the database until we absolutely were forced to implement it. If we were sure that we could release the first version of PSP Tools without a real database, we would have deferred it. But we were not sure and, if we did need it, it was important to get an estimate of how long it would take to get it working.

You may wonder how we would avoid creating the database. Java can "serialize" objects. The `java.io` package provides a `Serializable` interface. When your classes implement this interface, you are able to write objects of the class to some persistent storage, like a disk, and read them back later. We could have built a data model of the different classes and their relationships and serialized the data to a file, just as we ended up writing to a database. However, it seems much easier to let the DBMS worry about ensuring that the appropriate connections are made between objects and that two programs using the same database will not corrupt the database when they try to update the same information at the same time.

In this section we describe the physical layout of the database and look at how to access the database from Java. We will use some SQL (Structured Query Language) statements. If you are not familiar with SQL, there are many good references, but we will explain the statements we do use.

UML is a good language for describing databases, especially when you are working on an object-oriented system.[5] Even though our chosen DBMS is not an object-oriented database, we want to think of it as a data store that contains objects, not just tables.[6] We show the structure of the database and its objects in Figure 7.5.

Figure 7.5 is quite simple, yet it conveys a lot of information.[7] It tells us that there is exactly one PSPDatabaseInfo object in any PSP Tools database. It also tells us the different types of objects that are stored in a PSP Tools database. The asterisk (*) on the arrow end of each aggregation association tells us that there can be any number of that type of object (like PSPTask) in

---

[5] See *UML for Database Design* by Eric J. Naiburg and Robert A. Maksimchuk.

[6] An object-oriented database and an object-oriented database management system (OODBMS) offer advanced capabilities for storing and accessing objects. See "The Object-Oriented Database System Manifesto" by Atkinson et al. for one definition of an OODBMS. It is available on several Web sites. The easiest way to find the Manifesto is to use a search engine.

[7] We assume that readers of this chapter have a basic understanding of UML. If not, there are many good references and Web sites that will give you enough information to understand the little bit of UML that we use here. A good starting place is www.omg.org/uml.

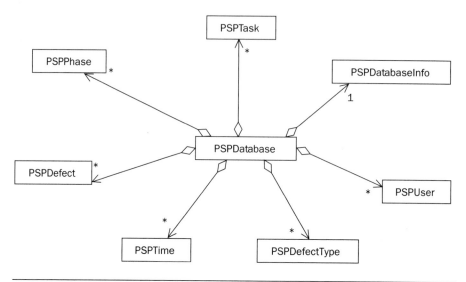

Figure 7.5 PSP Tools database structure

a PSP Tools database. The objects shown in the diagram provide us with the information we need to identify the tables in our database.

We could include more details in the diagram in Figure 7.5, but we think that more information would clutter it up. Instead, we chose to create another diagram that shows the different properties of the objects. It then becomes quite easy to use those properties to create the schema for our database. Figure 7.6 shows a diagram that describes our database in a different way, with more detail.

We use a class diagram to show the objects that are stored in the database. There is one table for each class in the diagram. By making the attributes of each class visible, we can see the specific fields that belong in each table.

The information we get from the diagram in Figure 7.6 lets us create a script that creates an initial database. We created such a script, `createdb.sql`, and used it to build our test database for use during early testing. It was trivial to recreate the database when we wanted to run a new set of tests or rerun previous tests.

Figure 7.7 shows the specific fields for the `PSPUser` class and the associated code in `createdb.sql` that creates and populates the Users table. You can easily create similar diagrams to show the other table structures. We created the diagram in Figure 7.7 with Rational XDE. The figure illustrates a feature of UML tools that we think is important—that tools such as

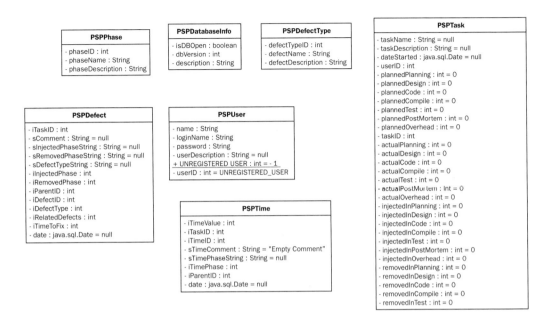

Figure 7.6 Diagram showing database tables and fields

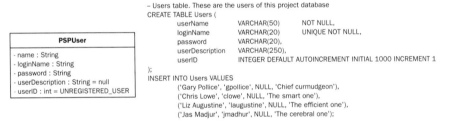

Figure 7.7 The PSPUser class and associated code from createdb.sql

XDE allow you to insert all kinds of information into a diagram in addition to the UML structures. In this figure, we placed the script we used to create the table in the database on the same class diagram with the associated UML class representation.

We used several scripts with the Cloudview tool to create, update, and clean up our database as we made our way through the Elaboration phase. They are all available on the book's Web site.

Unit Testing

Unit testing verifies that individual parts of the system comply with the requirements. With an object-oriented language, such as Java, the preferred unit for testing is the class. Typically, individual developers do unit testing, or at least they should do it. Far too many programmers today think that programming is just about coding and that someone else, the tester, is responsible for testing. Methodologies such as RUP and XP clearly identify different types of testing and place unit testing in the developer's set of responsibilities.

The Plan—Test-First Programming

We planned on using the practice of Test-First Programming (TFP). This practice requires that you write a test for the functionality *you are about to implement*. You then write the code to make the test pass. The theory behind this technique is that the test embodies the requirements for the code. By writing the test first, you ensure that you write the code to satisfy the requirements. When you write the test after the code, there is more of a chance that you will write the test to fit your code, which may not accurately reflect the requirements. If you are interested in Test-First Programming, which has evolved to Test-Driven Development, we recommend Kent Beck's book *Test-Driven Development: By Example* for an overview of the subject, and David Astels' *Test-Driven Development: A Practical Guide* for an excellent view of the details.

The Reality

TFP makes sense. There is not yet enough empirical evidence to make a definitive statement about its efficacy, but there seem to be enough testimonials and studies to suggest positive results in some situations. Chris and Gary both planned on adopting the practice.

Unfortunately, they didn't follow through on this part of their plans. Does this mean that they failed? No. They learned a lot about developing unit tests. They also learned that performing unit tests on certain types of classes and methods is much more difficult and time-consuming than on other types of classes—regardless of whether the tests are written before or after the code. They also learned that the practice requires a lot of discipline, which takes time to acquire.

The classes that required more effort for writing tests were the GUI classes, such as the windows and dialogs, and the classes that required database access. They required more effort than we were willing to expend on this project. We would have needed to research the different ways we might implement and automate the unit tests for these classes. The results of the research would have given us knowledge of how to do the job, and then we would have worked on our skills to do the job effectively. We chose not to pursue this path for the PSP Tools project.

Most projects face decisions such as the one just described. We all want to learn new skills and techniques. However, sometimes we make a decision based upon some criterion, such as the time we think it will take to master the skills enough to successfully use them, to defer the learning until another time. This is, in our opinion, part of being a professional.

In Chapter 11, both Chris and Gary lament their lack of follow-through on unit tests. They both believe that the code would have been better initially had they been more disciplined. They also agree that those classes for which they wrote unit tests before the code had few, if any, defects against them.

Tools and Techniques

When you write unit tests, you need a way to automate them. Every time you write new code, you want to have tests that exercise the code, and you want to execute all previous tests to ensure that you didn't make a change that broke some other code in the system. Manually executing unit tests every time you change the code is not practical.

Fortunately for most programmers today, a unit test framework is freely available for most programming languages. The framework defines a way of writing and executing tests, provides appropriate libraries to support writing and running the tests, and helps you view the results of the tests. The framework goes by different names depending on the programming language. For Java, it is called JUnit.[8] JUnit is available for download at www.junit.org. The Web pages for JUnit contain documentation and other supporting tools, many of them integrations with IDEs. We used the JUnit add-in for Eclipse.

---

[8] Other languages have unit test frameworks with names like CUnit for C and VBUnit for Visual Basic.

Anatomy of a JUnit Test

Writing JUnit tests is simple. You must follow just a few rules when you write your test code, for example:

- Each test method must begin with the string "test." JUnit uses the reflection feature of Java to identify the test case's methods that should be run when executing the unit tests.
- The test case classes can have any name, but we recommend that for any <class>, name your test cases either Test<class> or <class>Test. We chose the latter naming convention.
- If you have code that you want to run *before* every test method in the test case class, insert it into the setUp() method.
- If you have code that you want to run *after* every test method in the test case class, insert it into the tearDown() method.
- If you want to run just the tests of the test class, provide a main() method.

The easiest way to get started is to use a code template. Many of the JUnit IDE integrations come with templates for JUnit tests. Start with one of them and modify it for your needs. We used the template that came with the Eclipse add-in for JUnit. The JUnit integration for Eclipse makes it easy to follow the rules and guidelines.

You select the class for which you want a test case, choose the methods that require tests, and select a couple of other properties. The JUnit integration generates a test case source file as shown in Listing 7.5, with stubs for the test methods.

Listing 7.5 JUnit test case

```
package com.skunkworks.psp.main;

import junit.framework.TestCase;

/**
 * @author Gary Pollice
 */
public class PSPNewUserManagerTest extends TestCase {

    /**
     * Constructor for PSPNewUserManagerTest.
     * @param arg0
     */
```

```
public PSPNewUserManagerTest(String arg0) {
    super(arg0);
}

public static void main(String[] args) {
    junit.textui.TestRunner.run(PSPNewUserManagerTest.class);
}

/**
 * @see TestCase#setUp()
 */
protected void setUp() throws Exception {
    super.setUp();
}

/**
 * @see TestCase#tearDown()
 */
protected void tearDown() throws Exception {
    super.tearDown();
}

public void testPSPNewUserManager() {}

public void testDoNewUser() {}
}
```

Notice that the test methods in Listing 7.5 do not have a return value. Each test is self-contained and uses special functions for testing the correctness of the code. These methods are associated with the Assert class that is part of the JUnit framework. The Assert class is used to group static functions that allow you to code conditions in your JUnit tests. As long as the *assertion* is valid, the test continues. If the assertion is invalid, the test stops and reports an error. Listing 7.6, taken from the PSPUserTest class, illustrates the use of the assertTrue() method. We make two assertions. The first ensures that two PSPUser objects with the same user name and login name compare as equal. The second assertion ensures that when the user names and login names are different, then the objects are not equal.

Listing 7.6 Using assertions in unit tests

```
/** Test of equals method, of class PSPUser. */
    public void testEquals() {
        System.out.println("testEquals");

        PSPUser u = new PSPUser("Gary Pollice", "gpollice");
        Assert.assertTrue(u.equals(new PSPUser("Gary Pollice",
            "gpollice")));
        Assert.assertTrue(!(u.equals(new PSPUser("test", "test"))));
    }
```

The astute reader will note that we have not tested all possible conditions in Listing 7.6, such as the same user name, but different login names and so on. You have to decide when you have done enough, based on the possible damage an error in the method would cause.

Test Suites Group Tests

Sometimes you want to run one specific test, such as the one shown in Listing 7.5. More often, you want to run more than one test, so you use a *test suite* to collect the set of tests to run. For example, after you change your code, you usually want to run all your tests to ensure that you have not introduced regressions with the changes, and to ensure that the tests still run successfully.

The structure of a test suite is similar to that of an individual test, except that in the test suite you specify which tests to run (remember that in an individual test, you specify which methods to call). You can specify a combination of tests and other test suites. This allows you to have a single test suite file that runs all your tests. Listing 7.7 illustrates our top-level test suite. It simply runs all the tests specified in the test suites of the subpackages.

Listing 7.7 Main PSP Tools test suite

```
public class PSPSuite extends TestCase {

    public PSPSuite(java.lang.String testName) {
        super(testName);
    }
```

```
public static void main(java.lang.String[] args) {
    junit.textui.TestRunner.run(suite());
}

public static Test suite() {
    ///$JUnit-BEGIN$
    TestSuite suite = new TestSuite("PSPSuite");
    suite.addTest(com.skunkworks.psp.main.MainSuite.suite());
    suite.addTest(com.skunkworks.psp.util.UtilSuite.suite());

suite.addTest(com.skunkworks.psp.dataobjects.DataObjectSuite.suite()
);

suite.addTest(com.skunkworks.psp.database.DatabaseSuite.suite());
    //$JUnit-END$
    return suite;
    }
}
```

The layout of a test suite is very simple. The constructor and `main()` method are part of our template. The `suite()` method does the following:

1. It creates a new `TestSuite` object. The `TestSuite` is one of the classes provided in the JUnit framework.
2. It adds the tests returned by the `suite()` methods of the test suites in the subpackages to the `TestSuite` object created in Step 1. The `suite()` method in the `TestSuite` objects in the subpackages gathers the objects' tests and passes them back in the form of a `TestSuite`.

The test suites in the subpackages can further invoke test suites in their subpackages or specifically add the tests contained in their own packages. Listing 7.8 shows how the test suite for the `main` package adds the individual tests. The example has been shortened to just show it adding the tests from the `PSPNewUserManagerTest` class shown in Listing 7.5.

Listing 7.8 TestSuite class in the main package

```java
package com.skunkworks.psp.main;

import junit.framework.*;

public class MainSuite extends TestCase {

    public MainSuite(java.lang.String testName) {
        super(testName);
    }

    public static void main(java.lang.String[] args) {
        junit.textui.TestRunner.run(suite());
    }

    public static Test suite() {
        ////$JUnit-BEGIN$
        TestSuite suite = new TestSuite("MainSuite");
        suite.addTest(
            new
           TestSuite(com.skunkworks.psp.main.PSPNewUserManagerTest
              .class));
        ////$JUnit-END$
        return suite;
    }
}
```

Adding the tests from the `PSPNewUserManagerTest` class takes advantage of Java's ability to examine class contents dynamically. The second statement in the `suite()` method of Listing 7.8 creates a new `TestSuite` object that contains just the tests defined in `PSPNewUser-ManagerTest`. When we add code to bundle the rest of the tests into the test suite, we return the composite test suite to the caller, in this case the `PSPSuite` object.

Once you establish a method for using JUnit and you create the templates, it is easy to add to your test cases. You then can concentrate on the hard work of writing good tests.

Running the Unit Tests

You can run the unit tests by executing the `main()` method from specific test classes or test suite classes. Many IDEs have integrations that let you run your tests directly from them. The Eclipse platform provides a nice JUnit integration. We simply select the test case or test suite and run it as a JUnit test. The results are shown graphically. As long as you are not color blind,[9] the status of your tests is instantly obvious by glancing at the result bar—green means everything passed, red means something failed and requires investigation. The actual failures are displayed, with stack traces and other useful information in the error windows. Figure 7.8 shows the result of running just one of our test cases in Eclipse. The Hierarchy tab shows the single test that was run (`testMakeDatabase`) and the green bar tells us that the test passed.

Figure 7.8 JUnit test results viewed in Eclipse

---

[9] Red and green are the hardest colors for people afflicted with color blindness to distinguish.

Summary

This chapter describes some of the technical details of the PSP Tools project's Elaboration phase. Our purpose here is to convey our approach to developing a solution for Russell. We provide only a taste of the details. For more, see our code, models, and other artifacts on the book's Web site.

CHAPTER 8

Construction: We Build PSP Tools

Construction is the phase where development teams, especially the programmers, do what they know how to do best—implement the software. Some people think that the Construction phase is all about programming, but this phase involves more than just writing code. As described in the RUP hump chart, each discipline usually applies some effort in every iteration. During the Construction phase, the Implementation discipline is predominant, but significant work is done in analysis and design, testing, and configuration management. The PSP Tools project illustrates this point quite well.

This chapter describes our journey through the Construction phase. We started by examining our tools and fine-tuning our environment. We planned the iterations, started implementing code slowly, then developed our own rhythm and became productive.

Adjusting the Environment Again

The RUP hump chart illustrates an often-overlooked feature: At the beginning of each phase, there is a small spike in effort devoted to the development environment. In other words, don't set up your tools and procedures at the beginning of the project and expect them to remain static throughout the project. Even small projects completed in a short time frame are susceptible to changes in the environment.

Our project was more susceptible to changes because we were working on it part time and it took longer than it would have otherwise. Another factor that caused more changes to our environment was that for some of the time, we were working with early, unreleased versions of Rational tools because that was the environment we needed to work in for our regular

135

work (our day jobs). Because we worked on teams for our regular jobs, we needed to change versions of tools in synchronization with our teams. We did not have the "luxury" of staying with earlier versions until our PSP Tools project was finished.

In Chapter 6, we discussed the changes in our development platform: we switched from Forte to Rational XDE and the Eclipse development environment. In the Construction phase, we made additional adjustments to address the needs and limitations of our team.

We have already discussed some of the characteristics of our team—the geographical distribution, frequent traveling, and the fact that we did not all work for the same company. These factors affected our version control, defect tracking, and requirements management tools.

Version Control

Many artifacts *can* be placed under version control—requirements documents, designs, models, user documentation, and source code. Configuration management and version control are each processes. As systems become more complex and you begin to build multiple versions and derivatives, and you reuse components, your tools must be capable of supporting the development process. We were not at this point with PSP Tools.

ClearCase was initially much more than we needed for our project, but our project grew to need more of its features. The major problem we had to overcome was that not everyone on the team had access to the Rational tool set. Jas was no longer with Rational, and the company he was with did not use Rational tools. Even with access, and even with the ability to set up a multi-site implementation, we were not all sharing the same secure intranet. How could we make sure that everyone had access to the latest version of all of the artifacts they needed?

Our solution was twofold. First, we realized that only Chris and Gary needed to change source code. We set up a ClearCase VOB (versioned object base) on the Rational network to store the latest versions of our source code. This enabled Chris and Gary to work independently of each other and to check source code in when it was ready. ClearCase provides powerful merging features, so we didn't have to worry about whether we had the latest checked-in versions of our code when we did our individual builds and were connected to the network.

The solution didn't address the issue of Gary's frequent traveling. He needed to work when he wasn't connected to the Rational network, and he had to communicate his changes with Chris. Many of his trips were longer than a week and he often worked at home for long stretches, where he does not have high-speed access to the Rational network.[1] In order for Chris and Gary to frequently integrate their work and deliver builds to Liz and Jas, they needed access to changed code regularly.

The first part of addressing this issue was for Gary to create a *snapshot view*[2] of the source directory on his computer. ClearCase snapshot views are copies of files that can be used when are disconnected from the network. Gary would modify files while he traveled. You can change a file in a snapshot view without first checking it out. ClearCase calls a file in this state *hijacked*. When you reconnect to the network and update your view, Clear-Case lists all the hijacked files and allows you to check in or discard your changes. ClearCase even gives you the option to merge your changes with any others that have been made while the file was hijacked.

The second part of our version control solution was to use the Groove workspace. When either Chris or Gary made changes, they copied the modified sources to a separate Transfer location on Groove and left a message for the other.

Groove also provided a solution for Jas's inability to access the Rational network. We set up a special area on Groove, labeled *Drops for Testing*. Whenever we created an integration build for testing, we placed the files in this area and left a message. Jas and Liz could copy the build from this area and begin working with it. This solution worked very well for us. This area also served as a "poor man's" version control system. We kept as many versions of the files as we desired here. The only cost was the space we used on each team member's computer.

We should note that there are other solutions available to a small development team. Online communities such as SourceForge host open source development projects providing version control support as well as defect tracking. Whatever solution you choose, make sure that you select one that works for your needs and does not lock you into an approach that will make future change difficult.

---

[1] Despite the fact that Massachusetts is a high-tech hotbed, there are still pockets where high-speed Internet access is not available. Even satellite is not a possibility because he is surrounded by woods. There is a price to be paid for living in the country.

[2] ClearCase provides two types of views. With *snapshot* views, you copy files to your computer disk and you can work connected or disconnected from the network. To look at changes, you need to update your view. To use *dynamic* views, you need to be connected to the network, but you have instant access to all the changes made by your teammates.

Defect Tracking

With the end of the Elaboration phase and the start of the Construction phase, we needed the ability to report and track defects. There are many possible solutions available to software development teams. The solutions range from free, open source software to commercially available tools. For our team, being on different networks was the driving factor in our solution. As you might expect, we used Groove again.

There was no defect-tracking tool available for Groove when we developed PSP Tools, so we created a simple one.[3] The Groove discussion tool is a versatile workspace component. We created a new discussion tool, just as we did to handle our engineering backlog. The Defect tab on our workspace used stylistic conventions to identify the defects, priorities, and status. This was simple enough for all of us to use and it was always accessible. Figure 8.1 shows a snapshot of our defect-tracking tool.

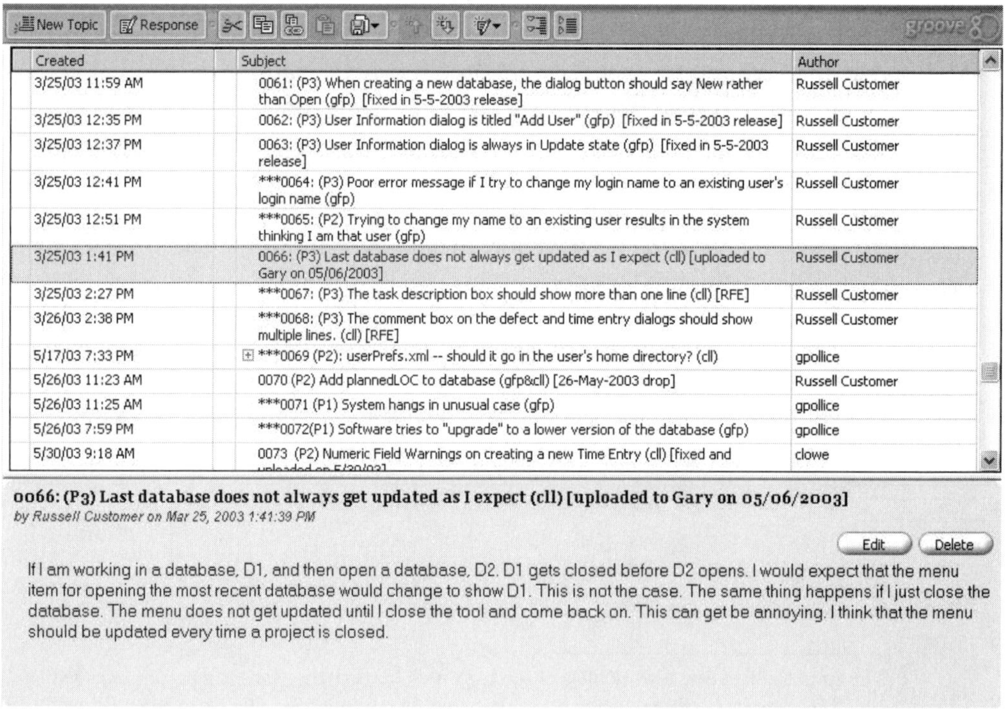

Created	Subject	Author
3/25/03 11:59 AM	0061: (P3) When creating a new database, the dialog button should say New rather than Open (gfp) [fixed in 5-5-2003 release]	Russell Customer
3/25/03 12:35 PM	0062: (P3) User Information dialog is titled "Add User" (gfp) [fixed in 5-5-2003 release]	Russell Customer
3/25/03 12:37 PM	0063: (P3) User Information dialog is always in Update state (gfp) [fixed in 5-5-2003 release]	Russell Customer
3/25/03 12:41 PM	***0064: (P3) Poor error message if I try to change my login name to an existing user's login name (gfp)	Russell Customer
3/25/03 12:51 PM	***0065: (P2) Trying to change my name to an existing user results in the system thinking I am that user (gfp)	Russell Customer
3/25/03 1:41 PM	0066: (P3) Last database does not always get updated as I expect (cll) [uploaded to Gary on 05/06/2003]	Russell Customer
3/25/03 2:27 PM	***0067: (P3) The task description box should show more than one line (cll) [RFE]	Russell Customer
3/26/03 2:38 PM	***0068: (P3) The comment box on the defect and time entry dialogs should show multiple lines. (cll) [RFE]	Russell Customer
5/17/03 7:33 PM	⊞ ***0069 (P2): userPrefs.xml -- should it go in the user's home directory? (cll)	gpollice
5/26/03 11:23 AM	0070 (P2) Add plannedLOC to database (gfp&cll) [26-May-2003 drop]	Russell Customer
5/26/03 11:25 AM	***0071 (P1) System hangs in unusual case (gfp)	gpollice
5/26/03 7:59 PM	***0072(P1) Software tries to "upgrade" to a lower version of the database (gfp)	gpollice
5/30/03 9:18 AM	0073 (P2) Numeric Field Warnings on creating a new Time Entry (cll) [fixed and uploaded on 5/30/03]	clowe

0066: (P3) Last database does not always get updated as I expect (cll) [uploaded to Gary on 05/06/2003]
by Russell Customer on Mar 25, 2003 1:41:39 PM

Edit Delete

If I am working in a database, D1, and then open a database, D2. D1 gets closed before D2 opens. I would expect that the menu item for opening the most recent database would change to show D1. This is not the case. The same thing happens if I just close the database. The menu does not get updated until I close the tool and come back on. This can get be annoying. I think that the menu should be updated every time a project is closed.

Figure 8.1 Our Groove Defects tab

---

[3] Like any product, Groove is continually evolving. Several new tools and product integrations have become available since we started. There may now be a defect-tracking solution.

Additional Requirements Management

In Chapter 6, we discussed how we used Rational RequisitePro to store the PSP Tools feature requirements. When you begin to implement the use cases corresponding to the features, you can add the use case requirements to the RequisitePro project.

On each project, you may be tempted to delay using RequisitePro. For example:

- You may be concerned that you won't receive enough benefit from the tool to outweigh the extra time you will spend managing the tool.
- You may feel that your project is small enough that you can keep requirements in your head.

Fortunately, RequisitePro adds very little overhead to capturing requirements, so it's easy to start using it early on your project.

Whether you adopt use cases or use some other format, such as user stories,[4] to capture requirements, you can use RequisitePro to collect valuable information about your requirements. For example, RequisitePro maintains information about the relationship between different requirements. (RequisitePro calls this *traceability*.) You can use this information to determine whether all the features you planned for the release are represented by at least one use case. If a feature has no associated use case, then there is a danger that the feature will not be implemented. If you do not keep track of this information, it is easy to miss a commitment and end up with an unwelcome surprise toward the end of the project.

Figure 8.2 shows a traceability matrix from RequisitePro. The columns are the features from the Vision that we designated for implementation in the first PSP Tools release. The rows are the use-case requirements from our use-case requirements document.

The matrix shows that feature requirement FEA2.3 doesn't have a use case traced to it. This indicates an omission. The user is expecting to be able to record size information but there is no functional requirement in the use cases that describes this feature. We need to add to the set of use cases, either a new use case, or a flow of events in an existing use case, to satisfy the feature requirement. In our case, we implemented the code and then later modified the use-case document. The important point, though, is to make sure that you implement all the required features in the code.

---

[4] See Appendix C for a description of user stories.

Relationships: - direct only	FEA2: Record Personal	FEA2.1: Record time	FEA2.2: Record Defects	FEA2.3: Record Size	FEA3: Create a project	FEA3.1: Personal	FEA3.2: Create a team	FEA4: Reporting	FEA4.1: Personal	FEA5.1: Data access	FEA6: Statistical	FEA7: PSP Level 1	FEA7.1: PSP Level 1
UC1: Open Project Database						↗	↗						
UC1.1: Basic Flow: Select Project...													
UC1.2: Alternate Flow: Add New User										↗			
UC1.3: Alternate Flow: Open Last...													
UC2: Record Personal Engineering...	↗											↗	↗
UC2.1: Basic Flow: Create New task												↗	
UC2.2: Alternate Flow: Update...												↗	
UC2.3: Alternate Flow: Enter Actual...		↗̸										↗	
UC2.4: Alternate Flow: Update...		↗̸										↗	
UC2.5: Alternate Flow: Enter Defect..			↗̸									↗	
UC2.6: Alternate Flow: Update...			↗̸									↗	
UC2.7: Alternate Flow: Time an...		↗̸										↗	
UC3: Maintain a Project Database													
UC3.1: Basic Flow: Create a New...					↗								
UC3.2: Alternate Flow: Edit a Project.													
UC4: Run Personal Reports								↗	↗			↗	↗
UC4.1: Basic Flow: Run Personal...											↗	↗	
UC5: Run Team Reports													
UC5.1: Basic Flow: Run Team...													

Figure 8.2 Traceability matrix from RequisitePro

One other feature of a traceability matrix appears in Figure 8.2. Notice the line through some of the arrows; for example, the arrow tracing UC2.3 to FEA2.1. This indicates that one of the requirements was modified. It means that we need to determine if the change has an impact on a part of the development effort. For example, we might have added additional data to the database identification information. This would require changes in both code and testing. Using a traceability matrix makes it easy to assess the impact of change.

We wrote and maintained a use case document starting early in the project. But because of the small size of the PSP Tools project, we didn't put the use-case requirements into RequisitePro until the later stages of the Construction phase. We weren't all connected to the same network and we didn't set up a Web interface for RequisitePro, so we felt that it was easier to maintain the use-case requirements document outside of RequisitePro for the majority of the project. We felt that it was important to put requirements into RequisitePro for Version 2, so that the people who worked on the next release would have a good starting place (even if we were those people).

Construction Phase Goals

As with other RUP phases, there is a milestone that signals the end of the Construction phase. RUP calls this the Initial Operational Capability (IOC) milestone. We worked toward two primary goals to reach the milestone: stabilizing the product enough to send it to the user community, and ensuring that the user community was ready to accept the product.

Often a project team does an exemplary job of creating a stable, mature product. Just as often, a team ignores preparing the user community to work with the product. Even on a small project like PSP Tools, it is important to consider how to guide users toward success with the product. RUP helps us achieve both goals.

During the Construction phase it is possible to create many artifacts. Regardless of the size or formality of your project, there is one artifact that must always be produced: the "system," that is, the working software that embodies the features of the release. Typically at the end of the Construction phase you are ready to enter the Beta testing phase.[5] That is, you have implemented the software features, produced and tested them, and the stakeholders agree that the product is functionally complete for the release.

Even after the Construction phase you will encounter some changes. Members of your Beta test community will provide feedback that uncovers problems and defects you never encountered during your testing. In the worst case, they will identify necessary features that are missing from the product. You mitigate this risk by ensuring customer and stakeholder involvement throughout the project and getting frequent feedback from them.

Construction Phase Planning: The Project Heartbeat

One reason to develop in iterations, especially short ones where you obtain rapid feedback from your stakeholders, is to get into a *rhythm* of delivering working software. This characteristic is emphasized by many of the agile

---

[5] Some people mistakenly think that the software is ready for deployment to the entire end-user community at the end of the Construction phase. This is not the case. The final stages of creating a product and deploying it to users occur during the Transition phase.

evangelists. RUP has implicitly endorsed it since its inception (pun intended). Some people talk about the rhythm as the *heartbeat* of the project. Every iteration, the project team's heart beats and pushes the life-blood, working software through the system. The cycle removes some of the bad blood (defects) and adds nutrients (features and fixes).

When you develop iteratively, you create detailed plans only for the next iteration. Because of the small size of the PSP Tools project, we found that planning became a *transparent* part of the process. We should explain what we mean by this term.

Discovering Our Own Rhythm

Because we were working on PSP Tools in our "spare" time, we were unable to time-box iterations and maintain reasonable expectations of what we could accomplish in a specific time period.[6] The problem we faced was that there were occasions when we would allocate a period of time, two weeks for example, during which we hoped to complete an iteration. But due to pressures from our real jobs and real lives, little or nothing would get done. We could have followed a true iterative process and developed a plan for what we expected to do, assess our progress, decide that we missed most of the objectives, and re-plan for the next two or three weeks. This would take time and, frankly, the effect on the team of missing the deliverables would take its toll on our morale.

Many of our meetings started with "Are we stalled again?" Feelings of guilt ensued; we beat our chests, put on hair shirts, embarked upon the next "iteration," and sunk deeper into the depths of despair.

We needed a change of attitude. We needed to feel good about what we were doing while recognizing the constraints on our time. Every one of the team members had a rich life outside of work. Our workdays were full. Sometimes we had little or no time to contribute to our project. Often, as soon as one person became available to contribute, the person on whom they depended entered into a crunch period. This specific problem might not occur on most of your projects. But often a team becomes demoralized for reasons that really are beyond any team member's control.

When something is not working, you need to try another approach rather than continue to do what doesn't work and hope for the best. During the Construction phase we found that by using the Engineering Backlog

---

[6] Many people, including us, have learned that iterations are usually fixed in time. While this is generally true, you can use some other measure, such as the functionality you are adding, and still follow an iterative development process. We recommend that you consider using other measures only when there is no way to time-box the iteration.

and Defects tools in Groove, we were able to make progress regularly, if not on a schedule, and the software took shape rapidly.

Chris and Gary talked several times a week, either face-to-face, on the phone, or through an online chat tool. Whenever one had a question, he was usually able to contact the other immediately. This communication and feedback allowed them to coordinate their work and deliver working features to the rest of the team. When they felt that PSP Tools had enough new features to make it worthwhile to run acceptance tests and get customer feedback, they built the `PSPTools.jar` file and copied it to the `Drops For Testing` folder. Then Jas and Liz could test when they had time. Russell could monitor the progress and provide feedback when he was available. This asynchronous style of working propelled us into a richly productive period.

Communicating by Release Notes

To facilitate this process, we needed to produce one document with every drop: a short set of release notes. If the release contained bug fixes only, we pointed to the Defects tool rather than describe the fixes in detail. If we added new features, we included enough information for Jas or Liz to begin testing them, perhaps by referring to a specific use case or scenario.

We had to make a small change to our Defects list. We originally forgot to number each defect, making it cumbersome to refer to a specific defect. One weekend, Gary spent about a half-hour adding defect numbers to the headers, and that made writing release notes much easier.

Figure 8.3 shows one of our more verbose sets of release notes. This drop contained some new features, but more importantly, it had some infrastructure changes that required explanation.

Figure 8.4 shows a much more succinct set of release notes for a drop. No one would consider either of these examples to be formal. They did, however, do the job we intended them to do—communicate.

Experimenting, Making Mistakes, and Arriving at Our Own Style of Planning

We don't want to mislead you into thinking that one day it occurred to us to plan based upon the Engineering Backlog and Defects tools. We tried several approaches—including cajoling and pleading—before we settled on one that suited our small team.

We tried, for a short while, to use well-formed requests (described in Chapter 3). We set up an area on Groove that we could use to create and track our requests. This approach also failed for us. Why? The technique is good and is proven. Some consider it a best practice for team empowerment. So what did we do wrong? Nothing. Using well-formed requests might be a best practice, but it wasn't suitable in our context. The practice

Merry Christmas! And since you've all been good, here's the Christmas drop.

There are a couple of significant changes to this drop, so make sure you read this document fully before running the new version.

Files in this build:
– PSPTools.jar
– dbupdate.sql
– createdb.sql
– this file of release notes

Changes:

1. I have changed the database schema so the DBInfo record now contains a database version number and a description. The version number will be used to automatically upgrade databases in the future.

   If you have an existing database that you are using for testing and you want to upgrade it, you can load the dbupdate.sql file into Cloudview and execute it on the database. That will add the appropriate fields and supply default values.

   For any new database you create, the createdb.sql script has been updated to include the new fields. Of course, you can always just create a new database using PSP Tools. This now asks you for a description.

2. I have added a database properties feature. Whenever you have a database open, you can use the Project>Properties menu selection and you will see the properties of the database, including a list of users for the database. Right now, you cannot change the user information. That will come later. You can, however, change the description. Once you change the description, the OK button is enabled. If you click it, the description will be updated. Canceling or closing the window does not update the description.

Figure 8.3 A "detailed" set of release notes for a drop

This release fixes defects 0054, 0061, 0062, 0063.

Figure 8.4 A typical set of release notes

proved to be another technique that depended on our ability to commit time that we weren't able to control. The result was more guilt for letting down our teammates. We removed our well-formed request area from Groove. We didn't need the reminder of our shortcomings.

There are a couple of lessons learned in this section. First, when you think about how your environment will change, don't assume that it changes only by addition; it can also change by subtraction. If a tool or technique isn't working, get rid of it. You don't need to clutter up your workspace, whatever form it takes.

The second lesson learned is subtler. Regardless of how good a practice is, and how well it works for someone else or has worked for you in the past, it may not work for you in your current context. The best you can do is learn as many practices as you can, understand when and for whom they work, and then try to adapt them to your situation. If they don't work, don't try to force-fit them—just discard them and move on.

Implementation Accelerates

One primary goal of the Construction phase was to produce a stable Beta release that we could deliver to our user community. The most important piece of the release was the working code. In PSP Tools, the code developed rapidly after we exited the Elaboration phase. For this project, we had already tackled the hardest work during the Elaboration phase. Now it was time to fill in the missing pieces. We had a couple of bumps along the way, but nothing that caused major rework.

Let's look at our starting point. Figure 8.5 shows the PSP Tools main window at the end of the Elaboration phase. You can see that the product is not fully functional. There are aesthetic issues. Few people would want to, or could, use this product.

With the pre-Construction phase version of PSP Tools you can:

- Open an existing project by selecting **File > Open** and following the prompts. A login dialog box, seeded with the login name you use for the system, prompts you to log in with a user name and password.
- View summary information about specific tasks, related to time and defect entries.
- Create a new task by selecting **File > New Task** and entering summary information in the appropriate fields.

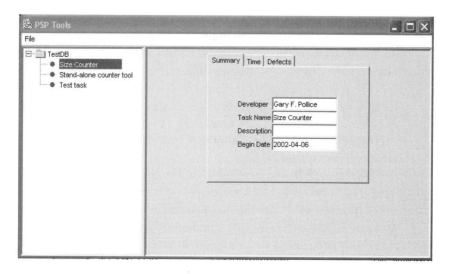

Figure 8.5 PSP Tools at the end of the Elaboration phase

At the beginning of the Construction phase, it felt like there was a tremendous amount of work left to do. Fortunately, Russell understood that this product wasn't ready to ship—it was in an early prototype stage. We were comfortable showing him our work and asking for feedback. Too often we hear stories of development teams who will not show early work to anyone, especially sales and marketing people. They are afraid that the people they show it to will start to sell it. Surely this happens, and it builds barriers of mistrust among people who should be working together as one team.

The Fear Factor—An Example

In contrast to the PSP Tools experience, Gary has experienced one of the ultimate forms of this reluctance to share early versions of a product. He worked in the compiler development group of a large company. This group had a reputation for delivering "world-class" compilers to its customers. The group consisted of a brilliant team of people with extensive experience in building optimizing compilers. At the time, the company was developing a new computer with a completely new architecture. This affected the compilers significantly because they had to produce object code for the new machine. So, the team used an architecture that took advantage of a common code generator, also called the *back end* of the compiler. This major piece of code needed to be ported for other applications to work. In order for the many company applications to be ported, the compilers had to be available.[7]

The group that was building the back end for the new computer was working on a highly optimizing back end. The company was making its first entry into the reduced instruction set computer (RISC) marketplace. The team knew that the success or failure of the computer hardware would be dictated by the ability of language tools to optimize their object code.

The back-end group was afraid to release early versions of the code generator, even to internal development groups. They were waiting until they felt it was completely ready for consumption by their internal customers. They were not developing incrementally or iteratively, so they could not release early results. Unfortunately, this meant that they could not get feedback until later in the project. It also meant that the groups dependent on them could not make progress. Why did this happen? In this case, it was fear.

Fear is a major problem for development teams and those managing the teams, and it can come in many forms. In this story, the team members knew that the software would eventually work. They were afraid that early in development, the software would not work as efficiently as it needed to at the final release. The team had a reputation of producing some of the best optimizing compiler technology in the world. Anything less—any intermediate result—felt like failure to them. They didn't want to risk tarnishing their reputation for excellence, regardless of their users' actual expectations.

The story has a happy ending, but it was achieved with much anxiety and tension. Gary was managing one of the projects that needed the code generator. He tried every one of his silver-tongued (said tongue-in-cheek) techniques to cajole the code generator team to deliver an early release to his project. Finally, in frustration, Gary offhandedly threatened to have one of his engineers write a "quick and dirty" code generator, using the API specification for the new code generator. Gary has experience building compiler back ends and knew it would be a small effort to produce something that would be good enough for early engineering efforts. The code would be horrible, the applications would run miserably, but they would run! That's all he wanted.

This suggestion got the attention of the code generation group. Reluctantly, the manager of that group had one of his staff "throw together" a

---

[7] This dependency chain is very common in companies that make operating systems and language tools to support hardware they build.

code generator. The manager felt it was better to have someone who knew the code build the generator. If one of Gary's engineers wrote it, there would be several undesirable effects. The code generated would be as bad or worse than what the back end team would produce and it would probably be buggier. The back end team would be blamed for it anyway. A fear might emerge that they would be unable to deliver the final code generator. Perhaps most disastrous to the back-end group's reputation would be the questions raised about what those developers on the back-end team were really doing.

As a result, a code generator was delivered for internal use within a week. It was good enough for the rest of the projects to use to ensure their product ported to the new hardware. A large amount of documentation accompanied the delivery, mostly consisting of disclaimers that the code generator was delivered "as is" with no warranties, guarantees, or support. Attorneys would admire the rigor of the documents and disclaimers. Gary sometimes wonders whether some of the engineers in the group have moved on to legal careers, or to writing disclaimers for adult Web sites.

A Better Way to Deal with the Fear

The story about the fearful compiler group provided a detour on our Construction phase journey. But it does illustrate a common problem that occurs on many projects. As a project manager or team member, how can you mitigate the risk of not delivering anything because of fear?

We have a few suggestions. Maintain continuous communication with your whole team, including stakeholders, customers, development team, and managers. If your team members can quickly assess the current state of the project at any time, they are more likely to have proper expectations about what each product build will deliver.

Developing your software iteratively and incrementally, and making it available for anyone on your team to use, is also important. Welcome participation, even if expectations are high. Offer to help users install or use the product. Listen to problems they have or expectations that aren't met. Help them understand exactly where you are in the project and what your goals are. Good communication is essential throughout the project; this is just another example of how it benefits your team.

Another Short Tale

When Bob Martin of Object Mentor gives presentations on XP and agile methods, he often uses a story about working on a project that would help architects draw designs on a computer. The team decided to produce weekly iterations. In each iteration they would add more functionality so that the product would continually evolve. Further, they would get user feedback at the end of each iteration.

For the first iteration, the team produced a blank screen with some color and a menu bar that did nothing. Bob showed it to the customer who repeatedly asked "Is this all it does?" and "It'll do more than this, right?" Bob explained that there would eventually be more, but that the team would value some feedback from the customer. Bob kept asking, "So what do you think about this?" Finally the customer settled down enough to look at the first iteration's build and made a couple of suggestions about the order of menu items and so on.

In the next week's release, the customer saw that the menu bar actually worked and the changes he suggested were implemented. You could click on menu selections, but nothing happened then. There was a little palette with icons on it that did nothing. The same scene took place. Again, at the end of it, the customer made some suggestions for the team and the next iteration began.

This was the rhythm of the project. As the customer got more familiar with the process, he became more comfortable. He was able to see real progress and he always knew what the product was capable of doing. On our own projects, we should all strive for this level of openness with our customers and stakeholders. Open communications help build and maintain one of the most precious elements for success—trust.

Moving Forward in the Construction Phase

We saw what PSP Tools was capable of at the end of the Elaboration phase. It is helpful to review some of the major limitations. You could not:

- Create a database from within the tool
- See the details of time and defects
- Count lines of code from any subtool in the product
- Create any type of report

There were also several tasks for which there was UI support only, but no implementation had been written. For example, you could type into several fields and the system appeared to record the changes. Or, when you typed a new time into the time summary data for a task, the data persisted if you viewed a different task and returned to the original one (see Figure 8.6). However, the information was not stored in the database.

The reason that the data persisted was that the displayed object had not yet been released for garbage collection. If you quit and restarted the application, the changes were lost.

At this point in the project, try to avoid features that "apparently work." Your team can spend a lot of time understanding them. On our project, the testers couldn't tell whether certain features were mocked up (and weren't supposed to work yet) or whether they were supposed to work but didn't because of bugs. Sometimes we ended up filing a defect against a feature that wasn't supposed to work in the first place. The developers then had to spend time figuring out whether someone had sneaked in a surprise feature that contained bugs or whether they were dealing with a feature that hadn't actually been implemented. It's worth spending time either to make sure that a feature works completely or that you add code to make it obvious that the feature isn't yet completely implemented.

Another example of this phenomenon occurred with the Elaboration phase release. We all implicitly understood that the database was not getting updated when we modified the fields. It was less obvious that the database was not being updated at all. If you added a new task, it showed up in the tree on the left and you could click on it to see the data. But when you exited the program and returned, the task was missing. A better solution would have been to display a message saying that changes to the database were not permanent.

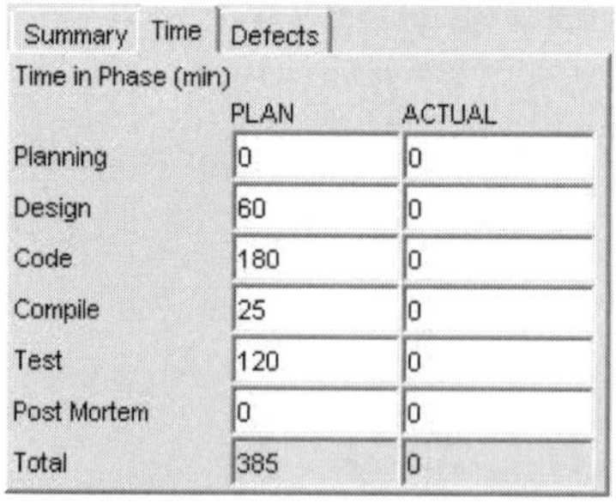

Summary	Time	Defects

Time in Phase (min)

	PLAN	ACTUAL
Planning	0	0
Design	60	0
Code	180	0
Compile	25	0
Test	120	0
Post Mortem	0	0
Total	385	0

Figure 8.6 Time summary tab for a task

Handling Database Changes

Early in the Construction phase we needed to change the database schema. We hadn't thought about database schema changes until this point—either the frequency or the method. An early solution was to use a database utility, Cloudview, to update the database schema with standard SQL statements. This approach required someone in a system administrator role to execute a script, or worse, manually enter SQL statements. For early development changes, this would be good enough, but it wouldn't be an acceptable solution for production.

The first time we changed the database structure, we used the Cloudview solution. We could continue to use this approach until the Beta release, but then what? Looking at our Vision beyond version 1, we expected to add several features. We weren't sure what form they would take, but they would have a significant effect on the database. After we thought about this problem for less than a minute, we rejected the option of relying on human intervention to keep a database updated.

We decided to record a version identifier in the database. This identifier corresponded to the database version, not the product version. When the software detected a version mismatch, it would ask the user if the database should be updated, and do so automatically. If the user declined—perhaps to back up the database first—the software wouldn't update the database, but also wouldn't let the user access the database. See Chapter 9 for details about our solution.

One nice feature of the solution was that users were required to update only once, even if their database was more than one delta from the current version. The solution we implemented handled the incremental updates.

If you are experienced with database applications, you have probably already internalized the need to provide for database migration. If you aren't so experienced, we suggest this lesson learned: *Consider how your database will be updated, because it is a certainty that it will need updating*.

Working Toward a Usable Product

Our first accomplishment in the Construction phase was to produce a version of PSP Tools that we ourselves could use. Gary had been using PSP for years, but had been manually tracking his work. He was eager for the tool to automate many of the mundane tasks that he had been performing manually. Specifically, he wanted the ability to enter the data and for the tool to perform most of the calculations. He also needed the ability to modify entries when he mistyped them. He wanted to see all the data in the database easily. Reporting was not as high on his priority list, and as it turned out, neither was it as high on Russell's.

Chris and Gary worked at a steady pace to implement the needed functionality. Every few weeks, they produced a build that was ready for testing. When the build was released, anyone could, and everyone was expected to, test it, and report any defects found. Russell or Gary often added requests for enhancement; after considering priority and effort, these became new requirements. Then Russell and Gary would reallocate work based on the priorities. We did all this without a formal planning cycle.

It didn't take long to create a usable product, what some projects call the *Alpha* release. At this point, Gary could use PSP Tools as his primary mechanism for recording PSP statistics. In the next few sections, we briefly describe the iterations added to each drop leading up to the Alpha release.

First Construction Phase Iteration

When we exited the Elaboration phase, there was only one working menu item, as shown in Figure 8.5. We placed our limited set of commands there. It was time to expand our repertoire. We concentrated on implementing a **Project** menu containing all the commands you could invoke on an open project. Figure 8.7 shows this menu.

The tabbed panes in the right panel take up more real estate than in the previous release. This was closer to the look we eventually wanted. At this point, the size of the panes was not consistent from one view to another. We found that working in raw Java without an IDE made it challenging to lay out user interfaces.

Introducing a Delighter

We made a change at this point that was not part of our requirements. One day Chris got frustrated when he was testing his code changes. Every time he wanted to open a database, he had to navigate to the directory containing that database. He usually worked on the same database for his testing, but the program always started in the user's home directory. We had previously discussed how to track user preferences and Chris was looking into the XML interfaces available in Java. Now he had the opportunity to implement something based on his research, starting with a simple example. His design statement was: "Whenever the user opens a database, record the database information in a user preferences file. Next time the program runs, put an

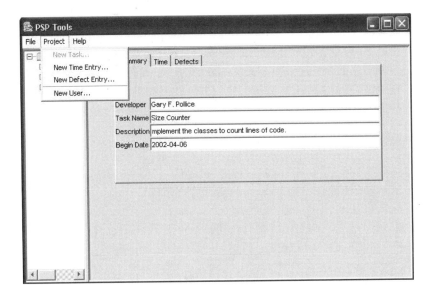

Figure 8.7 First Construction phase iteration—addition of the Project menu

entry into the **File** menu so you can directly open that database." The solution is shown in Figure 8.8.

Some people call this type of feature a *delighter*. Delighters cost little to implement and bring pleasure to the user, or make the user's job much easier. They aren't a substitute for required functionality, but they add to the user experience once the required functionality is in place.

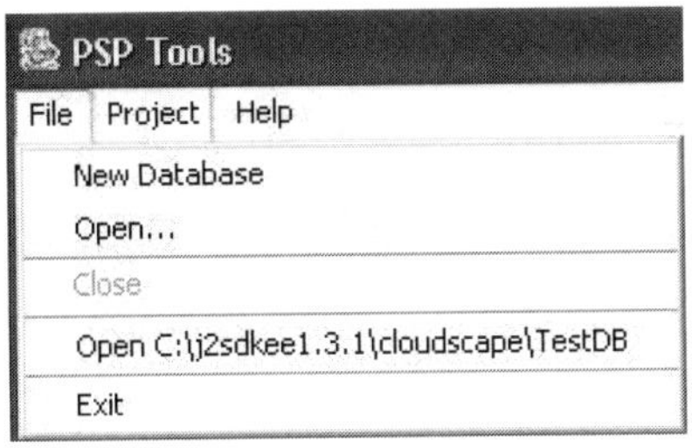

Figure 8.8 Open previous database menu item

John Whiteside, author of *The Phoenix Agenda*, related this story to a team he was coaching. He had purchased an expensive new car. The first time he had to change a tire, he went to the trunk, and in the tool case that held the jack and wrench was a very inexpensive pair of cotton gloves. The manufacturer had included the gloves so you wouldn't get your hands dirty. It cost very little for the company to add the gloves to the car's tools, but the value to the customer was significant. It showed that the company cared about the customer's needs.

This brings up another lesson learned (or one that we knew already and reapplied): *Throughout your development process, look for the opportunity to add delighters*. If you can identify something that costs almost nothing to add, and it will delight a user, consider adding it to the product. The danger, of course, is that you can convince yourself that your favorite feature is a delighter, when the reality is that you may be biased. Make sure the whole team agrees that the feature is truly a delighter if the cost of adding it, and perhaps having to remove it, isn't close to zero.

We added one more feature to this iteration—the ability to enter and view defect and time entry details. This gave us the basic functionality we needed to use PSP Tools to record our statistics. Figure 8.9 shows what we implemented for time entries.

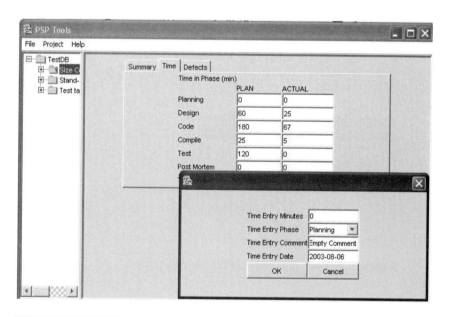

Figure 8.9 Time entry input dialog

Second Construction Phase Iteration

The first Construction phase iteration was a warm-up for us—it helped us get into the rhythm of delivering frequent releases. In just a couple of weeks, we released the second Construction phase iteration, adding significant new features:

- A simple **Help** menu item that displayed a build identification we could use when reporting defects
- A more robust and complete **Project > New User** interface
- Database updates (this was the first time we could see the effects of adding records and data to the database)

The **Help > About PSP Tools** dialog box is illustrated in Figure 8.10. Every program has a **Help** menu that usually offers more than the simple About box that we produced. In fact, the PSP Tools Vision shows our original intention to provide online help only and to omit printed manuals. The menu item we implemented in this iteration provided the placeholder for our online help system, and also gave us a quick way to find out what build we were working with. So at least defect reporting and tracking were easier from this point.

In the first Construction phase iteration, we implemented the ability to add a new user to the project database. However, the original implementation was simple and didn't allow the user to fill in all the data. The New User dialog box in that iteration just asked for the login name and password, if any. All other user data was set to default values, usually blank. Figure 8.11 shows the new dialog box from the second Construction phase iteration. Now a PSP Tools user could create a database for use by more than one engineer.[8]

Figure 8.10 Simple About dialog added in the second Construction phase iteration

---

[8] Any user could add another user, without needing special privileges. We originally planned to assign privileges to certain users, but never implemented that in the first release.

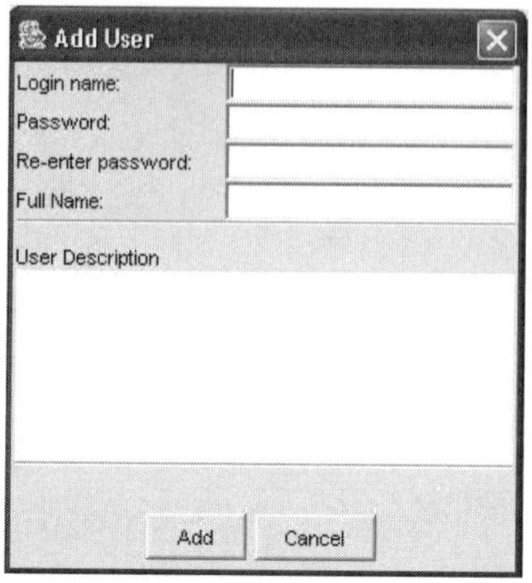

Figure 8.11 New user data entry dialog box

During this iteration, we became more comfortable with the Java layout managers, as reflected by the appearance of the dialog box in Figure 8.11. The field widths are uniform and they line up neatly along the vertical axis.

We knew we needed to make our dialog boxes more consistent and attractive, but early in the project beautifying our product was not a high priority. However, some of our stakeholders started to complain about the "ugly" appearance of PSP Tools. While this issue is not critical to product usability, it is still important. We recommend that you plan to spend some time working on the user interface aesthetics as early as possible. It is tempting, when time pressures intervene, to convince yourself that it really isn't that important. But it is important—it affects the user's experience of your product. First impressions do count, especially in software.

Third Construction Phase Iteration

We released the third Construction phase iteration only a week later. Until this release, you created a database by running the `createdb.sql` script in Cloudview. In this release, we implemented a menu item that allows you to create a database from within PSP Tools, making testing easier.

We also added the ability to right-click on the items in the tree, causing a shortcut menu to appear. The shortcut menu offers the same choices as those that are on the **Project** menu. The entries in the **Project** and shortcut menus are enabled based on what is selected in the tree. The shortcut menu shown in Figure 8.12 is an identical copy of the choices available on the **Project** menu at the time.[9]

Figure 8.12 Context-based pop-up menu

Once we wrote the code for the regular menus, it was easy to write the code to enable the shortcut menus. There was a problem with the initial implementation of the shortcut menus. They behaved in what felt like a buggy manner, but we didn't know exactly what the correct behavior was. We researched how other products behave and then followed what had become our usual approach—we asked Russell what he thought. We wanted to adhere to standard look and feel practices, but when there was a choice, the best place to seek guidance was with our customer.

Why Did Development Speed Up?

Two primary factors account for the acceleration in our development. In our experience, these factors are present in all types of projects, but their effect is greatest on small projects.

Beyond the Learning Curve

The first factor is familiarity with the code base. When a project starts, there is a learning period. This is true whether you are creating new software from scratch (called *greenfield development*) or whether you are adding to an existing system. Unless you have already worked with the existing code

---

[9] During the Construction phase we were continually adding new capabilities to the different menus. The set of features shown here is different than the **Project** menu features shown in Figure 8.7, because this figure is from a later iteration.

base, you need time to get used to the style, functions, and structure. To minimize learning time, organizations can establish (and adhere to) coding styles, and they can insist that developers document their code. But even in organizations where communication is consistent and useful, there is always a learning period.

By the time we started the Construction phase, we had written between three thousand and four thousand lines of code. Our architecture was stable enough that we made little structural change. We had reorganized the code—moved classes and renamed them. This effort, called *refactoring*,[10] results in better code, but the tradeoff is that it can cause a short-term reduction in productivity. After the refactoring, though, both Chris and Gary could easily navigate through the PSP Tools code and find the appropriate classes and methods in the classes.

Working with the Infrastructure

The other contributing factor to our improved delivery times was that we had already developed some of the application's infrastructure, so we didn't need to stop to work on it during the Construction phase. Engineers argue about how much infrastructure code you need to write and when to write it. Do you ignore future needs for infrastructure and develop it as needed, or do you plan ahead if you are fairly sure you will need a piece of infrastructure? We chose a mix of these approaches. In some cases, we waited to develop infrastructure until we needed it. However, there were some aspects that we addressed early, even though we were not ready to take advantage of our solutions at the time we implemented them.

We developed most of the infrastructure during the Elaboration phase. During the Construction phase, we used the infrastructure code so we were able to implement specific features more quickly than during the Elaboration phase. Here are two examples of our experience.

Examples of Working with the Infrastructure

Earlier in this chapter we discussed how we created a general-purpose solution to handle database changes. Once we established the mechanism to instantiate an appropriate *updater* class, it was trivial to create a new class to change the database. Writing the code for the new updater class usually

---

[10] There are many other types of refactoring activities. We only mention these two here. For a detailed reference on the topic, see *Refactoring: Improving the Design of Existing Code*, by Martin Fowler et al.

meant copying the code from another updater class and editing it. At the end of the project, when we had to add a field to the database, Chris and Gary implemented and tested it in less than an hour.

The second example involves the way we structured the database and the database code. As we mentioned in Chapter 6, the database contained a separate table for each data object class. One way of implementing the relationship is to have a class for each data object and a class for the database. In this case, the database is responsible for delivering the data objects to client classes that request them and updating the database when client objects send messages requesting the update. We initially implemented the database and data objects in this manner.

As the database evolved and the number of data objects increased, the database code grew until it was difficult to navigate and maintain. The eXtreme Programming community talks about the code *smelling bad*. The database code had a distinctly offensive odor. Our solution was to have an *accessor* class for each data object class, as shown in Figure 8.13.

The solution shown in Figure 8.13 provided a cleaner separation of concerns. The database class contains the necessary data and behavior to handle general database creation and maintenance operations. It also contains a field for each data object class. This field is an instance of the appropriate accessor class, and there is a getter method for each of these fields. When a client class needs a specific data object from the database, it requests the appropriate accessor from the database, and sends one or more messages to the accessor to get the actual data object.

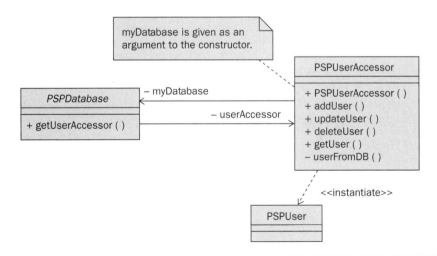

Figure 8.13 Database accessors for each data object class

See Chapter 9 for more technical details of this solution. The point is that by recognizing the "accessor pattern" as our software evolved, Chris and Gary were able to communicate more effectively about the work they did and the tasks that remained. This is a well-known advantage of patterns—when you can communicate better, you will work better.

Using Our Own Software

One more factor affected our productivity in a subtler way than the two primary ones described so far. We began to see results and were able to use the system we were building—it was good and we wanted more. When you build software that you might use yourself, a psychological lift occurs when you get to the point where you can actually use the software. Not everyone works on projects where they build such software. There may be a lift when a customer uses the software for the first time, but usually that occurs later than on projects where the programmers want to use the software.

Remaining Construction Phase Iterations

The remaining iterations in the Construction phase followed the pattern of the three already discussed. We observed a phenomenon that is typical of software projects as they get closer to their release date: The number of new features you add at each iteration decreases and you spend more of your time fixing defects and fine-tuning the code (see Figure 8.14). Regardless of the process you follow, this seems to be a recurring pattern. The actual shape of the curves will change, but the pattern occurs.

Table 8.1 shows the features we added in each iteration after the third iteration. We identified and fixed approximately fifty defects in these iterations. Only a few of these defects caused the program to be unusable, for example, by causing the program to "hang" and become unresponsive. None of the defects caused a loss of data. We feel that data loss is the severest type of defect because there is no good workaround for it. Most of the top-priority defects identified something missing in the database schema.

Most of the iterations shown in Table 8.1 are small. Yet, many of them represent a significant improvement in the user's experience. Gary and Russell used each iteration to track their own work and quickly returned feedback to the developers. We were fortunate that our customer wanted to participate in the development process. Russell says he was lucky to work with a team that wanted his participation.

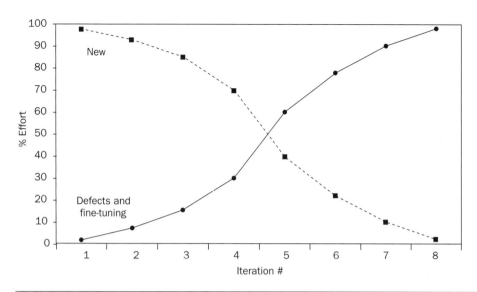

Figure 8.14 New functionality vs. fine-tuning as project progresses

Table 8–1 Features added in Construction phase iterations 4 through 12

Iteration*	Functionality Added
C4	Incorporated activity time and defect entries. Also implemented activity timer that updates the database directly. Implemented ability to update task summary information directly from the task summary panel.
C5	Added line counter tool to the program. Improved login dialog. Removed need to run with a Cloudscape database server.
C6	Installed database schema changes and automatic database upgrade mechanism. Added the Database Properties dialog box.
C7	Added basic export function. Made user information editable.
C8	Added program size and estimation tab.
C9	Added ability to delete a task.
C10	Delivered a self-extracting archive that unpacked the required files into a target directory and removed dependencies on the user's environment.
C11	Fixed defects. Released an initial *User's Guide*.
C12	Added an executable program for Windows that launched PSP Tools. Users no longer needed to run a batch file, and extra windows no longer appeared on the user's task bar.

* We identified our iterations by a letter representing the phase (I=Inception, E=Elaboration, C=Construction, and T=Transition), followed by the iteration number within that phase. For this project, only the Construction phase had more than one iteration.

We want to stress again how important it is to work closely with your user throughout the project. Gary once reviewed a book that described a development method in which there was a certain point "beyond which customers are no longer welcome to actively participate in the process." We strongly disagree with this approach. We want our customer with us, shoulder-to-shoulder, from the start to the end of the project. We want few or no surprises for both the customer and the rest of the team. We are one team, with one common goal defined in our vision.

Table 8.1 doesn't reveal a significant fact, one that is impressive when you remember that we worked on this project part-time. Sometimes we didn't work on the project at all when our real jobs took precedence. We delivered iterations four through seven in the span of sixteen days! That's one iteration every four days—developed, tested, and packaged. During this period, we worked at peak efficiency.[11] Imagine what your team can accomplish when working on a project full-time and operating at peak efficiency.

Iteration C5 was a significant milestone for the project. Until this point, you had to run a batch file to start the Cloudscape database server program. This was necessary to allow simultaneous access by multiple users. But Russell told us that each member of his staff would have his or her own database. This represented a change from the initial vision, proving once again that customers can—and will—change their minds. Gary did a little research and figured out how to access the databases in a single-user mode. He wrote very little code, less than twenty lines, to implement the change, and provided another delighter.

The export capability we added in iteration C7 was minimal. It simply added the ability to export user data to a comma-separated value file (CSV file) that could be read by Microsoft Excel. Our vision for this feature was grander, but Russell decided he didn't want to wait for us to implement a more elaborate solution. This is a reasonable tradeoff to make—request faster delivery of a product with a reduced set of features.

We followed the guidance in RUP: We removed the feature from the first release and moved it to an unspecified future release. With Rational RequisitePro, it took about a minute to make the change to the appropriate requirement attribute in the database. We always want to see where we stand with the planned work, and also see the work that has been scoped

---

[11] To be fair, this period was during the Christmas holidays, so we had a little more time to work on the project.

out of the current release. Change management doesn't have to be complex, but it does have to "*be*."

Gary finally addressed Jas's concerns about installation in iteration C10. The self-extracting archive satisfied Jas and the people he knew who wanted to try the software. Looking back, Gary can't believe how hard he resisted making it easy to install PSP Tools. In fact, creating a self-extracting archive required *no code changes*. Gary used one of the many available programs to create the archive for the Windows environment. To paraphrase a current commercial for a major credit card: "Total time: less than five minutes. Value to the customer: priceless."

Iteration C12 was the last iteration for the Construction phase. Russell and the rest of the team felt the software was ready to deliver to a wider group of customers. We made PSP Tools a real executable program on Windows platforms. Gary asked Chris to write the program that would replicate `runPSPTools.bat`. By making an executable, we avoided extra windows appearing in the user's taskbar.

Everyone Needs a Friend Sometimes: Programming in Pairs

eXtreme Programming had made the practice of pair programming popular. The practice is not new—programmers have been working in pairs for years. But XP adds discipline to the practice by defining how pair programmers work.[12]

An open question is whether programmers should pair up for all code they write. If you adhere strictly to the XP practices, every line of code is written by a pair of programmers. Chris and Gary believe in the value of pairing, but they aren't convinced of its necessity for all code. Programming is often a creative intellectual activity. At other times, it involves focused coding that is more detailed than creative. Some people are more creative when they reflect on the problem to be solved and others are more creative when they interact with others. We think most people need to work both independently and in pairs to maximize their creativity.

On our project, it was impossible to do all our work in pairs if we wanted to deliver a working product to Russell in a reasonable time. When you work on a distributed team, pair programming is often not feasible.

---

[12] See Appendix C for details about eXtreme Programming.

Instead of abandoning the idea entirely, we followed our customary approach and adapted the practices to the way we chose to work.

Much of the PSP Tools code was developed individually by Chris or Gary. They coded their components for particular features, using previously defined interfaces or infrastructure code. Even though they weren't working together physically, they were almost always in communication because they used instant messaging software. They periodically met for pair programming or design sessions. These sessions allowed them to address the difficult problems they were encountering and then implement enough code together for them to continue individually until the next meeting. These focused sessions were invaluable and kept us from getting hung up on any single problem.

For small, distributed development teams, we think instant messaging software is a critical tool. Many organizations have adopted messaging software as a standard communication mechanism. There are many choices available and all provide similar capabilities. We recommend that you choose one that has a logging, or history, function. This gives you the ability to record all conversations with your teammates. Regardless of how well you communicate, you will forget the details of conversations. The history gives you a *memory boost*.

Testing During the Construction Phase

Quality is a concern throughout the project. The spirit of RUP tells us that quality is a way of life. As your project progresses, you emphasize different aspects of the quality of your product. The Test discipline in RUP describes this approach to quality by recognizing that each iteration often has a different quality goal, or mission. At the beginning of each iteration you determine the mission for that iteration and decide upon the appropriate approach to fulfill that mission.

In the Inception phase we identified a general approach to testing the software and indicated who was responsible for each type of testing. In the Elaboration phase we focused on getting our unit test harness, JUnit, working and relied on manual use-case scenario testing. This was the state of the PSP Tools testing when we started the Construction phase.

For the first few Construction phase iterations we maintained the testing practices from the Elaboration phase. However, as we got closer to the Transition phase, we knew we would need more detailed testing and more types of testing. Gary and Chris were responsible for the unit testing, ensuring that the modules they created performed as specified. Liz and Jas initially ran the use-case scenario tests. But as we inched towards the Transition phase, Liz's time was occupied with documenting the product and Jas had significant time constraints because he had started a new job. Gary and Russell tested each drop, but Gary was too close to the code as one of the developers, and Russell had a business to run.

Gary used Rational PureCoverage to derive test coverage data from the unit tests and the manual use-case tests. He was already familiar with PureCoverage and we didn't need to run it that frequently. We used coverage tests to help us identify code that was either not needed, or that was never executed.

We needed to do something. We needed more automated tests. But we had a problem automating the use-case tests. We were unable to find the time, or experience, on the team to automate use-case tests.

The solution was to add a testing consultant to our team. Fortunately, Chris worked with a quality professional at Rational who volunteered to help us. Raj Srinivasan offered to set up an automated environment for us, using the Rational Java testing tools.[13] Our goal was to create a good set of automated tests by the time we entered the Transition phase. The automated tests would give us confidence that any changes we added late on the project, specifically in the Transition phase, did not cause regressions.

In retrospect, we should have addressed the test automation issue earlier. Our project was small enough, and simple enough, and our quality didn't suffer from this late start. However, we might have just been lucky. Our advice is to *have the test automation environment up and running, with the team trained on its use, by the end of the Elaboration phase*.

There is a lesson to learn from this tale. Many people think that you choose a team for a project and, barring people leaving the project for another job, the same team stays together for the project duration. This is seldom the case. You should plan for the team to change.

Anticipating Change of Team Membership

Figure 8.15 shows a common evolution of a team as a project moves through the phases. This diagram is for a larger project than PSP Tools, but the concepts apply to almost any project. The initial team will probably produce some code. Whether you call it a prototype, an early iteration, or some

---

[13] See Chapter 9 for more about the test automation.

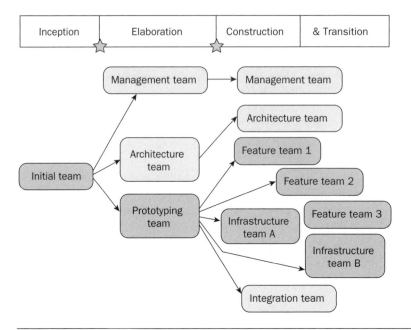

Figure 8.15 Team evolution through project phases[*]

[*] This figure was provided by Philippe Kruchten.

other name, whether it is real code that evolves into the final product, or throwaway code that helps you test ideas, it is code nonetheless.

There are many ways of organizing your project and, following the principle of configuring your process to fit the way you work, your team makeup might differ from the same type of team in another organization. The real lesson here is that you should plan for your team to change as the project progresses.

Summary

The Construction phase is what usually comes to mind when people think of software development. It is just one of the four phases that a project goes through in order to deliver a software product.

Construction is not just coding. There are many tasks that have nothing to do with coding. The whole team is involved in these tasks, including the customer. You continually manage the scope of the project, making tradeoffs based upon business and technical decisions. By following the principles of iterative development, however, you ensure that you are ready to deliver valuable software to your customer.

PSP Tools Construction: 8 weeks

CHAPTER 9

Construction Details

This chapter describes the technical details of the PSP Tools project during our Construction phase. The chapter is similar to Chapter 7, which describes the technical details of our Elaboration phase. If you aren't interested in the code or testing details, you can skip this chapter without losing anything from the "PSP Tools story."

The major technical issues discussed in this chapter are:

- *Fine-tuning the user interface*—As we progressed, we found additional surprises in the Swing classes and discovered new techniques for improving the user's experience.
- *Finishing the database*—We started by using the Cloudscape database in a "server" mode. We found out how to use it in single-user mode and then had to decide how to let the program decide which was appropriate.
- *Testing*—We added a tester at the end of the Construction phase. This section describes how we used testing tools, presents some of the scripts, and shows some of the results.

Fine-Tuning the User Interface

During the Elaboration phase we created a basic structure for the user interface and tested different ways of presenting the information. The user interface was "rough" at best. The menus were incomplete and many of the visual objects were not properly sized. At the end of the Elaboration phase, PSP Tools didn't feel like a finished product, nor was it supposed to.

In the Construction phase we needed to add new features and put some polish on the user interface. Version 1 still doesn't have the look and feel we hoped for, but it is completely functional and feels good enough for the first release. The following list identifies the major modifications and additions we made to the user interface during the Construction phase:

- Menus with appropriate functions
- Context menus on the tree items
- Tables to show the time entries and defect details
- User preferences

In the following sections we discuss each of these in more detail.

Dealing with Menus

Creating menus is easy. We showed the basic menu construction code in Chapter 7 in Listings 7.2 and 7.3. The tricky parts are separating the menu items into logical groups, giving the menus and menu items meaningful names, and making sure that the items are enabled or disabled at the appropriate times.

Naming and Grouping Menu Items

Determine the appropriate menu item groups for your application by following general standards and referring to your use cases.

Most applications have a **File** menu and a **Help** menu. These have standard items such as **New** and **About**, respectively. Use the accepted standards for your items. For example, to create a new project database with PSP Tools, you would probably look in the **File** menu because that's where most applications put similar functions. That's exactly where we put the **New Database** menu item (seeFigure 9.1).

The menu items shown in Figure 9.1 exhibit another important feature for naming menu items. When clicking on an item causes a dialog box to open so that you can complete the operation (other than a login dialog or

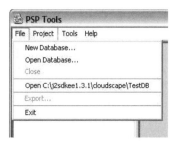

Figure 9.1 Standard File menu items

something of that type), place an ellipsis (…) after the item. This tells the user that more input is needed to complete the operation.

Notice that we chose to say **New Database** and **Open Database** rather than just **New** or **Open**. The additional information is especially important for the database creation command because the user will also create new tasks, new time entries, and new defect entries for a specific database. *Make sure that the context of any operation is clear from the menu command. When in doubt, add modifying words.*

We also use separators (horizontal lines) between groups of items in a menu. This is just a visual cue for the user. It helps us group those operations that we think are similar to each other.

When naming menu items, also refer to your use cases. Earlier in the project, you spent some time naming the use cases and the alternate flows. You can use these names to help determine what to call the menu items. For example, an alternate flow of events in the Record Personal Engineering Statistics use case is called Enter Actual Time. We could have created a menu item called just that—**Enter Actual Time**. However, we provided two ways to enter the time information: the user can enter the exact data needed or let the system record the data automatically through a timer. We decided to create two entries called **New Time Entry** and **Time Activity**.

The first command displays a data entry dialog box. The second invokes the activity timer tool (discussed later in this chapter). Both these menu items are under the **Project** menu. After you open a project, all of the actions that affect the data for that project are found under the **Project** menu.

Enabling and Disabling the Menu Items

As with creating menus, enabling and disabling menu items is easy. The tricky part of getting it right, however, is to toggle the availability at appropriate times. For example, it makes no sense to let the user enter defect data for a task if a database is not open or no task has been selected.

You can quickly make your code overly complex if you try to keep the menu items synchronized with the state of the application. Chris used a neat technique that kept the necessary code in one file, and kept most of the real action in one method. Let's look at the method that enables and disables the menu items. Listing 9.1 shows the beginning of the `setMenuFor()` method in `PSPMainFrame.java`.

Listing 9.1 Enabling and disabling menus at the proper time

```
/**
 * Enables the proper menu items
 * @param int menuType one of the defined values at the top of
 * this file
 */
public void setMenuFor(int menuType) {
    switch (menuType) {
        case PSP_CLOSED:
            fileExport.setEnabled(false);
            projectNewTask.setEnabled(false);
            projectDeleteTask.setEnabled(false);
            projectNewTime.setEnabled(false);
            projectNewDefect.setEnabled(false);
            projectNewUser.setEnabled(false);
            projectTimeActivity.setEnabled(false);
            projectProperties.setEnabled(false);
            toolsUserInfo.setEnabled(false);
            break;
        case PSP_TIMESUMMARY:
            fileExport.setEnabled(true);
            projectNewTime.setEnabled(true);
            projectNewUser.setEnabled(true);
            projectTimeActivity.setEnabled(true);
            projectProperties.setEnabled(true);
            projectNewTask.setEnabled(false);
            projectDeleteTask.setEnabled(false);
            projectNewDefect.setEnabled(false);
            toolsUserInfo.setEnabled(true);
            break;
        //...
```

The method takes a value that specifies the state of the application as a named constant like PSP_CLOSED, which tells us that a database has been closed and there is no active, open database. The code is one switch statement. For each state, we turn the appropriate menu items on or off. Whenever we added a new menu item that required enabling and disabling based on the application state, we just added a line to each of the cases. Each of the objects referenced in the cases, such as fileExport, are JMenuItem objects.

For a complex application, you probably want to create a document that indicates the specific menu configurations for the different states. You can easily do this with a matrix; we prefer using a spreadsheet application for this purpose.

The `PSPMainFrame.java` file contains all of the menu handling code. Each action invokes a menu handler that calls the appropriate private method. Once the action has been completed, we call the `setMenuFor()` method to synchronize the menus. Listing 9.2 shows the `doFileClose()` method. After the database is closed, we call `setMenuFor()` with an argument value of `PSP_CLOSED`.

Listing 9.2 Synchronizing menus after closing a database

```java
/**
 * Execute the Close command in the File menu.
 */
private void doFileClose()
{
    PSPDatabase db = PSPTools.getCurrentDatabase();
    if (db == null) {
        return;              // should never happen
    }
    try {
        db.close();
    } catch (PSPDatabaseException e) {
        //TBD
    }
    PSPTools.setCurrentDatabase(null);
    projectTree.setRootNode("No Project");
    fileClose.setEnabled(false);

    //select the root node
    projectTree.setSelectionRow(0);

    //disallow creation of new tasks
    setMenuFor(PSP_CLOSED);

    //blank the right side
    setRightPane(new JPanel());

}
```

Menu items also need to be synchronized when the user selects an item in the tree in the left panel. For example, if you select a task, you should be allowed to enter a defect or a time entry, or invoke the activity timer. If you select the root of the tree, it doesn't make sense to perform these actions because the application doesn't know what task to associate with the data. To handle this situation, we call the `setMenuFor()` method from appropriate places in `PSPTree.java`. This is shown in Listing 9.3.

Listing 9.3 Synchronizing menus after clicking on a tree item (excerpt)

```
if (nodeInfo instanceof Task) {
    ((Task)nodeInfo).setTopTab(getRequestedTab());
    JPanel newPanel = ((Task)nodeInfo).getPanel(nodeInfo);
    ((PSPMainFrame)getTopLevelAncestor()).setRightPane(newPanel);
    ((PSPMainFrame)getTopLevelAncestor()).setMenuFor(
PSPMainFrame.PSP_TASK);
    ItemID = ((Task)nodeInfo).getTaskID();
} else if (nodeInfo instanceof PSPTimeSummary) { ...
```

Perhaps in a future release we will find a way to synchronize the menus by making calls from just one place. Code refactoring will continue as long as we work on the project. The solution we have is good enough for our purposes. We can easily deal with two calling locations for this application.

Adding Context Menus

Most applications that provide a tree view of data allow you to perform some actions by right-clicking on an item and choosing an action from a pop-up menu.[1] We wanted PSP Tools to follow this convention when you right-clicked on a tree node, as shown in Figure 9.2. By design, the menu contents are the same as the **Project** menu contents. The **Project** menu items are enabled or disabled based on the type of item selected in the tree; the same rules apply to the items in the pop-up menu.

We had a choice at this point. We could have made the pop-up menu show only those actions relevant to the item clicked, or we could duplicate the whole **Project** menu. We chose the latter approach for these reasons:

---

[1] Other names for pop-up menus are *context menus* and *shortcut menus*.

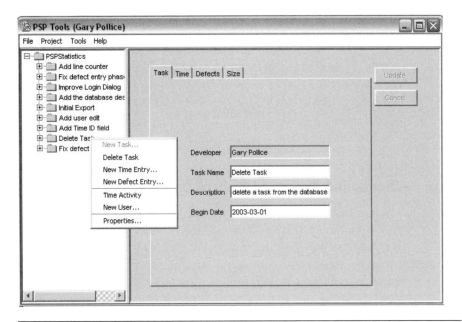

Figure 9.2 Pop-up menu for clicking on tree items

- It was much easier to display the whole **Project** menu. To show only those actions relevant to a particular item, we would have had to create separate menus for each item type and populate the menus accordingly.
- The code to create both menus was the same and made it less likely that the code would diverge if we made changes later.

Whenever the user right-clicks on a tree item, the code in Listing 9.4 is called. The `showPopup()` method gets the **Project** menu's contents and displays it in the pop-up menu as shown in Figure 9.2. The first two lines inside the condition select the item that was clicked. This is the expected behavior when you right-click an item. The remaining lines are responsible for displaying the menu.

Listing 9.4 Displaying the pop-up menu for tree items

```
private void showPopup (MouseEvent me) {
    if (me.isPopupTrigger()) {
        //find and set the corresponding tree item
        int index = getClosestRowForLocation(me.getX(), me.getY());
        setSelectedIndex(index);
```

continues

```
JPopupMenu popup =
((PSPMainFrame)getTopLevelAncestor()).getProjectMenu().getPopupMenu();
        popup.show (me.getComponent(), me.getX(), me.getY());
popup.setInvoker(((PSPMainFrame)getTopLevelAncestor()).getProjectMenu(
  ));
            }
        }
};
```

Displaying Time and Defect Details

For any task, the PSP Tools user must be able to enter details about the time spent in each PSP phase and the defects uncovered. Entering the data is straightforward: we use input dialog boxes for both types of entry. We also provide a timing tool that automatically enters the time details.

Presenting the data required us to think about how the PSP Tools user would use the information. Some data is *active*. For example, task summary data continually reflects the current state of work on that task. Time and defect entries contribute to the task summary. Once you enter a time you aren't going to update it, unless you entered it incorrectly. Once the entries are correct, you will mostly want to scan the entries for a task, perhaps to detect a trend or anomaly in the data. The best way to display this type of data is in a table. Yet, you still want to allow users to change some of the fields. Providing this capability, as shown in Figure 9.3, isn't a trivial task.

When you present data in a table view, you have to decide which of the cells can be modified and which of the modifiable cells require data validation. For the time entries shown in Figure 9.3, any of the cells can be modified. The Date, Time, and Phase fields must be validated. The comments have no restrictions (but we did have to modify the database code to allow any characters to appear).

Java provides special classes for certain data types such as dates. To install a date field in the table you need to develop a table model.[2] The Java Swing framework provided a default table model that can be easily extended. If you want to extensively customize the table presentation, you may need to write your own table model. This isn't a trivial task, and it's one that we didn't want to tackle for this release.

---

[2] Many of the Swing classes use the Model-View-Controller pattern to separate data from its presentation and logic. Table and tree models are two such classes that we used in PSP Tools.

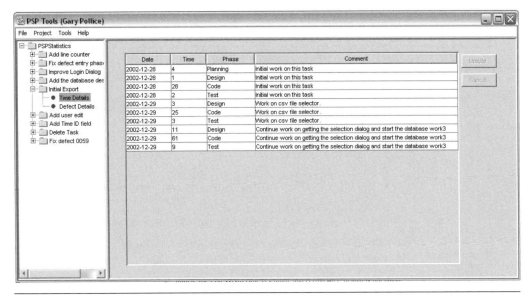

Figure 9.3 Presenting details in a table

The PSP Tools table model is defined in the `PSPTableModel.java` file. There are just a few methods other than the constructor. Most of the methods set up the table headings and insert a row of data. We used the same class for both time and defect data tables. As PSP Tools matures, we will probably refactor this class into two separate ones.

One method that we require is the `isCellEditable()` method. We want to make sure that the user is prevented from changing specific fields through the table interface. The `isCellEditable()` method takes a row number and column number and returns `true` if the cell at that location is editable; otherwise it returns `false`.

To understand how the tables work, look at the `PSPTimeSummary.java` file after you download the source files from the book's Web site. This file contains most of the interesting methods that you need to think about when you implement a table. Let's look at a couple of the more complex methods.

The largest method is `createInfoPanel()`, which sets up the panel with the table. It goes through the following steps:

1. Create a `JPanel` with a `GridBagLayout` as its layout. This is the most efficient way to create a table. This layout is more complex than a `GridLayout` but provides much more flexibility. If you

aren't familiar with `GridBagLayout`, you might find the time to learn it well spent.

2. Create a `PSPTableModel` and make it the model for this panel's table.
3. Make this panel the `TableListener` for the table. This adds extra responsibility to the panel and may be refactored into a separate class in future releases.
4. Install a `JComboBox` in the second column and make it the cell editor for that column. For time data, the second column represents the phase to which the time applies.
5. Load the data into the table. Read the time data for the selected task from the database and put it into the table.
6. Add the **Update** and **Cancel** buttons to the panel. These buttons are enabled once the user changes information in the table.
7. Position the visual items in the panel with appropriate sizes.

When you work with tables, setting different types of data in the cells can be confusing. To put the `JComboBox` into the table's second column, we call the private method `setComboBox()` in Step 4 above. Listing 9.5 shows this method. The trick is to set the `CellEditor` object associated with a column to be the `JComboBox`. We create the combo box and populate it with the phase names from the database. Then we call `setCellEditor()` on the specified column's model. Yes, there are other models to work with, but in most cases the default models are sufficient.

Listing 9.5 Inserting a JComboBox in a table

```
public void setComboBox(int column){
    TableColumn defectColumn =
            jt.getColumnModel().getColumn(column);
    JComboBox comboBox = new JComboBox();
    try {
        PSPPhaseAccessor tP =
        PSPTools.getCurrentDatabase().getPhaseAccessor();
        Vector vPhases = (Vector)(tP.getPhases().clone());
            for (int i = 0; i < vPhases.size(); i++) {
            PSPPhase phase = (PSPPhase)vPhases.get(i);
            comboBox.addItem(phase.getPhaseName());
            }

    }
```

```
    catch (PSPDatabaseException e) {
        System.out.println("Error getting Phases from DB");
    }

    defectColumn.setCellEditor(new DefaultCellEditor(comboBox));
}
```

The final part of implementing the tables is to install a listener to monitor when the user makes changes to the data presented in the table. When the code detects a change it enables the **Update** and **Cancel** buttons. When a user clicks the **Update** button, the changed data is written back to the database.

The `PSPDefectSummary.java` class is similar to the `PSPTimeSummary.java` class. There are two combo boxes for the defects: one for the phase in which the defect was injected and one for the phase in which it was resolved.

Adding User Preferences

When you think about user preferences, you probably imagine settings that the user can customize directly. For example, many applications allow the user to set font size, color schemes, and other visible characteristics of an application. In the first release of our application, we allow users to set preferences indirectly only, for example, to set the size of the application's window.

The initial users of PSP Tools quickly became annoyed that every time they opened a database they had to navigate from their home directory. They wanted to start from the directory with the last database they used. They also had to continually resize the windows. As an annoyed early adopter, Chris decided to find a solution. He created a user preferences file that contains an XML (eXtended Markup Language) file describing the preferences. His implementation is a very simple one taken from *The Java Cookbook* by Ian Darwin.

The utility class, `PSPUserPrefs.java`, implements everything needed to read or write user preferences. The class has three types of methods:

- The *getter* methods read values of the different characteristics from the file.

- The *setter* methods write the values of the characteristics to the user preferences file.
- The *I/O* methods perform all of the physical file access to and from the file.

For this release, there is one user preference file per computer. The file resides in the directory from which PSP Tools is launched. As a result, if multiple users are using PSP Tools on the same computer, they all have the same preferences. We discussed this with Russell. He didn't want to delay delivery, so he pushed the request for a single user preference file per user to a future release.

The implementation makes it very easy to add a new user preference. You write a getter method, as shown in Listing 9.6. You use helper methods to read and write string or integer values. Next you write a setter method, illustrated in Listing 9.7. Finally, you call the appropriate method whenever you need to access the value. Listing 9.8 shows how the user preferences are used to set the divider location for the split panel when we created the main window.

Listing 9.6 User preferences getter method

```
static public int getDividerLocation()  {
        return getIntValue("Divider");
}
```

Listing 9.7 User preferences setter method

```
static public void setDividerLocation(int newDivider) {
      setIntValue("Divider", newDivider);
}
```

Listing 9.8 Calling a user preferences method

```
JSplitPane createSplitPane()
{
      splitPane = new JSplitPane(JSplitPane.HORIZONTAL_SPLIT);
      splitPane.setContinuousLayout(true);
      int divider = PSPUserPrefs.getDividerLocation();
```

```
    if (divider == 0) {
        splitPane.setDividerLocation(0.25);
    } else {
        splitPane.setDividerLocation(divider);
    }
    projectTree = new PSPTree();
    leftPane = new JScrollPane(projectTree);
    rightPane = new JScrollPane();
    splitPane.setRightComponent(rightPane);
    splitPane.setLeftComponent(leftPane);

    return splitPane;
}
```

Using XML as the format for the user preferences file means that we can view the file with a text editor. Because there is a consistent, simple format, we can quickly see the settings.

The implementation we used is almost trivial. Every time you get or set a user preference value you read or write the complete file.[3] This is good enough for what we need now and, if the day comes when we need to expand the user preference capabilities, we can extend the implementation to take advantage of the latest Java XML technology. We think this is a fine compromise of implementing the simplest thing that will work and looking ahead to the future.

Finishing the Database

At the end of the Elaboration phase, the database was fairly stable. We added a couple of new fields during the Construction phase and had to make changes to allow single quote characters in the fields. In the following sections we describe how we addressed each of these situations.

Adding New Fields—Updating the Database Schema

You can add new fields by changing the schema. There is no effect on the user if the user creates a new database after receiving the new schema. But what happens to existing databases that contain valuable data? You don't

---

[3] A user preferences file is typically smaller than 200 bytes.

want to manually copy the data from the old database to the new one. Nor do you want to have to choose between using a new release of the software that supports the new database schema or staying with an older release that supports your existing database. You want the software to update the database when necessary with minimal intervention on your part.

We realized that PSP Tools users would face database update problems as new versions became available. Our early adopters, Gary and Russell, were already using the software. Although we could insist that they use the database utilities to update their databases, we knew we would have to address the database upgrade problem eventually. Gary developed a simple yet effective solution after studying the Cloudscape SQL documentation and prototyping a couple of ideas.

The solution to the problem requires that the database schema has a version. We added the version to the `DBInfo` table. Every time we change the database, we also do the following: we increase the database version number and we write a database updater class. The database updater class implements the `IPSPDatabaseUpdater` interface. The interface, shown in Listing 9.9, requires two methods, `initialize()` and `doUpdateDatabase()`. The `initialize()` method associates an open database with the updater. The `doUpdateDatabase()` method executes the appropriate SQL commands to update the database schema.

Listing 9.9 Interface for database version updaters

```
public interface IPSPDatabaseUpdater {
    /**
     * Update the database and return true if everything went
     * okay. Return false otherwise.
     */
    public boolean doUpdateDatabase();

    /**
     * Initialize the updater with the database.
     */
    public void initialize(PSPDatabase db);
}
```

Now let's look at an updater class. Listing 9.10 shows the updater class for updating a database from version 1 to version 2. The required change is to add a `timeID` field to the table containing detailed time entries. The `initialize()` method is trivial. We can add the `timeID` field with the SQL statement:

```
ALTER  TABLE  C16A  ADD  COLUMN  timeID  INTEGER
DEFAULT AUTOINCREMENT INITIAL 1 INCREMENT 1
```

The `alter` command adds the column and inserts appropriate values into the added fields for all records in the database. Using this technique, we avoid having to read and update each record after altering the schema. The only thing the `doUpdateDatabase()` method must do is execute the SQL command.

Listing 9.10 Sample database updater

```java
public void initialize(PSPDatabase db) {
    myDatabase = db;
}

public boolean doUpdateDatabase()
{
    String sqlUpdate =
        "ALTER TABLE C16A ADD COLUMN timeID INTEGER" +
        " DEFAULT AUTOINCREMENT INITIAL 1 INCREMENT 1";
    Statement stmt = null;
    try {
        stmt = myDatabase.getNewStatement();
        int rows = myDatabase.doUpdate(stmt, sqlUpdate);
        stmt.close();
    } catch (PSPDatabaseException e) {
        JOptionPane.showMessageDialog(
        null,
        "Unable to update the database.\n" +
        "SQL Error:\n     " +
        e.getSQLExceptionMessage(),
        "Database Update Error",
        JOptionPane.ERROR_MESSAGE);
        return false;
    } catch (SQLException e) {
        JOptionPane.showMessageDialog(
          null,
          "Warning: problem closing the statement\n" +
```

continues

```
                          e.getMessage(),
                          "Database Update Error",
                          JOptionPane.WARNING_MESSAGE);
                 return false;
         }
         return true;
     }
```

Each database updater is responsible for updating a database from one version to the next version. If, for some reason, your database is more than one version behind the current version, PSP Tools invokes a series of database updaters, each updating the database one version.

We check for an out-of-date database when we initialize a database in the PSPDatabase.java module after the connection is made, as shown in Listing 9.11.

Listing 9.11 Checking database version during initialization

```
public void initializeDB() throws PSPDatabaseException {

    try {
        // Get the database information
        dbInfo = dbAccessor.getDBInfo();
        if (checkUpgrade() == false) {
            close();
            throw new PSPDatabaseException(
                "Cannot work on the database until an " +
                "upgrade is performed");
        }
        // Get the phases (done for side effects only)
        phaseAccessor.getPhases();
    } catch (PSPDatabaseException e) {
        throw e;
    }
}
```

The checkUpgrade() method determines if the database is at the current version and, if not, updates it. Before updating the database, the user is asked to confirm that the update should proceed. This provides an opportunity to back up the database before upgrading it. The checkUp-grade() method is shown in Listing 9.12.

Listing 9.12 Method to determine whether the database needs upgrading

```java
private boolean checkUpgrade()
{
    if (dbInfo.getDBVersion() == DB_VERSION) {
        return true;
    }
    PSPDBUpdateManager updateMgr =
        new PSPDBUpdateManager(this, dbInfo.getDBVersion(),
            DB_VERSION);
    boolean result = updateMgr.doUpdateDatabase();
    if (!result) {
        return false;
    }
    // Update the dbInfo record.
    try {
        dbAccessor.updateDBInfo("dbVersion", "" +
            DB_VERSION);
    } catch (PSPDatabaseException e) {
        JOptionPane.showMessageDialog(
            null,
            "Unable to update the database info " +
            "after updating.\n" +
            "SQL Error:\n     " +
            e.getSQLExceptionMessage(),
            "Database Update Error",
            JOptionPane.ERROR_MESSAGE);
        return false;
    }
    return true;
}
```

After we determine that an update is required, we create an instance of a PSPDBUpdateManager object. The PSPDBUpdateManager performs the individual updates in the proper sequence. When the object is created, we call the doUpdateDatabase() method. After having the user confirm that the update should proceed, the code in Listing 9.13 executes.[4]

---

[4] We replaced some error-handling code with comments in this code example to make it easier to understand the core logic in the loop.

Listing 9.13 Database updating code in PSPDBUpdateManager.doUpdateDatabase()

```
// Now, iterate through as many updaters as needed.
int i = oldVersion;

Class updaterClass = null;
while (i < newVersion) {
    int j = i+1;
    // Get the appropriate updater class
    String className =
        "com.skunkworks.psp.database.PSPDBUpdate" +
        i + "to" + j;
    try {
        updaterClass = Class.forName(className);
    } catch (Exception e) {
        JOptionPane.showMessageDialog(
        null,
        "Unable to instantiate the class:\n" +
        className +
        "\nCannot update the database.\n\n" +
        "Error Message:\n    " + e.getMessage(),
        "Database Update Error",
        JOptionPane.ERROR_MESSAGE);
        return false;
    }

    // Now create an instance of it
    IPSPDatabaseUpdater updater = null;
    try {
        updater =
    (IPSPDatabaseUpdater)updaterClass.newInstance();
    } catch (Exception e) {
        JOptionPane.showMessageDialog(
        null,
        "Unable to create an instance of:\n" +
        className +
        "\nCannot update the database.\n\n" +
        "Error Message:\n    " + e.getMessage(),
        "Database Update Error",
        JOptionPane.ERROR_MESSAGE);
        return false;
    }

    // Now do the update
```

```
        updater.initialize(myDatabase);
        if (!updater.doUpdateDatabase()) {
            return false;
        }
        i++;
    }
    return true;
```

The main loop executes once for each update. Given the class name, it uses a Java feature to dynamically create an instance of a class. We create the class name based on the from-version and the to-version. For example, to update the database from version 1 to version 2, the variable className is assigned the value com.skunkworks.psp.database.PSPDBUpdate1to2. Similarly, to upgrade the database from version 1 to version 3, we call the doUpdateDatabase() method in a PSPDBUpdate1to2 object first, then in a PSPDBUpdate2to3 object.

Allowing Single Quotes in Fields

The SQL language uses single quotes to enclose strings. Some of the fields in the database are free-form and can include single quotes. For example, the database has a description. The first time we implemented the code to enter the database description, Gary typed Gary's database. SQL interpreted the apostrophe as the string terminator and deemed the SQL statement to be malformed.

The solution is to ensure that every embedded single quote is replaced by two single quotes (not the double quote character), forcing the single quote value into the field. We implemented the solution by creating a utility class, PSPSQLUtilities.java. This class contains two methods, as shown in Listing 9.14. One method converts every single quote character in the argument while the other method only converts embedded quotes. The appropriate method is called whenever we are about to perform an SQL operation. This is shown in Listing 9.15. Notice how we call the static method PSPSQLUtilities.prepareSQLString() when we insert the value of the login name into the user selection statement. This code is taken from PSPUserAccessor.java.

Listing 9.14 Utility methods to prepare SQL strings

```java
/**
 * Prepare a data string for inclusion in an SQL statement.
 * This routine replaces any single quote character by
 * two single quote characters.
 */
public static String prepareSQLString(String s)
{
    StringBuffer sb = new StringBuffer();
    for (int i = 0; i < s.length(); i++) {
        char c = s.charAt(i);
        if (c == '\'') {
            sb.append(c);     // append the single quote
        }
        sb.append(c);
    }
    return sb.toString();
}
```

Listing 9.15 Using the SQL utility methods

```java
public PSPUser getUser(String loginName)
        throws PSPDatabaseException
{
    String sqlGetUser =
        "SELECT * FROM Users WHERE loginName = '" +
        PSPSQLUtilities.prepareSQLString(loginName) + "'";
    try {
        Statement stmt = myDatabase.getNewStatement();
        ResultSet rs = myDatabase.doQuery(stmt, sqlGetUser);
        if (!rs.next()) {
            return null;     // not found
        }
        return userFromDB(rs);
    } catch (PSPDatabaseException e) {
        throw e;
    } catch (SQLException se) {
        throw new PSPDatabaseException(
                "SQL error getting a task", se);
    }
}
```

Testing

We continued to improve our testing during the Construction phase. Adding Raj to the team accelerated our adoption of automated tests. Raj created a test repository for automated acceptance tests and produced tests for the major use cases. This section shows an example of one such test, including the test script created by Rational XDE Tester and a test report.

Recording a test with Rational XDE Tester is similar to recording tests with other test automation tools. You simply walk through the test case in the software while the testing tool records what you do and how the software reacts. During the test recording session you identify those actions or values that determine the success or failure criteria. With XDE Tester these are called *verification points*. When you have finished, the testing tool writes a script that can be played back whenever you want to retest the software, in this case PSP Tools.

Listing 9.16 shows the script we created for testing the second use case. The script is written in Java. We are developing PSP Tools in Java, so reading and modifying the script requires little training time—we don't have to learn a special scripting language just for testing.

The code shown in Listing 9.16 performs the following operations:

- Opens the PSP Tools database, "project1"
- Logs in with a password of "psp"
- Creates a task called "task2"
- Opens the views for the time and defect details
- Removes the task

Any Java programmer should be able to easily follow the code.

Listing 9.16 Portion of test script for use case 2

```
package Folder1;

import resources.Folder1.UC2Helper;

import com.rational.test.ft.*;
import com.rational.test.ft.object.interfaces.*;
import com.rational.test.ft.script.*;
import com.rational.test.ft.value.*;
```

continues

```
import com.rational.test.ft.vp.*;

/**
 * Description    : XDE Tester Script
 * @author administrator
 */
public class UC2 extends UC2Helper
{
    /**
     * Script Name    : <b>UC2</b>
     * Generated      : <b>Jun 3, 2003 9:40:41 PM</b>
     * Description    : XDE Tester Script
     * Original Host : WinNT Version 5.0  Build 2195 (Service Pack 1)
     *
     * @since  2003/06/03
     * @author administrator
     */
    public void testMain (Object[] args)
    {
       // Insert Code Here


       try
       {
       // Frame: PSP Tools
       PSPMainFrame().click();
       PSPMainFrame().click();
       menubar().click(atPath("File"));
       menubar().click(atPath("File->Open..."));

       //
       Filename().click();
       JDialog().inputChars("d:\\pspproject\\project1");
       Open().click();

       //
       PSPLoginDialog().click();
       passwordtext().click();
       PSPLoginDialog().inputChars("psp");
       Login().click();

       // Frame: PSP Tools
       tree().click(atPath("project1"));
       menubar().click(atPath("Project"));
```

```
menubar().click(atPath("Project->New Task..."));
// TabbedPage: Task
text().click();
PSPMainFrame().inputChars("task2");
AddTask().click();
tree().click(atPath("project1->task2"));
tree().click(atPath("project1->task2->Location(PLUS_MINUS)"));
tree().click(atPath("project1->task2->Time Details"));
tree().click(atPath("project1->task2->Defect Details"));
tree().click(atPath("project1->task2"));
menubar().click(atPath("Project"));
menubar().click(atPath("Project->Delete Task"));

//
Yes().click();

// Frame: PSP Tools
menubar().click(atPath("File"));
menubar().click(atPath("File->Close"));

logInfo("Use Case 3 Passed");
}

catch(Exception Ex)
{
    logError("Use Case 3 Failed");
}
    }
}
```

When you finish running a test, a test report is written as an HTML page. See Figure 9.4 for a sample test report page. By creating HTML output, which many test tools do, you can make the results available to the whole team by publishing the results immediately on a Web site.

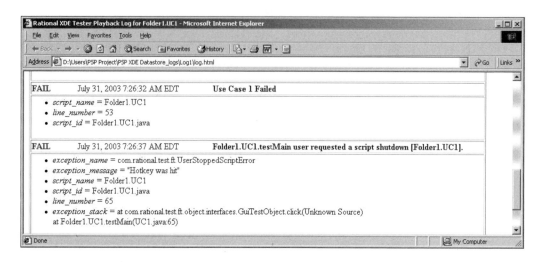

Figure 9.4 Sample test report

Summary

This chapter described a few of the technical details of our Construction phase experience. If you are interested in more such details, we recommend downloading the project from the book's Web site. If you have suggestions or find problems with the code or other artifacts we have posted, please let us know so we can make the appropriate corrections.

CHAPTER 10

Transition:
We Deliver PSP Tools

Transition is the last phase of the RUP lifecycle model. People differ about when the Transition phase begins, but there is little disagreement about when Transition ends. Small projects need only a simple, and preferably a short, Transition phase. The Transition phase for complex projects can require great expenditures of resources over a long time. For example, a complex project might involve installing software and hardware simultaneously at many sites, requiring careful planning, execution, and follow-up.

This chapter describes the simple Transition phase our project went through. Even for a small and simple project, the Transition phase doesn't just happen. We had to plan, prepare, and execute the plan to deliver the software to our customers.

What Is the Transition Phase?

What is the purpose of the Transition phase? RUP says that "The focus of the Transition Phase is to ensure that software is available for its end users. The Transition Phase can span several iterations, and includes testing the product in preparation for release and making minor adjustments based on user feedback."

It's easy to misunderstand the Transition phase. If you have followed the iterative development practice, your customer has probably already used the software before the Transition phase. If you follow some of the agile practices such as XP, your customer has been working with the product on a regular basis from very early in the project.

We have seen teams worry needlessly about whether they are in the Transition phase or still in the Construction phase. In many cases, especially

193

on small projects, the line between the two phases can be blurry. We believe that the key objective of the Construction phase is to iteratively and incrementally develop a complete product that is ready for transition to its user community. In other words, when you have implemented and tested all of the features as described by the use cases—or you've scoped features and use cases out of the release—you are ready to enter the Transition phase. The Transition phase is really about preparing the product and the customer so that the customer can use the product in a production environment.

One question causes much confusion—is Beta testing part of the Construction or Transition phase?

Philippe Kruchten, the thought leader of the RUP development group, says that by definition, Beta testing is part of the Transition phase. In RUP version 2003, the timing information on the Workflow Detail for Beta testing says that the work generally occurs during the Construction and Transition phases, but in some cases, you might perform Beta testing as early as the Elaboration phase.

Following an ancient tradition, we answer the question with another question: Does it really matter? Depending on which phase Beta testing belongs to, would you plan, code, or test differently? We don't think so, and we don't think it's worth worrying about. It's more important to ensure that you do have Beta tests. Here's a general guideline: *If you have implemented all of the use cases and scenarios and only need to fix defects and do minor cleanup, then you are ready to perform Beta testing, regardless of the phase you are currently in.*

Making the Transition to the Transition Phase

At some point, you and your customer decide that it is time to begin the transition. Usually, that time is based on the expected delivery date for the system you are building minus some amount of time to prepare. By the end of the Construction phase, you have finished most work on the software and you now need to package and deliver it. And, if you kept your customer involved throughout the project, you have implemented the most important and valuable features. Your Transition phase might be long, in which case you make several deliveries of code and supporting material to the user, or it might be short, in which case you prepare the software for deployment and support relatively quickly. To maintain control over the project, we recommend that you plan a short Transition phase. We discuss that topic later in this chapter.

Goals of the Transition Phase

RUP identifies several objectives for the Transition phase, as outlined in Appendix A. As we have said about other aspects of RUP, the goals aren't all appropriate for every project. For our project, we worked with the following goals:

- Beta testing to validate the system against user expectations
- Training users
- Tuning code and fixing bugs

We had other minor goals. We expected to do a final code refactoring, document the system for others who would work on it after us, and do a project post-mortem to improve our process on future projects. Commercial software development projects have more goals for the Transition phase, including training the internal support staff, preparing marketing and rollout materials, and manufacturing.

What About Requirements?

The RUP hump chart (see Appendix A) shows that even during Transition phase iterations you need to manage requirements. New requirements come in during all phases of a project. During the Transition phase, it's especially likely that you will see new requirements, because stakeholders have time to work with the product and to think about its implications. You need to manage the requirements carefully and thoughtfully. You don't need to implement each new requirement, but you do need to capture each one and use the collection to help you plan the next release.

Avoiding Late Changes

In our experience, most projects decree that during the Transition phase no new features will be added to the software. Compare this style to XP, where you welcome any change up to the final iteration. We find that the final packaging, documentation, manufacturing, and deployment of software to your customer community take time and benefit from stability. Significant changes at the project's end can cause delays in these non-coding activities.

And these activities are ones that can determine the success of your product.

How many times have you used software and found something that you couldn't quite get right, either during installation or the first few times you used it? Most of us have experienced this phenomenon. When that happens, what do you do? You avoid using the software and look for a different way to get your job done. If the software is a commercial product, you look at competitive products. If the software was developed by your in-house IT staff, you try to get help from the IT staff, usually starting from an adversarial position. In either case, you probably won't want to use software from them again.

This illustrates a truism about selling, in general, and selling software specifically:

It takes time to sell your product to a customer and earn his or her trust. It takes only one bad experience to lose that trust and the business.

Aiming for a Short Transition Phase

Sometimes you can't avoid changing the software just before you deliver it to your customer, but you can minimize the changes. We recommend that you make your Transition phase as short and as focused as possible. In this section, we outline a few techniques.

If you work closely with your customers during development, there should be few surprises at the end of the project. Your customers can evaluate the software from the early iterations through the final Construction phase iterations and, more importantly, provide feedback on whether the product is meeting their expectations and needs. During the project, you work with your customers to manage the project's scope and to prioritize work so you deliver as much value as possible in the time available.

By delivering working software at each iteration, you are already developing the non-code artifacts starting early in the project. You end up working on some of the less obvious code artifacts, too, such as install modules and programs. As a result, by the time you reach the Transition phase, you have made substantial progress toward this phase's goals, allowing you to shorten the Transition phase.

Compare this approach to a more traditional one where developers defer Transition phase work to the end of the project. At the same time, developers are fixing defects, and the documentation, quality, and release team members are scrambling to meet impossible deadlines. On a small team, this means that all team members are working ridiculously long hours, forgetting their life outside of work, in order to make the delivery.

There is a lot to do after you finish writing code and before you ship a complete software product, even on a small project like PSP Tools. No matter how short you make the Transition phase, you will get new requests and requirements. Manage them. If there is a good reason to satisfy a new or expanded requirement, do so. And make sure your stakeholders (including the development team) understand the cost and the benefit of satisfying the requirement. In most cases, given the choice to ship on time without implementing the requirement or to delay the release, your stakeholders will opt to ship on time.

Example

It is important to convey requirement changes to your team throughout the project, but the importance is amplified during the Transition phase. Before he took a job with Rational,[1] Gary was offered a position at a smaller company as a development manager. The offer was tempting and their product had great potential. Luckily, Gary knew many members of the development and QA team from a previous company and was able to learn how well they were meeting the business requirements.

Their first release was just weeks away and they had several major defects to address. They needed to release on time to display the product at a major trade show. Finishing the project was completely possible. There was still time to finish the work and produce a quality product.

Gary stayed in touch with the QA manager. In a three-day period, the number of major defects almost doubled. It didn't take long to figure out what was happening. One of the owners of the company was spending his evenings thinking up new requirements and implementing his "solutions" for those requirements. Most of the solutions caused integration errors with the rest of the product. Instead of a downward trend, the defect rate was going up because of the new requirements imposed, without any input from the rest of the development team or other stakeholders.

Gary realized that the company wasn't a good fit for him. He liked the people, and he liked the product. But he also knew that if he accepted the job, he would spend too much of his time managing the owner so his team could ship the product with the necessary commercial quality for each release. This was one of the better decisions Gary made in his career. He

---

[1] Actually, Gary was with PureAtria when Rational acquired them.

ended up at Rational and the small company lasted about nine months before it went out of business.

There is a simple moral to the story. If you have to meet an unchange-able date, then you simply cannot continue to accept requirements changes up to the end of your project. After a certain point, you have to defer requests, while keeping your team both informed and focused. Communication is perhaps more important in the endgame than at any other time during a project.

Defects Are Not Requirements

During the Transition phase, Gary and Russell met or talked frequently, sometimes daily, to ensure that everything was on track. Russell and his engineers started to use PSP Tools for their day-to-day work. They uncov-ered some defects that we missed in our testing.

Because we were in the Transition phase, it was important to decide which defects to fix before the release and which fixes to defer to the next release. Russell and Gary served as our change control board (CCB). They used two simple criteria to help direct their decisions:

- Did the defect cause the program to fail in such a way that data was lost or corrupted?
- Did the defect cause the product to become unusable?

If the answer to either of these questions was "yes," then the defect needed to be fixed. In all other cases the defect would be deferred.

Many of the defects could be fixed quickly. In fact, teams are often tempted to fix all the "easy" bugs. But remember that fixing a bug can have ramifications for other members of your team. For example, a bug fix might require changes to the documentation because screen shots can change or a sequence of actions might change. A bug fix needs to be tested; if it affects other code, your testers can spend extra time diagnosing the new bugs. And then your CCB needs to decide which of the new bugs to fix. Simple changes during the Transition phase can quickly become time sinks for the whole team.

Code Changes During the Transition Phase

We just said that we want to keep the code changes to a minimum during the Transition phase. But the fact is that there will always be some changes. Even if your customers have used the iteration releases regularly, they will exercise the final product much more. And they will uncover some new, and possibly serious, defects.

Regardless of how thoroughly you test at the unit or system level, you will not cover all of the possible ways your customers will use your software. Even if your customers help define acceptance tests, it doesn't mean that tests that pass indicate a lack of defects in your program. When acceptance tests pass, it does mean that you have created software that meets the expectations your customers were able to specify. Once customers begin to work with software, they will find ways of using it that neither you nor they ever thought about.

Here is a simple example to explain what we mean. Throughout the Construction phase, Russell and Gary used PSP Tools. Some of Russell's team used the product as well. Gary recorded his personal statistics using PSP Tools as soon as the database was implemented. Soon after we entered the Transition phase, a couple of significant defects were reported, saying that the program just hung in certain, repeatable cases. One of these occurred if you deleted a task while you were timing an activity for the same task. Even if you cancelled out of the activity timer, the program hung and you had to kill the process. Luckily, the database didn't get corrupted, but Russell and Gary decided that the behavior was unacceptable and needed to be fixed.

The defect just described is an example of one that might easily occur in real usage. But what is the chance that the exact sequence of actions that uncovered the defect would occur in the specifications, regardless of how you defined the specifications, use cases, and acceptance tests?

The Importance of Independent Testers

After reading the previous section, you might conclude that as long as your customers work with the product, and if you've tested the product continuously throughout the development during each iteration, you should be okay. All of this testing helps, and we believe that it is necessary. But you still need independent testers to test your software—as soon as possible!

Fortunately for us, Raj joined us at the end of the Construction phase, and he made an immediate impact. He uncovered defects that we might never have caught. He also automated the acceptance tests so we could easily determine when we were ready to deploy the software to the customer. More importantly, he provided an independent *voice of reason* for our group. (Of course, now we wish he had joined us much earlier in the project.)

The Brown Thumb

Some organizations mistakenly think that testing is all about putting quality into the code—at the end of the project! This is an impossible task. You have to build quality into the product from the start of the project. Testing is about verifying what the developers should already know (that the software works as specified), ensuring that integration issues are addressed, and about uncovering defects that might not be obvious. In other words, testing is about trying to break the software.

What does it take to be a good tester? One of Gary's teachers said it succinctly: A good tester has a "brown thumb." This means that a good tester can take software that people think is working and *turn it to crap* quickly.[2] The good tester uncovers huge numbers of meaningful defects in a short time.

Soon after Raj joined our team, we knew that he was gifted with a brown thumb. Gary used to have a brown thumb, but because he was out of practice, his thumb had become several shades lighter.

Testing Your Own Software

You might ask whether you can test software that you have also written, to determine whether the software is good enough to ship. In general, the answer is no. We know of only rare cases where this is possible. However, several factors can contribute to your ability to assist with testing your own software.

---

[2] The term came from Dr. Bill McKeeman at the Wang Institute of Graduate Studies. The brown thumb is the opposite of a green thumb. People with green thumbs have an uncanny ability to grow all kinds of plants, seemingly with ease, while those lacking the green thumb either grow plants with difficulty, kill the plants, or are most expert at creating compost.

Define Requirements

The requirements for the software you are building must be very well-defined. If you are going to do your own testing, or if your customer is paying you to deliver a specific feature set, there must be little or no doubt about what it means to satisfy requirements and meet customer expectations. The best examples we have seen of such software are compilers for programming languages. Most languages are formally specified and there is often an acceptance test suite for a given language.[3] Software that contains a considerable amount of graphical user interface is much more difficult to define unambiguously than a language processing program such as a compiler.

Have the Right Mindset

You need to have the right mindset. What does it mean to *have the right mindset?* There are people who firmly believe that they can produce defect-free software. Whether they are able to do so is not the issue. If you don't believe you can do something, you might as well not try. If you do believe that you can deliver defect-free code to your customer, then you must be willing to do whatever is necessary to make that happen.

Organizations can also develop the right mindset. The following example is a short side-trip that illustrates what we mean.

In 1984, Gary had the privilege of working at the Datapoint Technology Center (DATEC) in San Antonio, Texas. At the time, Datapoint was a leader in innovative computer technology. Although the technology center was a research group, its members took tremendous pride in delivering high-quality software to the rest of the company. Gary joined and worked on a compiler code generator for the company's programming language. He had never worked on a code generator up to that point, and he was about to build one from scratch. There were code generators he could study and colleagues he could consult with, but the responsibility to design and deliver the code was his.[4]

DATEC had an interesting tradition. When a staff member said that code was ready for release to the user community, there was an implicit agreement that accompanied the code. The first person to discover and

---

[3] Passing all tests in a test suite doesn't guarantee that you have implemented a defect-free compiler for the language, but it provides a minimum set of tests that you must pass to be *compliant* with the language.

[4] A code generator may not be specified quite as formally as the front-end of a compiler, but it is still fairly easy to determine if generated code is correct or not.

report each bug in the code received a free lunch at the expense of the staff member who released the code. This can be quite daunting, and very frightening. All Gary could think of was, "There goes the mortgage payment. There goes the house. My marriage is ruined...."

There were only three choices—never release the code generator, release it and hope there weren't too many defects in it, or do everything possible to make it bulletproof. Gary chose this last course of action. When he released the code generator, only three defects were discovered during the next year. Certainly, this was affordable. What is more amazing is that the three defects in a year was about the average for the group. The whole group had the right mindset.

Beware of the Hawthorne Effect

Sometimes you may think you are improving your work, but the improvement may only be temporary. For example, you need to know how to write good tests in order to improve your testing. We often overlook this need and think that as long as we perform a testing activity, such as unit testing, we will magically attain the hoped-for results of high-quality software.

Sometimes there is a benefit to just "going through the motions." For example, in a class on empirical software engineering, Gary's students conducted an experiment on Test-First Programming (TFP), which is a version of the XP testing practice (see Appendix C). A group of programmers were divided into two subgroups and given the same program specification. One group was asked to write their tests first and the other was asked to write the program using their normal (not test-first) approach. The results, while statistically inconclusive, indicated that TFP might be a valuable tool for producing higher quality code.[5] An interesting observation was that the tests written by most of the TFP group weren't good tests. The training provided for the participants was minimal. Yet, the TFP team seemed to produce better code. A possible explanation is that simply taking the time to think about tests, regardless of whether the tests were well-designed, decreased the number of defects found in the code. These results may simply be a manifestation of the Hawthorne Effect.[6] If so, the benefits realized from this study would eventually revert to earlier levels.

---

[5] For a result to be statistically significant, you need to have a 95% confidence that your prediction is correct. Our data, using a small sample size, indicated an 89% confidence level. We believe the results warrant more experimentation.

[6] The Hawthorne Effect was discovered in a study of workers at the Western Electric plant in Hawthorne, New York. Production increased, not as a result of actual changes in working conditions, but simply by the fact that the work was being observed.

The act of doing TFP might only provide a short-term increase in software quality, but lasting improvement requires more effort. If TFP is really useful in the long term, then it will only be useful if you write good tests. You need to learn how to write good tests, and then internalize that knowledge so that it becomes a natural part of your work. It takes time and perseverance to make any new skill a habit.

If you are lucky to have excellent requirements, the right mindset, and the ability to write good tests, you have a chance—albeit a slim chance—of testing your own work. On a small project, like PSP Tools, we thought it might work. It did not.

We should have realized sooner that we needed an independent tester, and then invited one to join us much earlier in the project. We were lucky that Raj was able to join us when he did. His participation and contributions helped us deliver better code.

Packaging the Product

Our customers had been working with PSP Tools for a while. Russell knew the product almost as well as the rest of the development team. What was the best way to deliver the product to our users? What exactly did we plan to distribute?

One possibility was to expend minimal effort and just package the Java Archive (JAR) file and other libraries, and then email it to the users. We could even post it to a Web site and let anyone download it. But would that be good enough? We believed that without support and training materials, new users would be stuck. We wanted to attract users who are not members of Russell's development staff.

We decided that our distribution package needed to contain the following items:

- The software product itself
- An introduction for new users
- Installation instructions
- Release notes to describe final changes for existing users of the software

Our Transition phase plan was simple. We gave everyone on the team a set of deliverables, let them think about how much time and effort they would need to produce the deliverables, added some additional time for fixing any defects that might crop up, and established a release date. If a feature isn't ready for release in an earlier iteration, you simply move it to a future iteration and perform the required scope management. During the Transition phase, the end date becomes more critical; you must plan and monitor the schedule and work products more carefully than in other phases. Your customers are waiting for delivery of the product and you've promised that they can have it. If you miss this date, most of the goodwill that you have gained from your customers will be lost.

Iterative development is great. It helps you focus on producing working software. As you reach the end of your project, however, you need to reserve time to work on the final packaging. You may have been extremely agile and responsive to changes during the project. We feel that at the end of the Transition phase, you shouldn't implement new requirements or produce new code. Instead, you should focus on packaging and deployment of your software. Similarly, your customers need to plan to accept and use the software, including any transitions from old systems or previous releases of the software. Planning, rather than responding to change, is critical for this part of the process.

If you restrict the Transition phase to work on the final packaging, support materials, and fixing only critical defects, you will find that you can meet the schedule you establish for your Transition phase iteration or iterations. When you add tasks that aren't in the established short list, you risk a delay in delivering the finished product to your customers.

User Documentation

We were very lucky to have Liz on our team. She's got a wealth of experience in producing documentation for many different types of users. Her ability to relate to the customer was valuable to the team when we worked on use cases and again when we designed the user interface. As a user advocate, she helped us think about what the customer might, or might not, understand about the product, or discover while using the product.

There are many books that say a lot about user documentation—how to write it, what it must contain, and different ways to present it.[7] We want to emphasize that unless you have designed the perfect program, or unless your program requires no user interaction, you need some type of user documentation. And your documentation should be useful to your end users.

---

[7] To explore this topic more fully than we can in this book, go to http://www.amazon.com and search under Books for "software technical writing."

The practice of writing user documentation has gone through several trends over the last few decades. Several years ago, the trend was to faithfully document every aspect of the user interface, leading to the following all-too-ubiquitous classic piece of "help": *Click **File > New** to create a new file.*

This type of user assistance isn't very helpful; it doesn't answer questions that real users might ask, such as:

- Under what circumstances would you want to create a new file?
- What are the alternatives to creating a new file (perhaps working in a temporary space)?
- Are there any restrictions (for example, on the length of the file name or the type of file)?
- What if something goes wrong while I'm creating a file?
- Are there related activities that I should know about (deleting a file, renaming a file)?

After just a few encounters with this type of documentation, most users learn to distrust, and eventually avoid, reading the very documentation that is supposed to be helping them effectively use the software.

Fortunately, a relatively recent trend in technical documentation has helped technical writers produce user assistance that is actually helpful. In the industry, this trend is called "task-oriented writing" or "user-centered information development."

The PSP Tools *User's Guide* follows this trend in that it is structured around the tasks that a user might perform to get value from using the software. Does this sound familiar? It should—it's one of the ways to define a use case.

We have already mentioned several reasons to work with use cases on your project, and using them as a foundation for writing effective user documentation is another one. If you structure the documentation by starting with use cases, you provide information that helps the users do their jobs, rather than documentation that simply describes the features of the product.

This approach fits neatly into Liz's philosophy about technical writing. She believes that most people don't use software for its own sake (because it's fun, for example); they use software so they can be more effective at doing their jobs. After all, most of us want to get our work done with minimal fuss. We want our tools to work, and when we need help, we want to find the information quickly and get back to the task. Liz believes that her job is to "help people go home at night." By organizing and presenting documentation in terms of what the user is trying to accomplish, she feels that she can be more successful at her craft.

Originally, we planned to deliver documentation as online help. Partway through the project, we decided to write a *User's Guide* instead, and not provide online help, at least not for version 1.[8]

Figure 10.1 shows the guide's Table of Contents. It is short but you can immediately see how to get value from the product. Notice that the headings

Table of Contents

Figure 10.1 PSP Tools *User's Guide* table of contents

---

[8] The full *User's Guide* is available on the book's Web site.

don't exactly map to the use cases, but they do follow the general scenarios in the use cases. If you aren't already producing user documentation based on use cases, try it and see how your users like it.

You want to involve technical writers in the project as early as you can hire them. Documentation work continues throughout the project. During the Transition phase, documentation work focuses on attending to the final publishing details to prepare the material for your customers.

Writers typically work with testers, engineers, product managers, and even customers to understand the goals of the product and how to use it. Writers can be excellent user advocates, and they can help develop use cases and assist with the design of user interfaces. As the writers learn the software (in preparation for writing about it), they can serve as an early warning system when the software doesn't work as expected or when it seems to veer away from the use cases. Writers can contribute a great deal to the project. We encourage you to get writers involved early in your projects.

Training the Users

Documentation is necessary, but it's usually not sufficient for training your customers. Actually, it's usually sufficient for training only some of your customers. On our project, we had a few options. We could send a team member to train the customers at their site. We could hold online training sessions. We could develop some training materials and let the customers learn on their own. We could hope that they would learn from the *User's Guide* or from each other.

We chose to let one of our team members train the end users for the initial release. The obvious team member was Russell. Yes, he was the customer, but he was an integral part of our team from the beginning. He had been using the product. He had access to all of the material that the other team members had, and he knew the end users better than anyone else on the team.

Russell was willing to do the training as long as someone was on call to help with any questions that he couldn't answer. He never had to use the lifeline, but he was reassured to have the option of using it. He spent about an hour training his team on how to set up a PSP Tools database and use the product.

During the session they also decided to use individual databases (one per user), rather than one single group database. They wanted the database to be portable so they could use it on different computers. For version 1, users need to copy the database. In addition to this overhead, they need to keep the database contents consistent across computers. Gary uses PSP Tools on three different computers and when he forgets to copy the database, he needs to manually re-enter data.

The feedback we got from the training session and our customers' subsequent product use resulted in more requirements for the next release. One of the high-priority changes we plan to implement in version 2 will give database access over the Internet, which will eliminate the need to maintain multiple copies of a database.

There was an additional benefit to having Russell conduct the training. Adopting PSP Tools meant that the engineers' process was going to change. Russell was part of the organization—in fact he managed the organization—so he was able to use the session to get buy-in from the engineers about how they were going to adapt to the changes. This made the changed process *their* process, not one that was imposed on them.

Training a Larger Group of Customers

We admit that the circumstances of our project are rare. It is fair to ask how you can help your customers learn your product. In a more typical situation, a representative from the customer's organization isn't available to help train users, or more than one small, co-located set of customers need to learn your software.

You need to balance the benefits of developing training materials and programs against the costs of not developing them. Consider the following points:

- How many users are there and where are they located?
- Are the users part of your organization or are they external to your organization? If they are external, it might be more difficult to gather them for a training session.
- Is there an economic advantage to offering training sessions? Especially when the customers are external to your organization, there may be an advantage to offering training sessions. Even if the basic use of the software is simple, it may be worth the customers' time and money to pay you to train them to become experts. Perhaps coupling teaching the tool usage with describing the underlying techniques (in this case, Personal Software Process itself), is valuable to the customer.

- Can training be delivered by interactive, remote sessions? Several networking tools (such as WebEx, at www.webex.com) allow you to conduct meetings and training sessions over the Internet. Consider some of these as possible alternatives to in-person training. These will not be as effective, but it may be more realistic to use them.
- Can training be delivered in self-study modules? If so, what is the cost of developing book-based or web-based training modules? This effort requires some special skills, but might be valuable to both you and your customer.
- If you decide to develop training materials, can your technical writers and trainers collaborate and possibly share material? We recommend that you develop user-centered training. One of the best places to start is with the use cases, the same starting point that we recommend for technical writers.

The size of the development project isn't a major issue here. The software you deliver, its complexity, and the value of training your customers are the major drivers when you consider the type and amount of training you will deliver.

Are We Done Yet?

We've packaged the software, developed documentation and training, and delivered the package to our customers. Can we declare victory and head off to the local pub for a celebration? Or is there more to do?

There are some other topics we at least need to consider. RUP provides an extensive list of items that you may choose to deliver as part of the Transition phase. We believe that every project needs to consider at least these:

- How will you provide support for your customers?
- What will you deliver to the development organization so that work can begin on the next version?

Supporting Your Customers

For PSP Tools, we made a simplifying decision about ongoing support. We decided that anyone could report problems to the development team, using email.[9] We will determine an appropriate action. This solution may be

---

[9] You can send feedback or problem reports to us at psptools@yahoo.com.

appropriate for some projects, like open-source software projects, but it's not good enough for commercial software. You have to design the defect reporting process, determine who is involved, and select the tools to use. If your organization has a separate support group, you need to ensure that its members are trained and qualified to handle customer inquiries. Further discussion of this topic is both beyond the scope of this book and the expertise of the authors. For more information, we recommend that you search for books about "customer support" on www.amazon.com.

Preparing for the Next Version

Many organizations begin to work on the next version before the current version is complete. Teams usually assume that the first version delivers a specific set of features that they can build on. Realistically, if you develop in this overlapped fashion, you need to synchronize code when the earlier version is finally complete.

Your approach to gathering the necessary project materials will vary depending on the individuals involved, the team, and the organization. On past projects, our most successful efforts have been to take time *after* the Transition phase to assemble the documents and artifacts that would help us move on to the next release of the project. We discuss this topic more in the next chapter on the project post-mortem.

Summary

The Transition phase is the culmination of the work that you did in the first three phases of the project. This is when you deliver the software release to your customers. On small, simple projects the Transition phase can be very short. You want to strive for as short a Transition phase period as possible to keep the customer expectations of the software product in line with what you deliver.

Whether you have a simple or complex Transition phase, you must plan for it and execute to that plan. Perhaps more than any other phase, the Transition phase requires planning and monitoring the plan. Project managers earn their money during the Transition phase. As projects grow, there are increasing avenues of communication and coordination the project manager must manage.

PSP Tools had a short Transition phase period. We addressed user documentation needs with our *User's Guide*. We ensured that the end users received appropriate training. We performed final testing, integration, and packaging and deployed the software to the customers. Finally, we made sure that the customers had a way to report feedback and problem reports to the team.

PSP Tools Transition: 3 weeks

CHAPTER 11

Post-Mortem: How Will We Improve the Next Version?

Post-mortem isn't a phase in RUP—it's an activity. Every project team deserves a good post-mortem review of the project. During this review, you try to learn how to improve your individual and team process in preparation for your next project. This chapter presents observations from the PSP Tools team's post-mortem. We also performed some activities after the Transition phase to clean up our artifacts so they are ready for the next release. The chapter also serves as a post-mortem for our story.

The actual PSP Tools project didn't happen in real time. Real life and real jobs intervened. At the end of each chapter, we have estimated how long it would have taken had we worked on the project full time. Someone asked us what we would do differently given the changes in technology and other areas that occurred during the period we built the product. We include a section that presents our ideas about these changes. We end, as all projects should, with our observations and a look to the future of PSP Tools.

Benefits of Conducting a Post-Mortem

The project is complete and customers are using the code you wrote. Reflecting on the individual and team experiences serves these purposes:

- It helps the team members better understand how they work as part of a team—specifically, how they worked as part of *this* team.
- It helps the team members understand their strengths and weaknesses in different technical areas and points out what they learned, and what they might want to learn.

- It gives the team a chance to improve their process by reflecting on the whole project.

There are several post-mortems throughout a project. Each iteration typically has a post-mortem—the Iteration Assessments. Part of each assessment is devoted to reviewing the process for the iteration and making mid-project adjustments. The post-mortem review at the end of the project lets the team take a more global view of the process, as a whole, and examine those process elements that worked and those that didn't work. From the viewpoint of process, the post-mortem review is one of the most important activities the team can do—*a process that doesn't change is a dead process!*

Conducting a Post-Mortem Review

Post-mortem reviews can be very casual, but in our experience they're much more helpful when you create an agenda and stick to it. Without structure, any meeting can become chaotic, but an unstructured post-mortem review can quickly devolve into a "bitch session." When this happens you get very little benefit from the review. People talk about what went wrong, which is cathartic in the short term, but no long-term improvements are realized.

From Gary's experience with moderating project post-mortem reviews, we present guidelines for making the review session effective.

Involve the Whole Team

While it seems obvious to invite all team members to the review, many post-mortem reviews are held without all team members present. Either members aren't invited, or they aren't available at the appointed time.

Sometimes a team doesn't invite certain people because they are perceived as disruptive or they didn't meet the rest of the team's expectations on the project. The team decides, incorrectly, that the missing member will add nothing to the meeting. It turns out that the team will often learn a lot by inviting this person. If nothing else, they will get a deeper understanding of why the difficulties existed, and perhaps what type of person isn't a good fit for the team in the future. Even better, they might learn how to work effectively with more and different types of people, so that in the future they can increase the diversity of the team.

Sometimes people aren't available because they are on vacation, or they have already started work on another project when the post-mortem review is scheduled. Make every attempt to change the schedule if necessary to accommodate these people. You just went through a project as a team, and you should review the project as a team. In the worst case, you can set up a phone link to let the missing members participate remotely. Remote participation is hardly as effective as in-person participation, but the team member is at least able to provide comments and realize that the team does value him or her.

There is one case in which it's appropriate not to invite a team member. Depending on the organization and the culture of the team, the project manager is sometimes a deterrent to openness. Some managers still rule by fiat and decree what the team will do, how they will act, and so on. These managers stifle honest criticisms of the project. You might ask how the team would even be allowed to have a post-mortem with such a manager running the project. Some organizations require a project post-mortem. Because it's required, the manager schedules the meeting, but ensures that nothing negative comes out of it.

Finally, remember that the whole team includes everyone who participated in the project, including the customers and other stakeholders. While you could have a post-mortem review without them, we strongly recommend that you invite them and encourage them to attend.

Provide an Agenda

Team members attending a post-mortem review should understand the purpose of the meeting, and what will occur. The agenda doesn't have to be very detailed, but there should be a clear purpose and estimated amount of time spent for each part of the agenda. The agenda is no different than an agenda you would publish for any other meeting, but you should make every effort to create one and publish it to the team well in advance of the meeting. Figure 11.1 shows a sample agenda for a post-mortem review meeting.

Establish Goals

Setting a clear goal for the meeting is important so that participants can tell if the meeting is successful. The purpose of the review is to improve the team's process for the next project. You may think of other goals that you want to express to attendees.

- Introduction
  - o Overview of the post-mortem review process
- Did we succeed?
  - o Actual results
- What went well and why?
  - o Every person provides their top three items
- What didn't go well?
  - o Every person provides their top three items
  - o What was the effect?
  - o What would we do differently next time?
- Wrap-up
  - o Would you join the project again?
  - o Action items

Figure 11.1 Sample post-mortem review agenda

Provide Preparation Guidelines and Activities

To have a successful and useful post-mortem, it's necessary for everyone to participate and not just show up because they have to. The best way to guarantee participation is to ask attendees to prepare for the meeting.

What type of preparation is most appropriate? That will depend upon the goals of the meeting, but in general we encourage you to ask these questions.

- From the customer's viewpoint, how well did we meet our objectives?
- From the company's or organization's viewpoint, how well did we meet our objectives?
- From the project team's viewpoint, how well did we meet our objectives?
- From my personal viewpoint, how well did I meet my objectives?
- Considering each viewpoint, were the objectives realistic?
- Considering each viewpoint, were the objectives clear?

After considering questions about the goals of the project, participants should answer the following questions and bring their answers to the review.

- What caused me, personally, the most difficulty during this project? Why? What could I have done differently to help alleviate the problem? What could others have done differently to help alleviate the problem? What was the net effect of this problem on the project?
- What went well during the project? Why? What was the net effect?
- What went poorly during the project? Why? What was the net effect?
- What things did we do that seemed to have no reason, but took up a considerable amount of my, or my team's time? How could we have reduced the time or eliminated these activities?
- How did I feel about the whole experience? Was it a positive or negative experience? Am I proud of the work I did? What did I learn? Would I do it again? What would I do differently?
- Did the team work well together? Why or why not?

Many of the items on this list are in the realm of the *soft side* of software development. As you know from reading this book, we think that the soft side is as important as any other aspect of software development. One of the early reviewers of our manuscript, Magnus Lyckå, said it eloquently: "Psychology is the trickiest part of software engineering." The post-mortem is like a group psychology session for the team. And like a group psychology session, you need to control it to make sure that you get results.

Employ a Facilitator

Meetings such as post-mortem reviews are best run by someone who isn't a part of the project team. Many meetings benefit from having an outsider facilitate because that person has no vested interest in the meeting and is viewed as impartial. The impartiality is an important factor in achieving open communication among the team members.

In a large organization, there are often several people who naturally make good moderators. You know who they are. They are the people whom everyone seems to respect and trust. They are the people who don't "flame" people whose opinions differ or who make "silly" statements. When you identify these potential facilitators, get to know them and establish a relationship with them. When it's time to hold your post-mortem review, ask if one of these people can facilitate the meeting.

There are times when no one from outside the project is available to facilitate the meeting. In such cases, ask the team member who comes closest to being the "facilitator type" to lead the meeting. This person must be comfortable with the role. This person also cannot participate in the session as if he or she were a regular team member. And it's best if this team member isn't in a management position.

When a team member facilitates the post-mortem review, there are times when he or she wants to contribute to the group's discussion in a more personal way. When this happens, facilitators must step out of the facilitator role, make it clear that they aren't speaking as a facilitator, get someone else to facilitate if possible, and clearly identify when they step back into the facilitator role.

There are many good references to how to (and how not to) run effective meetings. One of our favorites is a film called "Meetings, Bloody Meetings." This is a hilarious look at meetings starring John Cleese of Monty Python fame. It is perhaps the best training film ever made on the subject of how (not to) chair a meeting.[1] One book that describes how to facilitate meetings like the post-mortem review is *Facilitator's Guide to Participatory Decision-Making* by Sam Kaner et al.

The post-mortem is, in fact, a decision-making meeting. In it, the team members decide how they want to work in the future, as individuals and as part of a team. What could be more important?

Once you have facilitated a post-mortem review, or other meeting where the group is charged with making decisions, you will find your own style. Our observations are that you will be most successful if you can maintain a "gentle" approach to controlling the meeting, while actually having firm control of it.

Produce Action Items from the Review

The post-mortem review should be more than a time for everyone to get together and reminisce. There are many ways of eliciting, collating, and prioritizing the information the participants bring to the meeting. Many of these activities are similar to those described in RUP about how to run a Requirements workshop. If you think about it, this makes sense. During the project post-mortem, you are eliciting requirements for the next project—on the organization, the project team, and individuals. You are defining success criteria for the next project.

We recommend grouping the items in two dimensions. One dimension is a temporal dimension: short term to long term. The other dimension identifies the scope of the action: personal, project, and organization.

---

[1] This film is available from several sources. Use your favorite Web search engine to locate it.

Table 11.1 Format for action items from the post-mortem review

	Short Term	Long Term
Personal		
Project/Team		
Organization		

Table 11.1 shows an example of such a chart. Each action item produced from the meeting should be assigned to one of the cells on this grid.

Decide what your team considers short-term and long-term. We suggest two or three months as the boundary for most organizations. How you group the items really isn't that important, nor is the definition you give to each column and row heading. Some of these categories may not even apply to your project. Certainly for the PSP Tools project, the organization-level items weren't relevant. The important thing is that each person has at least one item on the board that she or he owns.

Act and Revisit Regularly

This guideline is critical. If you are just going to make the action items and then leave it up to individuals to "do the right thing," don't waste everyone's time. You would be better off buying each team member a good self-help book. Make a point to meet regularly to discuss how people are doing with their actions. You just finished a project as a team. Now continue to support each other (and the organization) to achieve the goals you've established for yourselves.

Do Something Fun

Either end the post-mortem review with a fun activity or plan such an activity for another time. The activity doesn't have to be elaborate or expensive, but it can serve as a nice acknowledgement of the humans who worked on the project. And it can be a creative way for the team to both bond and let off some steam. Suggested activities range from goofy (but not mean-spirited) awards to an ice cream party to an outing. Pick something that's right for your group and that your group will enjoy.

Our Post-Mortem Review

We held our post-mortem review by telephone and discussed these simple questions:

- What went well—what would you do more of on your next project?
- What went wrong—what would you do differently on your next project?
- What did you get out of working on the project?

We present the anonymous answers to the first two questions as simple lists. These are the items our group shared and agreed on. For the third question, we let team members write about what they got out of the project. Russell has nothing to say; at this point, the persona has served his purpose and it's time to bid him farewell until the next time we need him.

What Went Well?

We each described the top three things that went well. Some of us mentioned the same items. The following list collates our thoughts.

- Using Groove. Groove made it possible for us to collaborate in a way that would have otherwise been impossible.
- The team made the project fun. We were able to find ways to overcome many types of adversity. We didn't always agree with each other, but we still worked together effectively.
- Focus on the user experience. It was educational to see how focusing on the user experience and the users' problems directed our solution.
- Pair programming. It was effective to experience the benefits and the teamwork that resulted from pairing.
- Using Eclipse and Rational XDE. This IDE was the best one we've encountered in terms of the features it provided and the ease of use. The IDE helped us rather than got in our way.
- Russell. It was great to have "Russell" available to keep us on track and provide user input.
- The project wasn't a "death march." We had enough time to think about what we needed to do and then do it.

■ Just enough process. We didn't let the process get in the way. For some of us it was the first time we had the ability to do "the right thing" when it comes to process.

What Would You Change?

Another way of asking the question is: What didn't go well? Our list follows.

■ We should have found a way to get on track earlier. We spent too much time waiting for John to deliver something. We should have found a way to help him succeed on the project or provided him an opportunity to leave the team earlier.

■ We should have spent more time at the beginning on team building. We would have easily made up the time during the rest of the project.

■ Those of use who were co-located, even if in separate buildings, should have met face-to-face more often.

■ We should have spent more time on unit tests and been more serious about using Test-First Programming and JUnit for all of our code.

■ We should have all used PSP Tools for our work. The only one who really used it was Gary.

■ We should have enlisted a separate, experienced tester much earlier.

■ We shouldn't have had the same person fill the project manager and architect role.

■ We overused Groove. Groove is great for many things, but, for example, we quickly outgrew the benefits of using Groove for recording our defect tracking. We should have taken the time to install and use a real defect-tracking system.

■ We should have tried harder to get more Beta testers.

What Did You Learn?

In this section, we each contribute a personal note about what we learned on the project.

Gary

This project was my ideal type of project. It was fun, small, and successful. The bonus, and the thing that made this project special, was the team. I'm sorry that we've completed this. Maybe we'll work together on something else—I hope so.

I've been fortunate to have spent several years of my career working and studying with exceptional people. This team is a group of such people and I'm honored to be able to call them my teammates. I've always been saddened when the group breaks up—which is inevitable. I am saddened now, but value the time when we walked the same path together.

In the last few years I have gotten away from software development. I learned how many new things there were to learn and re-learn. I remembered how much I like building software. There is always something new to learn. When I stop learning, then I'll know that it's time to stop working. I can't imagine that happening.

If I had to choose one thing that I remember most about the project it's this: the PSP Tools project fits my definition of what meaningful work should be—useful to someone else, useful to me, something I want to do, and fun. It was all that and more.

Another thing that I treasure about this project is the fact that we were able to take it from start to finish. We didn't quite keep a complete record of the things we wanted to capture. We did deliver a product. As with most real projects, we didn't implement all the features we wanted to, and we did introduce a few minor defects that we didn't fix. That is always a humbling experience, but it shows how much opportunity for improvement we have.

When I looked back at some of the code I wrote, I realized how I could make it better. I think that is a good thing. It means that I'm learning still (or it means I have really gotten out of practice). Some of my code truly "smells," as the XP community might say. But, I can make it better, and I will. If you download the code from the book's Web pages, you may notice areas that we've improved since we wrote this book. The code is still not perfect, but we're improving it incrementally. I look forward to the challenges that await me on the next project. I hope I've learned something about people, process, and tools on this one that will serve me well. I think I did.

Jas

Looking back, a lot of life got in the way of our schedules; however, we did meet our overall plan to get to the end with a working product and, hopefully, a useful description of how we got there.

What worked well was having a shared workspace (Groove) to post our ideas, and our regular meetings to maintain the project momentum. Once we established the rhythm of meetings, our activities—the process of posting and testing builds, and creating issues for further work—fell into place. I was glad that Gary and Chris created the easy installs to facilitate the user experience with the product. On the negative side, I lost some would-be testers who got too frustrated with the product to give it another shot! As a tester, I must confess I was appalling—"forget the test cases… let me just have a go at the product." Exploratory testing is a lot of fun! However, when I did uncover bugs that way, it was often hard for me to retrace the steps that got me there, providing little value to Gary or Chris. Sorry, guys, I did say we needed a "video test lab"; then you could have seen what I did.

All in all it was a great experience. To paraphrase Christopher Alexander of "Pattern Language" fame, "It's not just the alphabetics of putting together the various bits and pieces to make the final product, but how much satisfaction people actually get from interacting with the result." From the outset I saw the book project as a journey and a team experience. We in the software business have our own "alphabetics." We created the various artifacts required to build the product. But much more than that, we kept together as a team across the continent and in different countries, through the dot.com and then the dot.bomb era.

Now that we're done I will miss the team, Gary's biannual visits, and our treks to various restaurants. It will be interesting some day to actually meet up with Chris. 'Til the next time.

Liz

For years, I'd read about, discussed, and even written about ideas and trends in the software development world. Now that I've worked on this project, I have actual experience with these ideas, and I can speak more knowledgeably about them. For example:

- RUP is a large knowledge base providing guidance to team members engaged in software development. However, it is just as reasonable to use RUP on a small project as it is to use it on a large project. The key is that for every project, you need to customize RUP to your own needs.
- Agile processes offer much of value, but again, you need to customize these processes to your project's needs.
- The real value for us was to customize a process that combined the best of RUP and agile processes.

In the tools arena, I of course felt comfortable using Rational tools. However, I was delighted to learn about other tools of use to members of small teams. Groove, of course, stands out as the tools workhorse. On future projects, I'd like to branch out and learn about other widely available tools that are useful to small teams.

And finally, a few observations about the people aspects (the "soft side") of the project:

- Life is about change, and we certainly experienced a lot of it during the project—deaths of several parents, layoffs, job changes, vacations, company buy-outs, completing our "real-work" projects. Some of these changes slowed us down, but they didn't derail us. I'm especially proud that in spite of real life's intrusions, and perhaps because of it, we maintained our focus and finished the project.
- The incident with our fifth member, "John," reminded me of a lesson I learned long ago—that sometimes you need to cut your losses and move on. I think that John and the rest of the team got stuck in the thought that we needed each other. Yet, when the time you're taking to manage a situation outweighs the benefit you're getting back, you need to recognize that you're not making progress and fix the problem. I was proud, though, that when we parted ways with John, we left things on friendly terms; his departure from the team didn't seem to affect our personal relationships with him.

Bottom line: Would I sign up again for a similar project? You bet. I had a lot of fun, learned a lot, and believe that I contributed substantially to the project.

Chris

I've created a simple list of the three main things that I took away from this project:

- Write unit tests as you code. Use Test-First Programming. Telling yourself that you'll write unit tests later rarely works. Write the tests and then write the code to make the tests pass. It's much easier to modify the classes later and know that they still work, because the tests still pass after you change the code.
- Plan a directory structure, and keep asking if this file belongs somewhere else. Be really tough on yourself about this. A well-organized file structure with good file names makes it easier to maintain the code.

- I am much more comfortable with Java. This was one of my stated goals. I took this skill back to my workplace and spearheaded Java efforts in my real job.

Conclusions

The post-mortem review is a time for closure. It helps the team tie up loose ends and get ready for the next set of challenges. It also gives the team time to say good-bye to those who will be moving on. Our review and the opportunity to share our comments with you have been important and cathartic for us; we hope our observations are helpful to you.

Tidying Up for the Next Project Team

Earlier in the book we said that we wanted to make it look like we did everything right. Now is the time to do it. The tasks are fairly minor, but this step takes a little time and effort. The sections that follow describe the tasks we wanted to complete to ensure that the next team to work on PSP Tools would have a clean starting place for working on the next version. This was especially important if *we* were that next team.

Refactoring

During the iterations we tried to keep up with maintaining consistent, documented source code. Of course, because of time and other pressures, the code degraded slightly over the course of the project. The post-mortem period is a good time to clean things up.

What type of clean-up activities did we do? Mostly, we added or revised comments and renamed variables or methods. Chris and Gary wrote their code slightly differently, yet within the guidelines they had established. They needed to take a last look at the source code and find places where their different styles clashed.

We also had to review the different error-handling and debugging mechanisms that we inserted in the code. Java is flexible about how you can handle unexpected situations in the code. You can use return values to signal special situations or you can use Java exceptions. We wanted to ensure that we addressed unexpected situations consistently and in an obvious way.

As we reviewed the error-handling code, we found two additional coding patterns we needed to clean up. There were some cases where we caught exceptions, but we didn't do anything with them. In many cases the code worked, but we needed to make sure that in the code we noted that the empty block was not an oversight.

There were other cases where we had inserted comments in the exception block indicating that we would add exception-handling code later. We did this because, at the time, we weren't sure what error-handling mechanism we needed or that we needed error-handling. Listing 11.1 shows a simple example from `PSPDatabase.java`. The code turns the database's `autoCommit` mode on and off. According to the API, this throws an exception. We weren't able to cause the exception to occur in our testing, and we weren't sure what to do if it did occur. In this case, we felt we could leave the catch block empty. If we left it empty, we needed more than a "TBD" (short for "to be determined") comment. Using the "TBD" string made it easy to locate these code segments and remove them from the final delivered product.

Listing 11.1 Incomplete exception-handling code

```
/**
 * Set the autoCommit mode.
 * @param boolean: true turns the mode on, false off
 */
public void setAutoCommitMode(boolean b)
{
    try {
        con.setAutoCommit(b);
    } catch (SQLException e) {
        // TBD
    }
}
```

During development, especially early development, we inserted statements to print informational messages to the Java console. These helped us ensure that methods were entered with the right arguments and so on. The messages were benign, but not appropriate in a finished product. We spent some of our refactoring time removing or commenting out these messages.

We thought of other refactoring activities that we could do. Had we followed our original plan and produced a better set of unit tests, we would have felt more comfortable performing these activities. We chose not to proceed after balancing the risks against the benefits of making the changes.

Reading this section, you may get two impressions. First, you may think that we wrote dirty code. We don't think so. The code is simple and easy to read (in our opinion, of course). But it could be better—it can always be better.

You might also think that we were reluctant to do substantial code refactoring. This is true. During the post mortem, both Chris and Gary said that they wished they had spent more time developing the unit tests. With a more complete set of unit tests, we would have felt more confident about refactoring more code. Without the tests, we were extremely careful to make changes that would not break the code. The lesson we learned from a technical viewpoint is: *The time you spend developing unit tests when you write the code will be made up many times over throughout the project.*

The XP community has been making this point with respect to Test-First Programming. We aren't sure if it matters whether you write the tests before or while you write the code. We are sure that *you must write the tests*.

The Final Diagrams

During the project, we designed most of the UML diagrams to provide information we needed at a particular snapshot in time. We drew some simple sequence diagrams to illustrate how the system would behave during a particular scenario (for example, see Figure 6.4). We sketched some simple class diagrams to show how the code was organized and the different layers and packages (see Figure 6.8). These diagrams don't necessarily reflect the final PSP Tools product.

At this point, automated tools that create UML diagrams from code can be useful. Several tools can reverse engineer the code; we used Rational XDE for Java development.

We were using the Eclipse IDE, so we used the XDE add-in to Eclipse. We had created a Java modeling project for some of the simple diagrams we created earlier in our development. Now we simply reverse-engineered the source code to create diagrams at any level of detail we needed. The total time to reverse-engineer the code to the model was less than five minutes, and it required just one mouse click. Figure 11.2 shows how we right-clicked on the project and selected **Reverse Engineer**. Now we were able to create class and component diagrams, and drag any of the classes and components onto them. With the appropriate visibility settings, we could provide high-level, as well as detailed, views of our code.

You need to decide how many diagrams are enough. In some cases, it might be enough to provide a simple overview and let future teams create

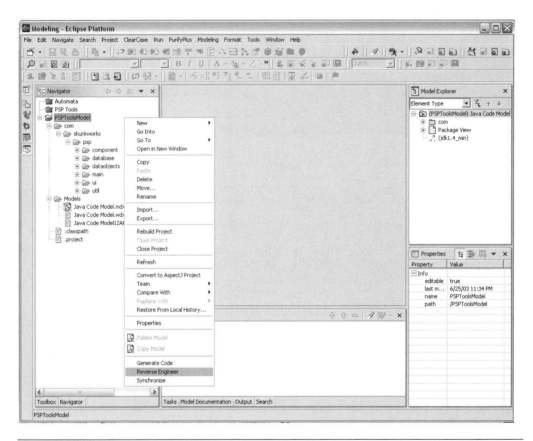

Figure 11.2 Reverse-engineering the code to the model

their own detailed diagrams as necessary. We thought it was important to provide an overview of the packages and how they relate, class diagrams for each of the packages to show the main classes and their relationships, and some patterns that we used in our code.

The complete model is available on the book's Web site both as an XDE model file and as a published Web site for readers who don't use XDE. Figure 11.3 shows the class diagram for our database package. It doesn't include test classes; it includes only those classes that provide information to help you understand the structure of the package and the general responsibilities of each class.

We chose not to show any associations in Figure 11.3. To show how the different accessor classes are used, we created one diagram showing the relationships between the database, the accessor, and the data object (see Figure 11.4). Here we show enough detail so you can see how the

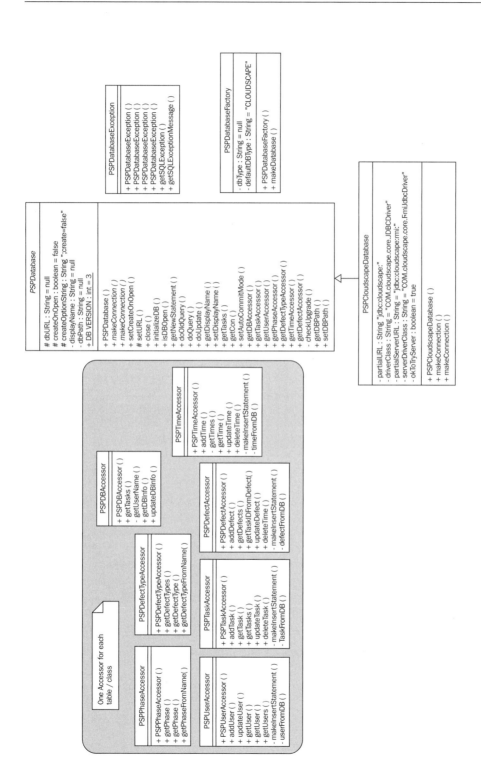

Figure 11-3 Class diagram for the database package

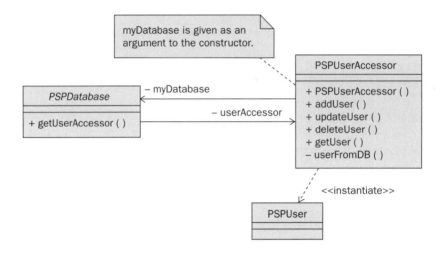

Figure 11.4 Relationships between database, accessor, and data object classes

three types of classes collaborate to get data in and out of the actual database.

How you choose to document your project is up to you. We found that spending a few hours creating a usable model that matched the code we delivered was valuable. It provided documentation for the next team, and gave us another perspective of the project and a final opportunity to review it a high level.

Other Project Documentation

It's always difficult to determine how much project documentation to produce. To reiterate our position, we recommend that you produce only as much as you need. We were undecided about whether to create a Software Architecture Document (SAD). The SAD is a composite artifact in RUP; it contains parts of other artifacts, or even whole artifacts. There are ways to automatically generate part of the SAD. We decided not to compose a SAD artifact. We think the model, requirements documents, code, and user documentation will provide enough information for the next team. Of course, we'll know if we're right when we hear from the next team.

The Changing Landscape

If we had the luxury of working on PSP Tools full time, the project would have lasted just a couple of months. Many of the issues we faced might not have arisen or they would have been much less important. But the fact is that it took us a while to complete the project. It took us over a year of starts and stops, stalls and accelerations. During that time, the technology and practices for developing software with the Java platform changed, as did the tools for many other parts of the software development process.

This part of the chapter discusses the main changes, as we see them, and how we might do things differently if we were starting over.

Team Communication and Collaboration

There are several tools to host projects for distributed teams. Today, we would select one of them at the beginning of the project. These were available when we began PSP Tools. We didn't make good use of them, in part because we didn't realize at the beginning of the project that we would need them.

Teams tend to overuse tools. Our team used Groove heavily. Groove is a great tool, but we used it in place of other, more appropriate, tools. In the next release, we will look for an open source community for hosting the code and artifacts, one that provides the capability for version control. A community such as SourceForge (http://sourceforge.net) would be our choice today.

One general guideline we can provide in the area of group tools is: *Make sure that all your team members who need to use tools for a specific purpose have access to the tools and to the artifacts the tools operate on.* For example, because Jas didn't have access to some of the testing tools the rest of the team used, it was impossible for us to have a consistent way to automate tests. When everyone works for the same company and uses the same network, this problem goes away. For us, not being on the same network was often a roadblock that we spent a disproportionate amount of time working around. If you are faced with this situation, consider adopting a tool that everyone can use, even if it has fewer features than another tool that isn't available to everyone.

Changes in RUP

RUP 2003 was released just before we finished the project. This version of RUP has more new features and improvements than any earlier version. In a future project, we look forward to using at least these features: more flexible plug-ins, Process Views and MyRUP.

Earlier versions of RUP allowed you to use RUP plug-ins to enhance the guidance in the knowledge base for specific domains, technologies, and tools. Until version 2003, you had to adopt all of a plug-in or none of it. This release lets you select specific core components of RUP and components of the different plug-ins when you publish a RUP configuration.

When you publish a configuration, you can also publish a *Process View*. A Process View filters the content of the RUP configuration to produce a view of the knowledge base appropriate to just one role or for one purpose (for example, you can create a getting started view). The Process Views let your team tailor views of the process to your needs, hiding those parts of RUP that you don't normally use (you still have access to the hidden parts). Figure 11.5 shows the standard Process Views delivered with standard RUP.

Gary says that he would create two Process Views for our team if we were starting with RUP 2003. He would create a roadmap to the parts of RUP that were appropriate for our team. Such a view would be analogous

Figure 11.5 RUP Process Views[*]

[*] © 2003 Rational Software Corporation. All rights reserved. This graphic is used with permission of IBM Corporation.

to our Development Case, presented as a set of specific pointers to the appropriate places in RUP.

He would also create a general practitioner view containing the minimal RUP content that everyone on the team would share. There would be a few links to specialized areas like modeling, design, and so on. Team members would start with that view and use the MyRUP feature to add useful links.

MyRUP is a personalization feature for RUP users. It lets you create a copy of a Process View and then modify it by adding or removing links. In addition to links to RUP, you can add links to anything on the Internet or on a file system.Figure 11.6 shows such a view.

With RUP 2003, we would also:

- Create a *thin plug-in* that integrates some of our material directly into RUP.[2]

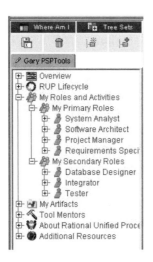

Figure 11.6 A personal view created with MyRUP[*]

[*] © 2003 Rational Software Corporation. All rights reserved. This graphic is used with permission of IBM Corporation.

---

[2] Thin plug-ins are produced with a small amount of effort using a tool called RUP Organizer. This tool lets you add or replace information in RUP as long as you don't change the underlining structure of the RUP model. To change the underlining structure, you need to use the RUP Modeler tool. RUP Organizer has more than enough capability for projects such as PSP Tools.

- Create a team Process View pointing to our artifacts, such as the RequisitePro database and XDE models. This would allow us to access artifacts immediately while using RUP to get process guidance.

IDE

There are many good IDEs available for developing software today. Eclipse, IBM WebSphere, Borland JBuilder, and Sun ONE studio are examples of ones we recommend for Java development. In many ways, selecting a development environment is like selecting a personal computer. Be happy with what you choose and realize that tomorrow, it will be superceded by a new model that costs less and has more features.

If your team is new to Java, or even to object-oriented programming, we recommend that you try the BlueJ IDE, available from www.bluej.org. BlueJ was developed at Monash University in Australia, with support from Sun Microsystems. While it doesn't have all of the special features for working with J2EE applications, Web services, and so on, it does present a simple, easy-to-use way of developing Java programs. Once you master the object-oriented concepts and Java, you can switch to a more full-featured environment.

Our advice is to choose an enironment that you adopt one that gives you full access to the underlying Java platform and one that doesn't lock you into using it forever. Remember our experiences with the GUI Builder in Forte. It was nice until we switched to Eclipse. We had to live with the Forte code, even though it wasn't implemented in the way we would have liked to write it.

If we were beginning PSP Tools today, we might spend more time testing the different IDEs than we did for this project. We are fairly certain that we wouldn't change IDEs in mid-project again.

The Future of PSP Tools

What is next for the PSP Tools software? There are several possible answers to this question.

- The answer we like the least is that nothing is next. This is it. This alternative happens if our team decides to disband rather than work towards PSP Tools version 2. It could also happen if none of the book's readers download the software and offer ideas for improvement.

■ Our team decides to produce version 2. We look at the known requests for enhancements, review user feedback, and build a better, more flexible product. We have talked about undertaking this project, but haven't committed to it yet.

■ Readers of the book take the PSP Tools software and improve on it. If you are such a reader, we would like to know what you've done, and ask that you share your changes with us. More information is on the book's Web site.

■ PSP Tools could be used as a starting point for projects in academic settings. At the time of this writing, Gary was about to start a new job in a teaching position as Professor of Practice at Worcester Polytechnic Institute and planned for some of his students to work on the project.

■ We build a community of PSP aficionados who want to work on PSP Tools as an open source project. We encourage you to join this effort. If you are interested in this option, we provide information on the book's Web site about how we can get started.

Summary

Every project team needs closure at the end of the project. We call this the post-mortem. Other people call it the project retrospective. It is a time for the team to reflect on their experiences—what worked and what didn't work. More importantly, it's a time to make things better for the next project. Take time to make your post-mortem valued by and valuable to the whole team.

Well, that's it. We have certainly enjoyed telling our story. We hope you have enjoyed reading it. More importantly, we hope that we have helped you appreciate how a process like RUP, along with a good set of tools and attention to people issues, can help you on your next small project. We encourage you to send us[3] your own success stories and lessons learned. Good luck on your future projects!

---

[3] Send us email at psptools@yahoo.com.

An Introduction to the Rational Unified Process (RUP)

This appendix provides a brief introduction to the Rational Unified Process (RUP). Our intention is to give you some context for the discussions in this book about RUP. Today (as of RUP version 2003), RUP is a complete process platform that contains a knowledge base and tools for authoring, configuring, and deploying the configured process. Consult the Rational RUP pages[1] for information about the complete RUP product. This appendix just describes an overview of the concepts in the RUP process framework, one part of the complete RUP product.

The Gateway to RUP

We like symbols, icons, and logos, and the first RUP icon that comes to mind is the "Hump Chart" (see Figure A.1). The "Hump Chart" is a gateway into RUP and the generic disciplines that describe best practices for object-oriented software engineering.

Disciplines, listed to the left of the chart, group related activities pertaining to major areas of concern within the context of a software development project. If you read down from Business Modeling to Environment, you might get the impression that RUP is a traditional "waterfall" development methodology. This isn't the case.

Most software development projects aren't clearly defined at the beginning of the project, and require several cycles to arrive at the ultimate solution. So RUP is an iterative and incremental software development process.

---

[1] See www.ibm.com/software/awdtools/rup.

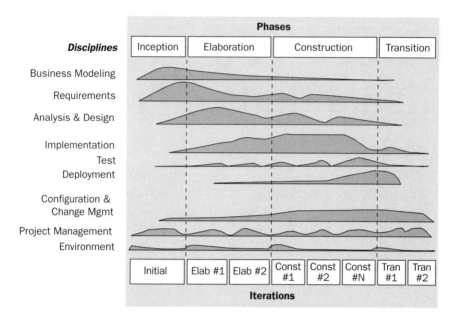

Figure A.1 The RUP "hump" chart*

* © 2003 Rational Software Corporation. All rights reserved. This graphic is used with permission of IBM Corporation.

RUP suggests that software is developed over a number of phases, each of which consists of one or more iterations. The humps suggest the level of effort required over time for each of the disciplines.[2]

For example, the Requirements discipline requires much effort in the Inception and early Elaboration phases, but dwindles in the later phases as build targets are set and requirements are frozen. However, RUP doesn't close the door on Requirements activities in the later phases when change requests, or real changes to the customer needs and business conditions, happen. The amount of effort you put into managing requirements should decrease as the project proceeds, but not always. A spike in Requirements activities towards the end of the project may mean that the real customer requirements weren't understood until late, when it may be expensive to

---

[2] These are *examples* of the effort you might expend on a project. Every project is different. People have told us that their projects had different effort profiles and they wondered what they were doing wrong. We gently told them to use the humps on the chart as guidelines, not as rigid prescriptions for every project.

make structural changes. To draw on a house-building analogy, it's much better to decide where to locate kitchens and bathrooms early in a construction project; it can be devastating (to schedules and budgets, at least) to make this decision late in the project. But, in software projects, it's quite possible that the changes are necessary and your process must be configured to adequately deal with them.

Phases

RUP describes four phases (Inception, Elaboration, Construction and Transition) that a project goes through. The Inception phase is about creating a vision, developing a business case, and assembling a software prototype—or partial solution—so that the endeavor gets support and funding. The Elaboration phase ends with an executable architecture where the key architectural decisions have been made and risks have been mitigated. The executable architecture is working software that exhibits an implementation of the key architectural decisions. The Construction phase is about filling out the functionality identified in the architecture, and the Transition phase focuses on delivering the software to its users.

Phases are divided into iterations. Iterations are "time-boxed" and have specific goals. The iterations are kept as short as possible, but long enough for you to implement complete use cases or use-case scenarios that provide real value to the user. At the end of each iteration, you hold an assessment where you adjust plans for future iterations, based on the results of the current iteration. During the assessment, your team also reflects on the efficacy of the process and adjusts it as necessary. RUP is all about creating a vision of what you want, creating a framework for getting there, and assessing at given points whether you are headed where you intend to go.

RUP Key Concepts

RUP is a software engineering process that describes the "general order" of "who" needs to "do what" in order to "create what." The key concepts are shown in Figure A.2.

Roles

RUP refers to the "who" entities as *roles*. RUP identifies over 30 roles that fall under broader categories such as Analysts, Developers, Testers, and

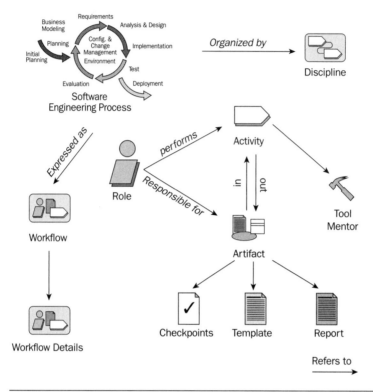

Figure A.2 Key RUP concepts*

Managers. The same person on a project can fill many roles. For example, the Project Manager can serve as a Use-Case Specifier, Requirements Reviewer, and a Testing Professional. On large projects, several people might perform the tasks described by one role; for example, your team might include several architects.

Activities

The "do what" part is covered in RUP as activities. Activities are associated with roles (see Figure A.3), and have inputs and outputs. Activities are often composed of steps that help the role achieve the purpose of the activity. The purpose of activities is to achieve observable results by creating, changing, or reviewing "artifacts." RUP provides guidelines and checkpoints that help you perform specific activities.

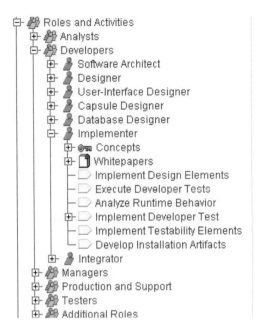

Figure A.3 Roles and their activities[*]

Artifacts cover the "create what" aspect of RUP as a software engineering process. Sets of artifacts are associated with each discipline and the workflows and workflow details that describe the discipline. For example, there is a set of Requirements artifacts, and similarly there are Deployment artifacts. RUP artifacts are typically models, model entities, tool-generated reports, and documents. Figure A.4 shows the artifacts that belong to the Analysis & Design discipline in RUP. Although artifacts are associated with particular roles, those in other roles may be able to modify artifacts as required when performing their given activities.

The "general order" in which activities are to be performed is described in the activity diagrams of each workflow. Figure A.5 is an activity diagram of the Requirements Workflow. Depending on your specific needs, there are a number of ways you can navigate through the activity diagram (which you read like a flowchart). Each visiting point is a "workflow detail."

Workflow details within each workflow show groupings of activities that can be performed simultaneously. These diagrams show the roles involved,

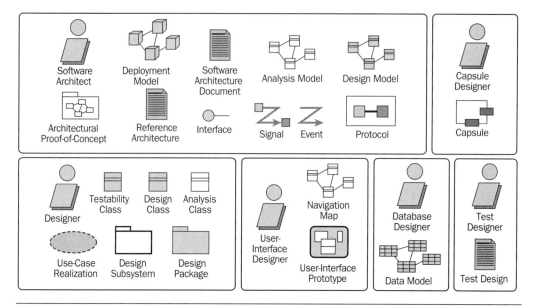

Figure A.4 Artifacts in the Analysis & Design discipline*

input and output artifacts, and activities performed. Figure A.6 is a workflow detail for Perform Architectural Synthesis.

The key RUP role associated with Perform Architectural Synthesis is the Software Architect, who is responsible for performing the three activities shown. However, none of these are mandatory, and may depend on when in the development cycle the workflow detail is invoked. The workflow detail shows the associated artifacts, and other information to help you understand the scope and context of the workflow detail.

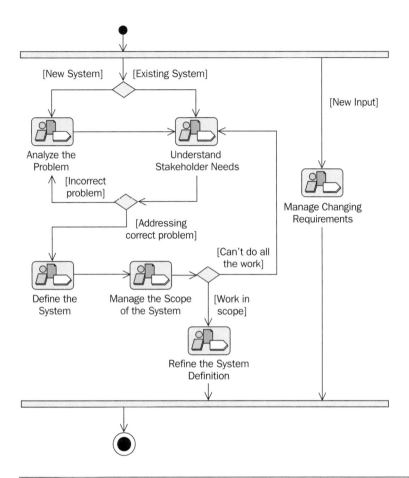

Figure A.5 Requirements workflow[*]

RUP Milestones

Each of the four phases (Inception, Elaboration, Construction, and Transition) of the RUP software development lifecycle has distinct milestones and objectives that mark their endpoints. Objectives for each milestone should be met as a way of mitigating risk before moving on to the following phase (see Figure A.7).

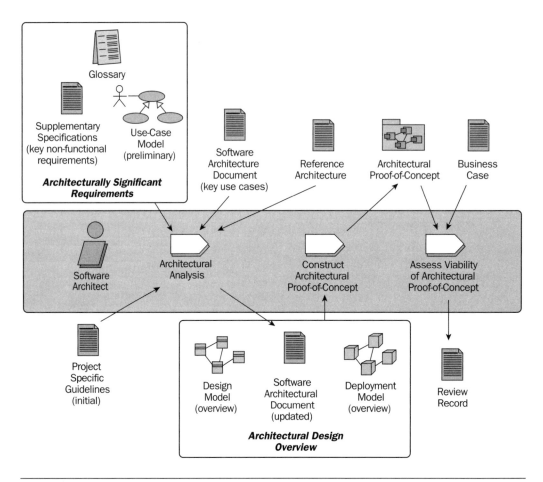

Figure A.6 Workflow detail for Perform Architectural Synthesis*

Goals of Inception

The objectives of the Lifecycle Objectives (LCO) milestone at the end of the Inception Phase are as follows:

■ The people who will use the final product, and the buyers, developers, and project managers (the stakeholders) have "bought into" the project. All stakeholders understand and agree about what needs to be done (scope), how long it will probably take (high-level schedule), and what it will probably cost (budget).

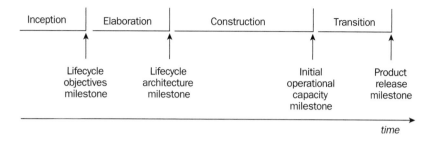

Figure A.7 Each phase has objectives

- The stakeholders agree that their expectations and priorities (requirements) for the product are correctly captured and understood by the others.
- Everyone has had the opportunity to flag perceived concerns (risks) and has devised a way to handle each of them should they arise (mitigation strategy).

The artifacts developed to support the LCO review are:

- *The Vision*—"What are we trying to accomplish?"
- *Business Case*—"What is this going to cost, and is it worth the effort?"
- *Risk List*—"What could derail us, and how are we going to stay on track?"
- *Software Development Plan, Tools, Templates and Environment*—"What do we need, and when, to get the product built and rolled out?"
- *Iteration Plan*—"What are our immediate development goals?"
- *Product Acceptance Plan*—"How do we know we built the right product?"
- *Use-Case Model*—"How will users interact with our product to get something useful out of it?"
- *Glossary*—"What are the objects in our domain?"

Goals of Elaboration

The objectives of the Lifecycle Architecture (LCA) milestone at the end of the Elaboration phase are as follows:

- We know exactly what we're going to build (stable architecture), and end users agree that it will support their needs (stable requirements).
- We have described the key scenarios that the product needs to support to be considered successful, and we have proved through a series of executable prototypes that we have made the right tradeoffs, and can meet the "success criteria" (mitigated architectural risks).
- Our overall and iteration plans for the Construction phase are realistic enough for work to begin (stable plans).
- Our budget "burn rate" to date has been realistic.
- We have established a suitable supporting environment and infrastructure to develop the product.

The artifacts developed to support the LCA review "now that we know better" are:

- Updated Vision Document.
- Updated Risk List.
- Updated Software Development Plan.
- Updated Iteration Plan.
- Updated Use-Case Model.
- Supplementary Specifications—These capture the nonfunctional requirements (performance, reliability, "we want it in pink polka dot," and so on).
- Prototypes—Quickly slapped together experimental executables used to explore software ideas (exploratory) on what parts are going to hang together (structural), or demonstrate specific behavior (behavioral), or even parts that may be scaled up into production code (evolutionary). Usually this is throwaway code.
- Software Architecture Document—This describes the key design elements and mechanisms (Logical View) needed to support the functional requirements (Use-Case View), and how the components will work together (Process View) and execute on their target platform (Deployment View).
- Design Model—This captures the product design, ensuring that the design meets user requirements and that the path to implementation is clear.
- Implementation Model—An organized collection of components, data, and subsystems that express the product design.
- Project Specific Templates and Tools to support product development.

Goals of Construction

The objectives of the "Initial Operational Capability (IOC) Milestone" at the end of the Construction phase are as follows:

- Produce an Alpha version of the product that is sufficiently mature to be released to "first-adopter" users.
- Ensure that users are ready to test and use the product.
- Validate that there is sufficient budget to complete the project.

The artifacts developed to support the IOC review are:

- Updated and expanded Implementation Model.
- Updated Design Model based on new design elements identified during the Construction phase.
- Test Model including test designs and harnesses required to validate the executable.
- Deployment Plan describing the tasks and resources required to install and test the developed product so that it can be effectively transferred to the user community.
- Preliminary draft of "use-case based" user manuals and training materials.

Goals of Transition

The objective of the Product Release Milestone (PRM) at the end of the Transition phase is as follows:

- The end users are ready to take delivery of the product.

To support that objective, activities such as the following need to have been completed:

- The users have validated and accepted the product, and are on their way to supporting the product in-house.
- The users are trained and know how to make the transition from their legacy system to the new one.
- The product is packaged for pricing and promotion rollout to the marketing, distribution, and sales forces.
- The product has been handed over to support engineering, which has been trained for tuning, bug fixing, and enhancing the product.

- The team has met the Vision and the acceptance criteria for the product.

The artifacts developed to support the PRM review are:

- The product build
- Release notes
- Installation and setup instructions and scripts
- End-user support material including training materials

Summary

RUP provides tremendous flexibility and can be used on a wide range of projects. At first blush, it may seem impossible to get started with RUP. However, the spirit of RUP is to take from it whatever is of use to you at any given time in the project.

Overview of the Personal Software Process (PSP)

The question "When are you going to be done?" plagues software developers. Everyone, from the Board of Directors, which safeguards investor interests, to line managers and individual developers needs the answer. Yet it remains difficult to predict the schedule and level of quality for a software release.

As practitioners we have tried various techniques. We have "time-boxed" and "dollar-boxed" releases so that we know we are done when either the final bell rings or the money runs out. Nevertheless, we continue to issue caveats about software releases, such as "It's good enough." We write release notes describing known defects, and, to our continued shame, wait for users to find and complain about what they want fixed.

In 1986, Watts Humphrey of the Software Engineering Institute (SEI) at Carnegie Mellon University (CMU) decided to develop a process program to help tackle the "software crisis." His work produced the Capability Maturity Model (CMM), a framework that organizations use to measure their software process. We refer you to books about the CMM, and the SEI Web pages about CMM at www.sei.cmu.edu/cmm/cmms/cmms.html.

The CMM provides a five-level process improvement framework. The model describes the attributes of organizations at the various levels in the maturity framework. A Level Five organization has more "mature" software development processes than those at lower levels. The model is inclusive; the default level for any organization is Level One, and most software development organizations are at this level.

The Personal Software Process

Humphrey turned his attention to the individual software developer in the early 1990s. He considered how to apply a model such as CMM at the individual practitioner level. The result of this effort is the Personal Software Process (PSP). PSP is fully described in Humphrey's 1995 book, *A Discipline for Software Engineering*. Web pages devoted to PSP are on the SEI site at www.sei.cmu.edu/tsp/psp.html.

The overall goals of PSP are to enable software engineers to develop defect-free products, on schedule and within planned costs. Like the environmentalists who encourage us to "think globally and act locally," Humphrey helps fix the "software crisis" at the individual level. Humphrey's idea is that engineers will plan and track their work, use defined processes, establish measurable goals, track against these goals, and analyze and improve for the next round. The net effect will be that improved individual practices will benefit teams, which in turn will benefit organizations. The theme of plan, track, measure, and improve is intended to scale up from individuals to organizations.

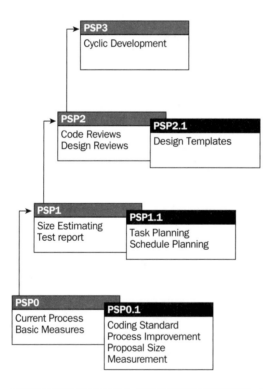

Figure B.1 PSP levels*

* Figure from www.sei.cmu.edu/tsp/psp.html.

PSP describes a four-level model, starting at PSP0 and progressing to PSP3. Each level builds on the practices of the previous levels. Figure B.1 shows the PSP levels.

Goals and Focus

The focus of the Personal Software Process is the individual developer. The promise of PSP is higher software productivity, quality, and timeliness. The PSP defines a way of working where the individual developer:

- Estimates the effort required to complete a given software task
- Tracks personal progress against the plan in terms of time and defects raised and removed at each stage

The goal is that the individual developer will produce better schedules and plans, detect and resolve errors earlier, and exploit opportunities for personal improvement.

The PSP structure, shown in Figure B.2, describes the methods that PSP uses for planning, estimating, data gathering, quality management, and design.

The PSP process elements consist of the following components:

- *Scripts* serve as activity checklists (short and precise instructions) for ensuring consistent application of each step in the process phases, and provide pointers to templates.
- *Logs* provide templates for recording and storing time, defect, and issue tracking data.
- *Forms* consist of design templates, review checklists, plan summaries, and estimating forms.
- *Standards* provide guidance on defect, coding, and lines-of-code (LOC) counting.

In his book, Humphrey presents data that supports his claims that following PSP will help individual software developers improve their effectiveness. Since its introduction, the SEI has built up a significant body of data that continues to support the claims.

Humphrey has now turned his attention to the next step up the organizational ladder—the software development team. He has defined a Team Software Process (TSP) that is built on his previous work.

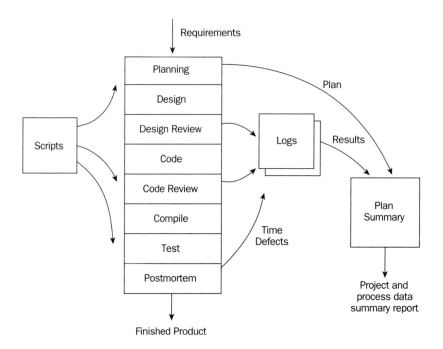

Figure B.2 Process Structure*

* From *A Discipline for Software Engineering* by Watts S. Humphrey.

Conclusion

The PSP mantra is quite simple: follow a defined process, plan the work, gather data, and analyze the data to improve the process. However, this mantra, like most others, can sound tedious. It's easy to drift back to tried and proven bad habits if you don't apply backbone, conviction, and discipline to the effort.

Results from PSP suggest that individual engineers can, through practice, become better estimators, produce better code, and remain productive. At long last, the question "When are you going to be done?" may even elicit a reasoned response.

Introduction to eXtreme Programming (XP)

eXtreme Programming (XP) is one of the best-known "agile" methods. XP was primarily developed by Kent Beck and Ward Cunningham. XP came together as a tightly knit set of practices, based on a few guiding principles, as part of a payroll project at Chrysler Corporation in the mid-1990s. Since then, it has captured the imagination of programmers throughout the world. There are many books devoted to XP—there is even an XP series of books published by Addison-Wesley. Nearly every software development conference today offers sessions on XP.

Teams that have adopted XP and have been successful report reduced defects and higher satisfaction from customers and developers on their projects. We are beginning to see some empirical data supporting the value of many of the XP practices.

Kent Beck says that XP is "a lightweight, efficient, low-risk, flexible, predictable, scientific, and fun way to develop software."[1] This appendix briefly describes XP. For information about why XP works, and details about XP itself, we refer you to the XP references in the Recommended Reading list at the end of this book and to any of the numerous Web sites devoted to XP.

The Primary Values

XP advocates these primary values:

- *Communication.* Software development is a team effort. Effective teams must communicate well. XP focuses on open, effective communications.

---

[1] Preface to *Extreme Programming Explained*.

- *Simplicity.* In XP, it is better to do a simple thing now, and tomorrow pay a little more if a more complex solution is needed.
- *Feedback.* Feedback goes hand-in-hand with communication. When you communicate, or perform some action, the sooner you receive effective feedback, the more effective you are. XP promotes rapid feedback.
- *Courage.* To use XP, the team must have the courage to do the right thing, even when there is pressure to do otherwise. You must have courage to throw away code when such actions are warranted. You must have the courage to take appropriate risks and the courage to admit when you have gone into a blind alley and need to back up.

XP Practices

There are a small set of practices defined by XP. As with any live methodology, the number of practices, and how they are defined, is evolving. Here we present the original set of practices identified by Kent Beck.

- *The Planning Game.* A simple, effective way of determining the contents of a release by combining business value and technical estimates. The plan is constantly updated.
- *Small Releases.* Based on short iterations that deliver working software to customers.
- *Metaphor.* A simple, shared story of how the whole system works.
- *Simple Design.* Do the simplest thing that can possibly work. Let the system's complexity evolve only when absolutely necessary.
- *Testing.* Programmers write complete unit tests for all their code. Customers write acceptance tests.
- *Refactoring.* Programmers continually refactor the code to make it simpler, clearer, and more flexible.
- *Pair Programming.* Two programmers *actively* develop and test production code at a single machine. This promotes instant review and feedback, and decreases the likelihood of defects.
- *Collective Ownership.* Anyone has the right, and everyone has the responsibility, to change any code in the system when they need to.
- *Continuous Integration.* Integrate and build the system as often as possible, usually several times a day. Some projects have developed ways for their configuration management tools to perform the integration builds, continuously, whenever new code is checked in.

- *40-hour Week.* Overtime is rare and not allowed for two weeks in a row under any circumstances.[2]
- *On-site Customer.* A real customer is a member of the team and is always available to help define requirements, develop acceptance tests, and answer questions from the developers.
- *Coding Standards.* The programmers adopt a set of rules for emphasizing communication throughout their code.

If you consider the XP practices and how they might apply to your project, you can see how the practices are designed to support each other. This key strength of XP requires significantly more discipline than you might first realize.

---

[2] This practice is usually stated today as "sustainable pace," since most people have trouble believing that anyone in the software industry actually works only 40 hours a week.

Recommended Reading

Books

Astels, David. *Test-Driven Development: A Practical Guide*. Upper Saddle River, NJ: Prentice Hall PTR, 2004.

Barnes, David J., and Michael Kölling. *Objects First with Java: A Practical Introduction Using BlueJ*. Upper Saddle River, NJ: Prentice Hall, 2003.

Bass, Len, Paul Clements, and Rick Kazman. *Software Architecture in Practice*, 2nd Edition. Boston, MA: Addison-Wesley, 2003.

Beck, Kent. *Extreme Programming Explained: Embrace Change*. Boston, MA: Addison-Wesley, 2000.

Beck, Kent. *Test-Driven Development: By Example*. Boston, MA: Addison-Wesley, 2003.

Beck, Kent, and Martin Fowler. *Planning Extreme Programming*. Boston, MA: Addison-Wesley, 2001.

Boehm, Barry. "A Spiral Model of Software Development and Enhancement." *ACM SIGSOFT Software Engineering Notes*, August 1986.

Booch, Grady, Ivar Jacobson, and James Rumbaugh. *The Unified Modeling Language User Guide*. Reading, MA: Addison-Wesley, 1999.

Brooks, Frederick P. *The Mythical Man-Month, Anniversary Edition: Essays on Software Engineering* (2nd Edition). Reading, MA: Addison-Wesley, 1995.

Clements, Paul, Rick Kazman, and Mark Klein. *Evaluating Software Architectures: Methods and Case Studies*. Boston, MA: Addison-Wesley, 2002.

Cockburn, Alistair. *Agile Software Development*. Boston, MA: Addison-Wesley, 2002.

Cockburn, Alistair. *Surviving Object-Oriented Projects*. Reading, MA: Addison-Wesley, 1998.

Cooper, Alan. *The Inmates Are Running the Asylum: Why High Tech Products Drive Us Crazy and How to Restore the Sanity*. Indianapolis, IN: SAMS, 1999.

Darwin, Ian F. *The Java Cookbook*. Sebastopol, CA: O'Reilly & Associates, 2001.

Demarco, Tom, and Timothy Lister. *Peopleware: Productive Projects and Teams*, 2nd Ed. New York: Dorset House, 1999.

Eeles, Peter, Kelli Houston, and Wojtek Kozaczynski. *Building J2EE Applications with the Rational Unified Process*. Boston, MA: Addison-Wesley, 2003.

Fowler, Martin, Ken Beck, John Brant, William Opdyke, and Don Roberts. *Refactoring: Improving the Design of Existing Code*. Reading, MA: Addison-Wesley, 1999.

Gamma, Erich, Richard Helm, Ralph Johnson, and John M. Vlissides. *Design Patterns: Elements of Reusable Object-Oriented Software*. Reading, MA: Addison-Wesley, 1995.

Glen, Paul. *Leading Geeks: How to Manage and Lead the People Who Deliver Technology*. San Francisco: Jossey-Bass, 2002.

Grand, Mark. *Patterns in Java: A Catalog of Reusable Design Patterns Illustrated with UML*, 2nd Edition, Volume 1. New York: John Wiley & Sons, 2002.

Grand, Mark. *Patterns in Java*, Volume 2. New York: John Wiley & Sons, 1999.

Highsmith, James A., III, and Ken Orr. *Adaptive Software Development: A Collaborative Approach to Managing Complex Systems*. New York: Dorset House, 2000.

Highsmith, Jim. *Agile Software Development Ecosystems*. Boston, MA: Addison-Wesley, 2002.

Humphrey, Watts S. *A Discipline for Software Engineering*. Reading, MA: Addison-Wesley, 1995.

Hunt, Andrew, and David Thomas. *The Pragmatic Programmer: From Journeyman to Master.* Boston, MA: Addison-Wesley, 2000.

Jeffries, Ron, Ann Anderson, and Chet Hendrickson. *Extreme Programming Installed.* Boston, MA: Addison-Wesley, 2001.

Kaner, Sam, Lenny Lind, Catherine Toldi, Sarah Fisk, and Duane Berger. *Facilitator's Guide to Participatory Decision-Making.* Gabriola Island, British Columbia: New Society Publishers, 1996.

Kroll, Per, and Philippe Kruchten. *The Rational Unified Process Made Easy: A Practitioner's Guide to the RUP.* Boston, MA: Addison-Wesley, 2003.

Kruchten, Philippe. *The Rational Unified Process: An Introduction,* 2nd Edition. Boston, MA: Addison-Wesley, 2000.

Kruchten, Philippe. "The 4+1 View Model of Architecture." *IEEE Software*, November 1995.

Larman, Craig. *Applying UML and Patterns: An Introduction to Object-Oriented Analysis and Design* (2nd Edition). Upper Saddle River, NJ: Prentice Hall PTR, 2001.

Larman, Craig. *Agile and Iterative Development: A Manager's Guide.* Boston, MA: Addison-Wesley, 2004.

Martin, Robert. *Agile Software Development: Principles, Patterns, and Practices.* Upper Saddle River, NJ: Prentice Hall, 2002.

Martin, Robert C. *UML for Java Programmers.* Upper Saddle River, NJ: Prentice Hall PTR, 2003.

McBreen, Pete. *Software Craftsmanship: The New Imperative.* Boston, MA: Addison-Wesley, 2001.

McCarthy, Jim, and Michele McCarthy. *Software for Your Head: Core Protocols for Creating and Maintaining Shared Vision.* Boston, MA: Addison-Wesley, 2002.

McConnell, Steve. *Code Complete: A Practical Handbook of Software Construction.* Redmond, WA: Microsoft Press, 1993.

McConnell, Steve. *Rapid Development: Taming Wild Software Schedules.* Redmond, WA: Microsoft Press, 1996.

McConnell, Steve. *Professional Software Development: Shorter Schedules, Higher Quality Products, More Successful Projects, Enhanced Careers.* Boston, MA: Addison-Wesley, 2004.

Naiburg, Eric, and Robert Maksimchuk. *UML for Database Design.* Boston, MA: Addison-Wesley, 2002.

Parnas, David, and Paul Clements. "A Rational Design Process: How and Why to Fake It." *IEEE Transactions on Software Engineering,* Vol. 12, Issue 2, February 1986.

Poppendieck, Mary, and Tom Poppendieck. *Lean Software Development: An Agile Toolkit for Software Development Managers.* Boston, MA: Addison-Wesley, 2003.

Rakos, John J. *Software Project Management for Small to Medium Sized Projects.* Upper Saddle River, NJ: Prentice Hall, 1990.

Schwaber, Ken, and Mike Beedle. *Agile Software Development with SCRUM.* Upper Saddle River, NJ: Prentice Hall, 2001.

Shalloway, Alan, and James Trott. *Design Patterns Explained: A New Perspective on Object-Oriented Design.* Boston, MA: Addison-Wesley, 2002.

Shavor, Sherry, Jim D'Anjou, Scott Fairbrother, Dan Kehn, John Kellerman, and Pat McCarthy. *The Java Developer's Guide to Eclipse.* Boston, MA: Addison-Wesley, 2003.

Weinberg, Gerald, James Bach, and Naomi Karten, Eds. *Amplifying Your Effectiveness: Collected Essays.* New York: Dorset House, 2000.

White, Brian. *Software Configuration Management Strategies and Rational ClearCase: A Practical Introduction.* Boston, MA: Addison-Wesley, 2000.

Whiteside, John. *The Phoenix Agenda: Power to Transform Your Workplace.* New York: John Wiley & Sons, 1995.

Articles

Articles in *The Rational Edge* are available from the archives at www.therationaledge.com:

Kroll, Per. "The Spirit of the RUP." *The Rational Edge,* December 2001.

Pollice, Gary. "RUP and XP." Parts 1 and 2. *The Rational Edge,* March 2001 and April 2001.

Pollice, Gary. "Involving Your Customers in Your RUP Project." *The Rational Edge*, April 2002.

Video:

"Meetings, Bloody Meetings." John Cleese/Video Arts.

Index